Little Miss Dynamite

Little Miss Dynamite

THE LIFE AND TIMES OF BRENDA LEE

Brenda Lee

with Robert K. Oermann
and Julie Clay

HYPERION
NEW YORK

Mass Market ISBN 0-7868-8558-0

Hyperion books are available for special promotions and premiums. For details, contact Hyperion Special Markets, 77 West 66th Street, 11th floor, New York, NY 10023-6298, or call 212-456-0133.

FIRST MASS MARKET EDITION

10 9 8 7 6 5 4 3 2 1

Book design by Casey Hampton

For my husband, Ronnie, my daughters, Julie and Jolie, and my granddaughters, Taylor and Jordan. I sing for you.

Acknowledgments

I'd like to thank all the people around the world who ever bought a Brenda Lee record or came to see a Brenda Lee show. You gave me a career. You're the reason there is a "Little Miss Dynamite."

There is no way to repay Julie Clay and Robert K. Oermann for their tireless research, able writing skills and steadfast companionship throughout the creation of my book. We truly had a ball writing this story together.

The reason you hold it in your hands is due to the efforts of our dear, wonderful and caring agent, Sarah Lazin, and our enthusiastic, supportive and insightful editor, Leslie Wells. Thanks also go to Bob Solinger and to the late Sam Hughes, who both helped jump-start this project.

Reconstructing the details of a six-decade career, even if it's your own, means a huge gathering of facts, figures, opinions and reminiscences. Add on top of that the checking and rechecking of every piece of information, and you have an enormous undertaking. Fortunately, I had some experts on my side.

I want to acknowledge the contributions of Jon Nickell, Pat O'Leary and Bob Borum, who helped compile my discography. John Smith's research about the use of my music in motion pictures was also invaluable.

For film and television footage, I am indebted to Alan Stoker and the staff of the Country Music Foundation. He spent hours providing us with TV memories.

The archivists at *The Tennessean* and at the Davidson County Courthouse were also kind enough to help locate vintage clippings and data. This helped me piece together the early years of my career.

Since so much of my professional life happened at such an early age, I relied on the memories of many, many old friends and colleagues to refresh my own recollections of important milestones and incidents. For generously donating their time, I sincerely thank Bob Beckham, Harold Bradley, Odell Braswell, Buzz Cason, Ron Chancey, Duane Eddy, Peanut Faircloth, Jim Foglesong, Freda Garrett, Emory Gordy Jr., Buddy Harmon, Jimbeau Hinson, Charlie Lamb, Sandy Ferra Martindale, Kay Meadow, Jackie Monaghan, Tony Moon, Bob Moore, Louis Nunley, Ben Peters, Boots Randolph, Billy Smith, Mel Tillis, Bob Tubert, Charles Warfield, Richard Williams and Sonya Worsham.

Thanks also to music scholars Mary Bufwack, Diana Reid Haig, John Lomax III, Jay Orr and Holly George Warren, who helped put my career into historical perspective.

Perhaps most important were the contributions of my family. My mother, Grayce Rainwater, my sisters, Linda Hutchison and Robyn Rainwater, and my brother, Randall Tarpley. Thank you for your loving memories.

These hundreds of hours of recollections were transcribed by the hardworking Christine Gruen, to whom I owe another big thank-you. Throughout the writing process, Agnes Bufwack kept us going with her delicious home-cooked lunches.

Finally, love and gratitude go to my husband, Ronnie Shacklett. He stepped into this crazy world of show business and gave me guidance and stability through it all—the highs, the lows, the joys and the sorrows. Not only that, he has faithfully maintained the Brenda Lee Archives, which provided the basis for the telling of this story. In addition, his help as a raconteur, Nashville historian and careful proofreader were priceless. Without his unflagging support, I would have been unable to complete such a monumental task.

ONE

Georgia on My Mind

All my life, whenever I'd go back to Georgia, I would get this feeling of sadness, like I'd lost something and could never find it again. It's been so long; there have been so many miles. Don't get me wrong—I love Georgia, and I love seeing my people. But for years I had so many conflicting emotions about my background and my family.

I grew up so poor, and it saddens me to see the poverty that is still there. A lot of my family have never done any better. Some of them are just exactly where they were when I was a kid. And, in a way, there is still something inside me that is part of that, the part that doesn't expect much. Little things make them happy, and that's the same with me.

I have been around the world, so to me their horizons seem limited. Those trips home always remind me that some people just don't get an even break in life. If you asked my family if they were deprived, they'd tell you that they're not. And now I know, they're right.

I left Georgia at such an early age. It's something that's hard to explain. Georgia's home, but it's not. My emotions are so complicated, so mixed up, about the world I came from. It almost aches to even talk about it. I crawled out of that red Georgia clay as a baby and never had time to look back, until now. And the emotions that it stirs in me are so confusing and intense that I can hardly express them.

I never thought of myself as being ashamed of that background, but I did run from it. I escaped and got to fulfill my dreams, and I left my family behind. I always felt guilty about that. Why was I the one who got to live this blessed, fairy-tale life when there are so many who never even get to hear applause?

I thought I could never go home again. But I finally have.

So that I could tell my story, I went back to my red-clay roots, back to my family and back to the world that I left so far behind. It was a journey of discovery and healing for me. I have a new understanding of where I came from and who I am.

Best of all, I've finally come to appreciate, understand and embrace the people who gave me my start in life.

♪

If you drive far enough east out of Atlanta, the city's vast suburbs finally disappear. The hills drop behind you and the land begins to undulate with softly rolling contours. The earth is colored in that russet shade described as "red clay." Pine forests cover the land that is not under cultivation. As the miles slip by, the road becomes straighter. Nowadays, it is Interstate 20, with its endless march of franchise restaurants, discount stores, gleaming service stations and prefab motels clustered at its exit ramps. But back when I was born, this was U.S. Route 278, the two-lane blacktop that connected Georgia's metropolitan capital with the bustling Savannah River town of Augusta on the state's boundary with South Carolina.

Exactly midway between the two cities is Greene County in the heart of the state's old cotton belt. Greensboro, the county seat, was historically a key trading center for the old plantations. But the days of antebellum homes, blooming magnolias and

moss-draped trees are long gone. After the Civil War, the plantations were chopped up into sharecropper farms. Erosion and the
nutrient-leaching cotton fields eventually turned the soil parched
and barren. My relatives remember that the boll weevil arrived
like a plague in swarms during the 1920s and 1930s, doing the
rest to decimate the land and its people.

. During the Great Depression, survival became a day-to-day
crisis in this desperate region. Out of this seemingly unblessed,
unforgiving earth came two Georgia clans who were my ances-
tors: the Tarpleys and the Yarbroughs. The fact that I rose from
this suffocating landscape of despair to achieve my dream of
singing is nothing short of miraculous.

Both sides of my family tree came from the Greene County
area. My paternal grandparents, Richard Andrew Tarpley and his
second wife, Nannie Lee Almond, raised seven children. He was
a struggling farmer who later found work as a guard in the Greene
County Jail. Nannie Lee was said to be a strikingly handsome
woman who tended to their old farmhouse in Maxeys, Georgia,
and minded her brood of children. I never knew my grandmother
and grandfather Tarpley. They both died before I was born.

My father, Ruben Lindsey Tarpley, was their sixth son, born
in 1908. Like his older brothers, he quit school at a young age to
help the family work their small farm. Daddy grew to become a
slim, athletic boy with almond-shaped brown eyes, long eyelashes and wavy black hair. He and his brothers all excelled at
sandlot baseball when they were growing up.

It was also a tradition in the Tarpley family for the sons to
have careers in the military. Daddy's older brother Charlie, for
instance, was gassed in World War I and spent the rest of his life
on military disability. His brothers John and Ivan both enlisted in
the then-new Army Air Corps as teenagers. Daddy followed their
lead when he enlisted in the Army Infantry at age twenty.

During his eleven years in the service, Daddy made his mark, not surprisingly, as a company baseball player. The Schofield Barracks in Honolulu still have the trophies to prove his prowess. Although only five foot seven, he excelled as a left-handed pitcher and fantasized about a professional career with his dream team, the New York Yankees, when his tour of duty ended. He rose to the rank of sergeant but decided not to reenlist when his superiors couldn't guarantee that he'd remain in Hawaii. So Daddy returned to Greene County in 1939.

That's where he met my mother. Her name was Annie Grayce Yarbrough. She was a petite, gray-eyed brunette, thirteen years his junior. Mother was born in 1921, just a few years before the Depression.

Mother told me that her father, Randall Isaac Yarbrough, tried anything and everything he could to make a living. He cut stone in the quarries; he farmed. Times were hard when she was small. After the stock market crashed in 1929, Mother said, "You couldn't hardly buy a job."

Because Mother's father had no brothers and sisters, there was no family to fall back on. He and my grandmother, the former Lucy Emma Wilson, had ten children to raise. Granny was a strong country woman, one quarter Cherokee, with a deep, sustaining faith. Mother and her siblings were raised with a powerful work ethic, a will to survive and an abiding, bedrock Baptist religious foundation. They grew up singing in church, and other members of the Yarbrough clan played guitar and piano.

Like the Tarpleys, most of the Yarbroughs had little formal education.

"I went as far as the eighth grade in school," says Grayce Tarpley, "but that was further than any of my brothers and sisters. Back then you had to buy your books. And as the grades got

higher, the books got more expensive and you needed more of them. And my parents couldn't afford it.

"We all had to go to work as kids. I went to work right away after I left school. I clerked in the five-and-dime store in downtown Greensboro; I babysat; I did gobs of things. Then I'd give all the money to Mama so she could buy material—she was a wonderful seamstress, and she made all our clothes.

"I met Ruben when I was babysitting his little sister. He had just got out of the service. I guess I was eighteen or so; and he began to take me out. My parents would let us date, but we weren't allowed to go to dances or anywhere where alcohol might be served. We'd go to friends' houses or to church functions. He didn't have a car, so we walked everywhere we went. He was about thirteen years older, but that didn't make no difference. It's been a long time ago—I don't remember how, but he just asked me to marry him, you know? My parents didn't say anything, so I guess it was all right. We went to South Carolina—he had some cousins that lived there—and went to a justice of the peace. Nobody but me and him. It was February 15, 1940."

Like thousands of other rural folks, my parents headed to Atlanta as newlyweds. The city had hosted the gala premiere of *Gone With the Wind* just two months before their arrival. The thunderclouds of World War II were rumbling now; and that conflict would bring previously unheard-of prosperity to the city. During the next four years, new industries flowed into Atlanta, creating thousands of jobs.

My parents lived in various small apartments while Daddy worked at Nabisco, doing everything from packing cookies in boxes to working on the loading dock. By the time their first child, my older sister Linda, was born in 1941, they were living in the central business district in a sparsely furnished apartment on Edgewood Avenue, next to the heart of the historically black neighborhood known as "Sweet Auburn." I've since learned that just one block north of Edgewood was the Auburn Avenue home of the Reverend Martin Luther King, whose Ebenezer Baptist Church was just two blocks further on. His son, the future Reverend Martin Luther King Jr., would grow to become that same church's pastor and would eventually help change the face of race relations in America. But in 1941, he was a twelve-year-old boy playing just blocks away when Mother and Daddy were beginning their family there.

I think it must have been a sobering experience for Daddy when he brought Mother and baby Linda back to the bustling neighborhood from Grady Hospital on that chilly March morning. The medical facility was only six blocks away, but it must have seemed like a million mental miles from the tradewinds, palm trees and Polynesian beauties of Hawaii, where he'd been just twenty-four months earlier. Daddy was thirty-three years old and facing real family responsibility for the first time in his life. His brothers John and Ivan would retire to Georgia from their military careers with steady pension checks to last the rest of their lives. I feel sure he wondered what would have become of him if he had done the same. What if he had stayed in the Army? What if he had never come home? What if he had remained footloose and single? That little Edgewood Avenue apartment had probably never looked so confining to him.

If he dared to dream of his lost island paradise, Daddy would have had a chilling awakening later that year. On December 7, 1941, the Japanese attacked Pearl Harbor, killing 2,400 servicemen and obliterating many military installations. If he had stayed there, he might have become a statistic instead of a new father. John, his brother, was discharged in 1944 because of arthritis. But his brother Ivan, who'd been stationed in Hawaii at the same time as Daddy, was captured by the Japanese in the Philippines and spent 1942–45 in a prisoner-of-war camp.

With America aflame in a national emergency and with little more than their clothes as possessions, Mother, Daddy and baby Linda left Atlanta.

"We kind of felt out of place in Atlanta," Grayce reports. "Life in the city wasn't as bad as it is today, but neither of us was really comfortable there. So we headed back east on Highway 278. Ruben didn't own a car, so one of my brothers came to get us."

Mother and Daddy went to work in cotton mills, and during the next few years they lived in various small towns around central Georgia. Cotton mill work was long hours, low-paying and monotonous. With wartime prosperity at a peak, Daddy eventually thought another move to Atlanta might be the smart thing to do. So about a year later, Mother, Daddy and Linda returned to the city. This time, they settled in the southwest part of downtown in yet another small, furnished apartment on Windsor Avenue. Jobs were plentiful, and Daddy had learned carpentry from Mother's brother-in-law, Harry England. That meant he could easily land jobs in construction in the booming wartime metropolis.

Atlanta. World War II. Poverty and promise. Lost dreams and wishful thinking. A cold winter with hopes for a warm tomorrow. This is the backdrop for the start of my story.

♪

I was born Brenda Mae Tarpley on December 11, 1944, in the charity ward of Atlanta's Emory University Hospital. I was premature by a month and weighed a big, fat four pounds, eleven ounces.

They took my middle name from my mother's oldest sister, my aunt Aeola Mae. She was a fiery, determined kind of lady. I remember her as a big, robust woman who always had a welcoming smile and a bosom you could get lost in when she hugged you. She was constantly cooking something for everybody in the family. Mother says she picked "Brenda" for my first name because she wanted something special and different for me. That wasn't a common name back then. Daddy nicknamed me his "Bootie Mae."

"Don't Fence Me In" was at the top of the Hit Parade in December 1944, and that might have been our family theme song. During the next nine years, we would move eight more times. The first destination was back to Mother and Daddy's hometown of Greensboro. Although Daddy's parents had died by this time, his brothers still lived there; and besides, he and Mother were both able to get jobs in the local cotton mill. Once settled back in Greensboro, Daddy returned to his love of the national pastime.

"I remember that time so well," says sister Linda Tarpley. "I recall going to see my father pitch for the cotton mill baseball team. And I have even more vivid memories of little Brenda, because it was amazing that she started to sing. It's hard to say when Brenda first started singing, because she sang from the time she could talk. She liked music even when she was a baby. When she was eight months old, she just loved listening to music on the radio. But it was something really amazing when she started actually singing. When she was about two years old, she could hear a song once on the radio and then whistle the tune perfectly. And sing all the lyrics, too. She did it so easily. Mother was sure it was a God-given talent.

"There was an old country store down the road from our house in Greensboro. I would take three-year-old Brenda by the hand, and we would skip along to its front steps. Inside, tiny Brenda would be picked up to stand right beside the candy jar on the rustic wooden counter. She'd sing happily while I collected

pockets full of change that the amused customers would toss. Afterwards, we would run home excitedly to dump it out on our old kitchen table. Then we'd head back the very next day to play this fun game all over again."

One of my earliest memories is of going to that hot, dusty ballpark near the Greensboro mill to sing "Take Me Out to the Ballgame" for Daddy and his teammates. Daddy always had the biggest smile; he'd scoop me up into his arms and put me on his shoulders while everyone clapped. I couldn't have been more than three or so.

The other thing I remember about music and entertainment was our old radio. I don't remember what kind it was, but it was a plastic table model that ran on a battery. It would fade in and out with static when you turned it on. It was a big deal at our house when the Yankees and Dodgers used to play. Mother was the Dodgers fan, and Daddy was for the Yankees. They'd get so worked up, the house would be foggy from the chain-smoking of Mother's Pall Malls and Daddy's Lucky Strikes.

But I also looked forward to Saturday nights. That's when we'd all listen to the Grand Ole Opry. In those days, Eddy Arnold, Bill Monroe, Minnie Pearl, Grandpa Jones, Ernest Tubb and Roy Acuff were the big stars of the show. So was Red Foley, who would later mean so much to me. Ball games, news reports, *Amos 'n Andy* and the Opry—those were the favorites at our house.

By 1945, cotton was gradually fading as the South's cash crop, making my parents' mill jobs ever more tenuous. Daddy took us to the stone quarries of Elberton to seek other work. That's where my little brother Randall was born in the summer of 1949.

I had been the baby of the family now for nearly five years and was wildly jealous of my new baby brother. I didn't like him one little bit. Any time I got the chance, I made his life miserable. I picked on him constantly. My mother remembers one particularly funny story.

"She didn't care for Randall too much," Grayce recalls. "An insurance agent came around one day. I was standing there on the porch trying to talk to him. The next thing I knew, out of the clear blue sky, Brenda interrupted.

" 'Do you have any goats?' Brenda asked him.

" 'No, I don't have any goats,' the startled agent replied. 'What do you want to know about goats for?'

"Brenda answered, 'Oh, I thought if you had a goat, I'd trade you this baby for it.' "

Around this time, Daddy moved us to Conyers, where he found work as a carpenter. Home construction was beginning to accelerate everywhere as thousands of GIs returned from the war. But although he was working steadily now, Daddy's financial situation never really improved. No matter where we moved, we never occupied more than a three-room rental house with no running water or indoor toilet.

And every time our family would get the least bit ahead, it seemed as though something set us back, like a medical bill. I still have a scar on my forehead as a souvenir of one catastrophe.

I climbed on the kitchen counter trying to reach for something and fell. I hit my forehead on the metal spiked spigot of an old-fashioned kerosene can that sat next to the oil stove. My face was covered in blood, and I was screaming bloody murder. Mother was terrified that I'd put out an eye. She rushed me to the local doctor, and he hastily closed the gaping wound with only two stitches.

They weren't big on cosmetic procedures in those days. So to this day I have a scar, right between my eyes. You can still see it in my publicity photos, unless they do some serious airbrushing.

Around the time of my accident, my mother was just a young

woman of twenty-eight, pinching pennies to raise us all; but she and Daddy eventually paid the doctor in full. In 1949, the median income in Georgia was $1,902 per year, and my family was nowhere near that. Mother told me that an income of $20 a week was not uncommon for us.

Things became really bad in 1951 when Daddy broke his arm at work. Our family hit rock bottom. Unable to do carpentry work, he moved us to a tenant farm in Conyers. One-handed though he was, he was right there with us as we all picked cotton side by side on the Turner Farm. This was grindingly menial work. When you pick, your back aches from constantly bending over and then from lugging the full cotton sack. No matter how careful you are, your hands bleed from being pricked by the thorny cotton bolls. And in Georgia, the sun is merciless during picking season. But Daddy did what had to be done. When my ten-year-old sister Linda needed a flute for her school music lessons, he toiled even longer in the fields to earn the $5 to buy her one.

Daddy eventually recovered and got together enough cash later that year for us to move off the tenant farm and go back to our own rental house in downtown Conyers. Us kids have especially vivid memories of this place, since this is where Daddy brought home the family's first clunky black-and-white TV set. This was the first house we ever lived in that had electricity. But the "bathroom" was still outside.

As always, Mother scrimped and somehow made do. Her mama, Lucy Emma, sewed dresses for Linda and me so that we were presentable for our first day at Conyers Elementary School in the fall of 1951.

Linda learned of an annual talent contest that pitted all the schools in the county against one another. Although only a child herself, when she heard her teacher talking about finding talented students, she says she immediately thought of me.

"I knew she could sing, so I thought, 'Well, why not her?'" Linda recalls. *"So I told them I thought my sister ought to be in it. They had a trophy among the schools, and whichever school won it got to keep that trophy for a year, until the next competition. Our school really wanted that trophy bad. They'd never won it.*

"I'll never forget that night of the show. It was the fall of the year and the school's auditorium was packed with people— adults and kids. There was a microphone and stage lights and lots of little performers. But after Brenda sang, the place just went nuts. They were really cheering."

Mother had rolled my curly hair into even tighter pin curls the night before. And, for a change, I got to be the first one in the washtub—while the water was all clean—for my bath. I wasn't a bit nervous. I just thought it was going to be fun. They dressed me up in a puffed-sleeved, bright pink dress that Granny had sewed for me. And I tried desperately not to get it dirty before it was my turn on the stage.

I sang Pee Wee King's Grand Ole Opry favorite, "Slow Poke," then the Nat King Cole ballad "Too Young," both of which were high on the record charts in 1951. Actually, I was vying for two awards at the school contest, one for beauty and one for talent. A cash prize went to the winner of the beauty competition; and that's what I desperately wanted to win. But I lost out to a cutie-pie eighteen-month-old baby. Instead, I brought Conyers the trophy for talent. My reward was a box of King Leo Peppermint Sticks. I was bitterly disappointed—I knew my family needed the money more. To this day, I won't eat peppermint sticks.

There was another talent prize, however, and it would have longer lasting repercussions. I was also invited to appear as a guest on an Atlanta Saturday morning radio show called *Starmakers Revue.*

♪

As the 1950s began, the United States tumbled into modern life as Sony tape recorders, Miss Clairol hair dye, Minute Rice and Diners Club credit cards all hit the market. In Washington, Senator Joe McCarthy was conducting a Communist witch-hunt, and Senator Estes Kefauver's commission was investigating organized crime. In Korea, United Nations forces started suffering setbacks at the hands of the Chinese. On Broadway, *Guys and Dolls, Call Me Madam* and *Peter Pan* premiered, and I grew to love all those shows. In Hollywood, *All About Eve* and *Sunset Boulevard* were the hot, inside showbiz, movie hits. They became favorites of mine, too.

Can you believe that a three-piece Sears bedroom set retailed for $49.98 in 1950? What's more, you could buy a four-door sedan for $2,250, and a brick ranch home in the newfangled communities called "suburbs" sold for $10,000. The minimum wage at the time was 75 cents an hour, but Daddy and the rest of our neighbors didn't even make that much. You have to remember, my parents never owned a home. They didn't have a telephone. They could never buy a car.

The house we lived in on the Covington Highway in Lithonia was made of weathered clapboards. There wasn't any paint on the house and the yard was mostly dirt. It had three rooms with an outhouse. You drew water out of the well, and the ice man would come by in a truck once a week with the ice. See, we had electricity, but we didn't have a refrigerator or anything like that. We had one common bedroom, and all us kids slept together on this sagging old iron bed. We had a primitive fireplace in one room with a big iron grate, and that was our heat source. If you wanted to be cooler in the summertime, you just raised the windows and prayed for a breeze. But that's the way my parents had been brought up. You had a washtub, and you took a bath in that. You didn't stay up late at night and waste electricity; the day was sunup to sundown.

There were kids in my school who had a lot more than we did, and probably not many were worse off than us. But I don't remember anybody making fun of us for being poor. I made friends with girls who lived in town who had running water and refrigerators—much more than we had. But we were clean, and we didn't go raggedy or anything like that. Granny made the most beautiful dresses; and, to us, they looked like they'd come out of a fancy department store.

I tore mine up all the time. No matter how hard I tried, I couldn't keep my outfits clean. My sister Linda and I were truly opposites. Linda was the neat one. She would come home from school looking just like she did when she'd left the house that morning. I'd come home, and my sashes would be torn and my dress would be dirty from playing with the boys. I was definitely the tomboy type, climbing trees and getting on top of barns and everything else. Linda was into the frilly things. Linda had shoe boxes full of paper dolls; I had boxes full of marbles.

There was a pair of blue denim overalls that I loved to wear, the first ones I ever had. As quick as Mama would wash them, I'd grab them off the clothesline and put them back on. One day, Linda brought the measles home from school and gave them to everybody. I happened to have the overalls on when I broke out in spots, and I refused to take them off until I got well. By that time, Mother said they were so dirty that they could stand up on the floor by themselves. To this day, I don't know why I connected those overalls with the measles. Maybe it was just an excuse not to get back into a dress.

Mind you, I didn't have that many dresses to my name. So I'll never forget the night that Daddy burned some of them up. I guess he was what you'd call today a binge drinker. I don't remember him drinking during the week, but on the weekends he and his brother Ivan would sometimes get together and drink whiskey. They'd get all tipsy and Uncle Ivan would say to me, "Bootie Mae, I'll give you a quarter if you'll get me a glass of water" or whatever little thing he wanted at the time. They'd give us so much money that they'd be broke the next morning, and Mother would have to give them the money back.

One night Daddy and Uncle Ivan were really "feeling no pain." There was a fire going in that living room fireplace, the one that kept us warm. The fire got kind of low, I guess, and they didn't feel like getting up to go out and get some wood. We were all in bed. Daddy took two new store-bought dresses that my mother had saved up so hard to buy and burned them for kindling. Mother cried and cried.

Looking back now, I can't believe that I didn't know we were poor, 'cause we really were. You spell that "p-o-o-o-o-r," with four "o's." We knew what it was like to do without. Fruit was practically unknown to us. The only time we'd get oranges was maybe at Christmas. I remember that a lot of the time for lunch, we'd have grease sandwiches. And you know what? I actually liked them. At the time, I was happy; I had people around me who cared about me and loved me; I guess I felt I had all I needed.

The only folks a rung below our family in Lithonia might have been the town's African American residents. Linda, Randall and I probably socialized more with their children than other classmates did, since our threadbare house was on "the wrong side of the tracks." Those were the days of rigid segregation. I remember there were signs everywhere instructing the populace which facility was "white" or "colored"—public toilets, railway station entrances, drinking fountains, theater doors, bus seats.

Blacks attended separate churches and schools and were buried in separate graveyards. Invariably, the "colored" facility was the more rundown and ramshackle. Maybe because we'd lived our lives in similar circumstances, our family was considerably less racist than many other Georgians of the day.

There was a black family up the road, and Linda and I used to go up there and play with their kids. Their mama was a big woman who wore floral housedresses and a handkerchief wrapped on her head. The kids had a homemade contraption they called a "Flying Jenny." It was a piece of wood on a post that spun 'round and 'round, like a spinning seesaw. I loved that thing. Sometimes if it got late, we'd even eat up at their house.

I don't know how I skipped the fact, but as a child, I wasn't aware of the inequality. The separate school was just a fact of life. And the black folks we knew in Lithonia were just part of our daily landscape.

There was an old black man who sat on the porch of a little general store on the edge of town. He played guitar and sang what I now realize was the blues. I don't know where he was from or if he even had a home. And I never knew his name. But I was fascinated with him and would stand there and listen to him whenever we went up there to shop. He was always in tattered clothes but seemed content to be there playing for tips. And, boy, could he sing and play.

I'd stay outside and listen to him for as long as Linda would let me. Then I'd go inside. There'd be people in there and the store owner would say, "C'mon, Brenda, sing us a song." I'd stand next to those old rickety grocery shelves and sing their requests. Then they'd give Linda and me pieces of candy.

I never did sing with that old man outside on the porch, but his music left a deep impression on me. If I had to point to two major influences on whatever my singing style turned out to be, it would be rhythm and blues and the old-time Southern gospel music.

Life in Lithonia for us Tarpley kids was a carefree round of schoolwork, playtime and chores. Since he was a carpenter, Daddy made almost all of our toys. I particularly remember slingshots, wooden cars, boats and little whittled figures. Every Friday on payday, he brought home three packages of pink Kitt's candy taffy, one for each of us. Mother and Daddy were affectionate parents, seldom physically disciplining us children. They particularly encouraged us in our studies. Linda was and still is especially smart. And since she's the oldest, she also has the most vivid memories of our father.

"I'd describe him as quiet man," Linda reports. "He wasn't antisocial or withdrawn, but more like simply quiet. He liked music a lot—his daddy had played the fiddle some. And he placed a lot of importance on reading. Daddy read a lot, and he always told me that if I read my local newspaper every day, I could keep up with the world. And every payday, he'd buy me a book. I remember having stacks and stacks of children's books."

Linda was Mother's little helper. She enjoyed the household chores of washing clothes, scrubbing floors and cooking simple meals. Even as a ten-year-old, responsible, conscientious Linda was placed in charge of my little brother Randall—especially on weekends. Because that's when Mother and I would have our "day out."

Each Saturday, we would board the bus in downtown Lithonia to travel to Atlanta for my radio appearances on *Starmakers Revue*. These appearances had come about after I won the Conyers school talent contest the previous fall. Despite my initial disappointment at not winning any cash, these weekly trips turned out to be a big treat for me. I wasn't paid for the radio show, but the sponsor was Borden's Ice Cream. And they gave me all the ice cream that I could eat. I was in hog heaven.

In addition to the Saturday radio performances in Atlanta, I was expected to be up bright and early every Sunday to sing solos at East Lithonia Baptist Church. The tidy, picture-postcard, white clapboard house of worship was across the railroad tracks on the other side of town from our modest home. "Uncle Rob" Wilson was the preacher.

He was Mother's first cousin. His church wasn't exactly a Primitive Baptist congregation. It didn't involve speaking in tongues or any of that kind of stuff, either. But they had ritual foot washings, like Jesus had at the Last Supper, and we baptized in the river. That's the way I was baptized, dressed in my little white dress, submerged in the running waters.

Church was a big part of Mother's life. That was our socializing—Wednesday night prayer meetings, Sundays and other days. So my background as a singer has a lot of gospel influence. Mahalia Jackson was an idol of mine. And my mother used to sing me Hank Williams gospel songs all the time.

Going to church was like going to a family reunion. Afterward, there were often long stay-overs at my cousins' houses. Big evening meals with kinfolk and large get-togethers were common within our extended family. Mother's brother Cecil and her sister Irene were particularly close to us. In fact, Uncle Cecil often drove Mother and me to my weekend shows.

At the time, Atlantans amused themselves at what were called "family dances." These weekly occasions were designed so that parents could take their children with them to evening outings. Boots Woodall and his band the Wranglers were the stars of these festive get-togethers. Dashing, single Cecil Yarbrough was right in the middle of it all. And because of him, so were Mother and I.

Recalls Grayce, "My brother Cecil went up there one week-end and told them, 'How about letting my little niece sing? She can really sing.' Well, you know how they are. They said, 'Oh, a little girl can't sing.' But after Cecil kept after them, they finally said, 'Well, what can she sing?' And my brother said, 'Anything your band can play.'

"So we took Brenda and she sang there at the Sports Arena in Atlanta. Then they wanted her to come back again, you know, because she was drawing people into the place. So we started going there on Saturday nights."

Because of my popularity with the Wranglers at the Sports Arena, the musicians invited me to appear with them at a concert at the Tower Theater. This glittering old movie house was one of the city's more prestigious venues. Lots of big touring stars stopped there to put on shows. I wasn't a big name act, of course, but every time I roared into my Hank Williams repertoire, people seemed to really love it. Before long, the band invited me to become a regular on its weekly television show, *TV Ranch*.

The influence of radio as a talent showcase was waning. The new craze was television. The first commercially available sets flickered to life in 1947–48. On June 20, 1948, *The Ed Sullivan Show* debuted. It would become a staple of Sunday night variety programming for more than two decades to come and would have an incredible impact on my career.

In 1951, all three of Atlanta's television stations launched country variety programs. I really lucked out by landing on the best of them. WAGA-TV's show, *TV Ranch* on Channel 5, was the first to go on the air. Hosted by the genial John Farmer, it became by far the most popular and lasted the longest. It debuted on January 15, 1951, with an act that was already a hit with Atlantans, the Radio Wranglers. Dennis "Boots" Woodall was the band's leader and steel guitarist. By the time I met Boots and his buddies, they'd changed their name to "TV Wranglers" to reflect their new renown as idols of the small screen.

In the fall of 1952, I made my debut on *TV Ranch* with the jaunty Hank Williams bopper, "Hey, Good Lookin'." I was seven years old.

"Viewers were doubtless stunned," observes author Mary Bufwack. "Brenda Mae Tarpley was one of those extraordinary, once-in-a-generation individuals, a prodigy so gifted that melody was as natural to her as breath," Bufwack wrote in her ground-breaking survey of women's music, Finding Her Voice. *"Her performances were not little-kid, wobbly-pitch, wispy-thin attempts. Even as a tot, she delivered full-throated, adult-strength songs. Brenda had a naturally chesty tone with decided blues shadings. She was armed with the booming power of Mahalia Jackson and the hillbilly heart of Hank Williams; and she attacked each number as if it were her last. A natural showman, she'd sometimes allow a growl or a clever hiccup vocal effect to punctuate her performances. She had an innate sense of timing, rhythm and finesse."*

"She never showed one sign of stage fright or self doubt," Grayce remembers. "On the other hand, there was nothing 'showbizzy' about her. Brenda seemed completely unaffected by her talent and the way people responded to it. She'd play little-kid games on the way to the shows, sit quietly on the side of the stage waiting for her turn, get up, do her showstopping song and just matter-of-factly return to her doll or comic book."

I'm sorry that no shows survive from the live *TV Ranch* broadcasts—local shows were seldom saved. But Mother recalls my repertoire at the time consisting of Hank Williams tunes, "Take Me Out to the Ballgame," gospel numbers, Eddy Arnold's tearjerker "My Daddy Is Only a Picture" and pop favorites by Frank Sinatra, Tony Bennett or Peggy Lee. I also loved to sing the songs I heard on the Grand Ole Opry radio broadcasts from Nashville.

The first major Opry star I met was Faron Young, who was the headliner at the Tower Theater concert with the TV Wranglers. Faron had recorded his first top-10 hit that fall, the toe-tapping song "Goin' Steady." But just as his fortunes were rising, he was drafted and sent to Ft. McPherson, Georgia. He once told me, "I cried like a rat eating a red onion when I was drafted." He was always the life of the party. Faron talked the Army into featuring him on recruitment shows with the Wranglers. So he'd perform in uniform, as he did at the Tower Theater show when both he and I sang with the band.

I thought he looked so important in his uniform. Of course, I was only seven at the time, but he treated Mother and me like queens. Mother always liked Faron a whole lot. They'd always joke backstage, and as everyone knows, Faron had that wickedly bawdy sense of humor. No matter where or when I saw him throughout my career, he'd always ask about Mother. He always thought she was such a beautiful woman.

We became lifelong friends. Faron always sang such great songs—"Sweet Dreams," "Hello Walls," "It's Four in the Morning" and all of those. I loved doing shows with him. Over the next thirty-five years, we worked shows together off and on. I was always close to his wife and kids, too. And after I married, he and my husband Ronnie became good friends and hung out together.

In the 1980s after I started having big country hits, I'd see him backstage at all kinds of events. We'd go Christmas caroling together with Hank Williams Jr. and go bug Mel Tillis and Webb Pierce. Half the time, when they saw it was Faron coming, they wouldn't open the door. So we'd sing louder and bang on the door until they came. That's one of my fondest memories, going Christmas caroling with Faron.

So, I'll never forget it. I'd just come in off the road when I heard the news that Faron had shot and killed himself on December 10, 1996. It was the day before my birthday. I felt so empty. Maybe a lot of us had let him down. How could we have not known that he was in such a state of mind for something like that to happen? He was so vital, one of the most alive and zany people I've ever known. They say he left a note, but the family never made it public. I don't know for sure, but maybe he thought that the business he loved so much had forgotten him, that his career was over.

The only thing that did my heart good about it all was when I got to announce him as an inductee into the Country Music Hall of Fame in 2000. I just wish he could have gotten that during his lifetime. Maybe it would have saved him. Or at least he would have known how much he mattered in my life and in the lives of so many other fans.

In addition to Faron Young, there were other country celebrities that I got to meet on the *TV Ranch* shows in 1952 and 1953. The Master Workers Quartet sang the gospel music that I had learned to love back home in Lithonia. After meeting them in Atlanta, I began traveling with the group to its performances.

I sang gospel with them, and they'd harmonize behind me. We'd go to high schools or VFW halls. I wasn't paid; we more or less did it just for the love of singing. Besides, a lot of it was in churches.

Another *TV Ranch* star who became particularly important to me was Joseph A. "Cotton" Carrier, who was practically a legend to Atlanta's country fans by then. The radio veteran joined *TV Ranch* just months before I became a regular on the show at age seven. He and his wife, country performer Jane Logan, took Mother and me under their wings. After the TV show aired live in the early afternoon, we would spend the remainder of the day at the Carriers' house in Atlanta. I would play with Cotton's daughters all day, then we'd all head for the Sports Arena together for the Wranglers' night show.

The TV Wranglers were paid for their Sports Arena concerts. But for me, the band would simply "pass the hat" for donations. It was like playing for tips, but Mother says she figured the stage experience was worth it. She was right. I could hardly wait to get up there on that stage.

The Sports Arena was this huge ballroom-style dance hall with colored lights. The stage was pretty high up, or at least it seemed like it to me. The band guys treated me like I was one of their own. They looked after me and were so sweet and protective. I remember the owner of the Sports Arena built me a little step stool so that I could reach the water fountain. And they always had Coke boxes for me to stand on when it was my turn to sing, because the microphone wouldn't go down low enough to reach me. I really looked forward to those trips to Atlanta.

I loved it whenever Uncle Cecil would drive us to a show, because then I'd get to jitterbug with him, and I loved to dance. He could dance up a blue streak and was movie-star handsome. The women were all over him.

Those Saturdays in Atlanta must have seemed like another world to Mother, too. From our meager three-room house in Lithonia and her grueling workweek of household drudgery, she was transported to a weekly vacation where people laughed and sang, audiences cheered, couples danced, musicians joked and the lights shone brightly. For a few hours, at least, I think life was merry for her.

Back home, Daddy was bursting with pride. Brainy Linda won a slot on an Atlanta TV quiz show called *Juvenile Jury*. Mother says that his watching that and seeing his "Bootie Mae" singing on TV were as much a highlight in his life as her travels were in hers.

Daddy used to say to me, "You're going to be a big star one day, Bootie Mae, but I won't live to see it." Looking back, I wonder if he had some sort of premonition. Did he know he was sick? I guess I'll always wonder about that.

He was a tough, tough, tough guy. He was like Mother. They were both tough—whatever came their way, they faced it. They were people with a lot of resilience.

Mother would need all the strength that she could muster in the months to come. In May 1953, Daddy and his brother-in-law Harry went to work like they had so many days before. The construction job was over near Atlanta. During that seemingly ordinary workday, our world turned upside down. A worker on a scaffold above Daddy accidentally dropped a hammer. It struck Daddy on the head, knocking him unconscious. He was rushed to St. Joseph's Hospital, where emergency surgery revealed a brain abscess. Doctors told Mother afterward that the blow had fatally disturbed a preexisting condition. My daddy, Ruben Lindsey Tarpley, age forty-four, died on May 23, 1953. I was eight years old.

The funeral was held at Mann-Walden Funeral Home in Lithonia. Most people who packed into the place mourned in stunned silence. It was such a shock to the community, because he was so young.

"They had shaved Daddy's head during the brain surgery," says sister Linda, *"so I remember Mother had put a Yankees ball cap on him in the casket, in honor of his favorite team. Uncle J. B. in Elberton carved the headstone—he was in that business—it was gray Georgia granite. We buried Daddy in the East View Cemetery in Conyers."*

I just remember being so terribly sad. One of my biggest sorrows is that I never had the chance to really get to know my fa-

ther. Even today, I literally dream of what it would have been like
to have him in my life.

Mother was pretty much devastated, especially because of
the way it happened. I was only a child, but I distinctly remember
that none of us had any good clothes to wear to the funeral, and
there was no money to buy anything. Mother had to borrow
money from her relatives to outfit us. I don't know how long it
took, but somehow Mother eventually paid them back.

*"We were broke," says Grayce. "It took six weeks to even get
Social Security. That's why we went to live with my sister Irene,
because we didn't have anywhere else to go. The insurance company tried to take Ruben's life insurance policy away from me, so
I couldn't get as much as my policy said I should. I had to fight
them to get the $500, even though it was there in black and white.
While that was going on, my sister and I went to see if I could get
some help, like welfare, but they wouldn't do it because of the Social Security. So we were never on welfare. Just the families taking care of each other.*

*"We also settled with the construction company about the
accident. They offered us a lump sum, I don't remember how
much. But I took a long-range payment of $20.40 a week for so
many years. And that was it."*

Mother, Linda, Randall and I moved into Aunt Irene's two-
story house on Chupp Road in Lithonia. We occupied three of the
downstairs rooms. Nothing fancy—it had electricity, but still no
running water or indoor toilet. Always determined and plucky,
Mother somehow talked the local bank into giving her a loan to
build her own little brick house on Klondike Road in Lithonia.
This one had plumbing, a Tarpley family first.

Mother has great tenacity. She's always been tough and
doesn't let anything get her down. She's had a hard life but has

never dwelled on that. Looking back, I think I got my grit and my strength from watching her. I found out early in life, you just do whatever has to be done. Mother has always had a great attitude.

My mother, Grayce Tarpley, was a thirty-two-year-old widowed mother with no means of support and no prospects for the future. Except one. Sometime during this period, I was paid for the first time for singing. Family members' memories differ regarding the exact occasion. Some say it was a Shriners' Club luncheon. Some say it was a political rally. Others recall it as a Poultry Convention. But we all agree that at least one of the earliest paying gigs was $35 for performing for a civic group in Swainsboro, Georgia. That would be the equivalent of more than a week's wages for any working man in rural Georgia at the time.

After my father died, it became necessary for me to help out. I was the only one making any money. But I was having a ball doing the thing I loved best. I wasn't making any great amounts or anything like that. But it was better than my mother having to work in a cotton mill every day.

Mostly the shows were on weekends, but sometimes we'd be asked to appear on weeknights. I'd be so tired some mornings that Miss Norton, my third grade teacher, would let me put my head down on the desk and sleep.

The bus driver who made the regular run between Augusta and Atlanta along Route 278 had become familiar with Mother and me, because we boarded his bus every Saturday morning. I don't know how he knew this, but one day he suggested to Mother that the producers of *Peach Blossom Special* on Channel 12, WRDW-TV in Augusta, would be willing to pay for me to become a regular cast member there. Up to this time all my appearances on *TV Ranch* in Atlanta had been done for free.

An offer for regular money sounded awfully good. So while us kids were out of school in the summer of 1954, Mother went to

Augusta and approached television personality J. T. "Pee Wee" Devore during a rehearsal of *Peach Blossom Special*. He agreed to listen to me and in turn approached WRDW program director Sammy Barton about it. That's when Mr. Barton suggested I change my name from Brenda Mae Tarpley to "Brenda Lee," an abbreviation of my last name.

So on August 27, 1954, at age nine, "Brenda Lee" was booked to debut on *Peach Blossom Special*. Our family headed out Highway 278, this time out of Lithonia, past Conyers, past Mother and Daddy's Greensboro homeland and all the way to the end of the line, Augusta.

The Ozark Jubilee

I didn't know it, but a musical explosion was about to detonate in American life. In 1954, the year that I headed for Augusta, the Georgia music scene was alive with promise. Such talents as Ray Charles, Gladys Knight, Jerry Reed, Bill Anderson, Little Richard, James Brown and Otis Redding were all beginning their careers in the Peach Tree State at the same time I was.

But in my opinion, no other musical event of the year would transform the culture more than the release of "That's All Right Mama"/ "Blue Moon of Kentucky," the debut single by Memphis truck driver Elvis Presley. Although the nation at large would not take notice of him for many months to come, we Georgians and the rest of the South immediately began rocking to "The Hillbilly Cat." Elvis had a new sound that was soon dubbed "rockabilly," a style that combined the roadhouse rawness of honky-tonk music with the upbeat tempo of rhythm and blues.

My bopping Hank Williams tunes seemed to fit right in with the musical climate of the day. To my delight, I was an immediate hit with *Peach Blossom Special* TV viewers in Augusta. Mother says that offers began coming in from throughout the region for me to perform at regional concerts on weekends. So I began to tour as an entertainer.

But Mother missed her family. She'd held on to our house
in Lithonia and thought she could parlay my status as an Augusta professional into making even more money in Atlanta. So
we moved back to the familiarity and security of the Lithonia
house on Klondike Road. And our commuting to Georgia's capital resumed.

This move turned out to have quite an impact on our lives.
Late that year, Mother met twenty-year-old Buell "Jay" Rainwater at one of my Sports Arena shows in the big city. A speedy
courtship ensued.

The product of a successful dairy farming family in southern
Ohio, Jay was a natural salesman who was drawn to show business as a result of his teenaged employment at the Jimmie Skinner Music Center in nearby Cincinnati. Thirteen years Mother's
junior, tall and charismatic Jay swept her off her feet. Within two
months, they were married by a justice of the peace. There was
no honeymoon.

The newlywed Rainwaters immediately moved to Cincinnati
with my five-year-old brother Randall and me in tow. I had just
turned ten; Linda, who was thirteen, opted to stay behind with
Mother's sister Irene in Georgia. She disliked Jay and was tired
of changing schools.

In Cincinnati, Jay went back to work at Jimmie Skinner's and
quickly tried to take charge of my career. Naturally, he booked
me to perform at the record shop every weekend. Jimmie Skinner's radio broadcast came from his store on the powerful
WCKY station, whose signal reached throughout the South and
Midwest. The show was pretty influential in country music, so I
know I must have had some kind of audience.

I don't remember a whole lot about Cincinnati, because we
were there such a short time. I do remember that the record shop

was long and narrow, with a small stage set up at the back. We'd do the broadcasts from there. Then I'd travel with Jimmie Skinner and his band to do shows in nearby Kentucky towns like Covington and Newport.

We lived in a high-rise apartment building close to the downtown business district. The thing I recall most about the whole experience was that we were still poor, and that I got to see a really big snowfall for the first time in my life. It was bitterly cold.

Me singing in the Ohio River town might have seemed like a good idea to Jay, but it essentially meant starting over. In Cincinnati, I was a complete unknown. So within a matter of months, it was back to *Peach Blossom Special* and weekend shows around Georgia. Appearing on a competing TV show in Augusta was Charlie "Peanut" Faircloth. He'd had a regional hillbilly hit with "I'll Sail My Ship Alone," and I'd performed with him on *TV Ranch* in Atlanta.

"Oh, she was red-hot down there," recalls Peanut. "I moved to Augusta in the summer of 1955. Went to work at WRDW, the same radio station that James Brown later bought. While I was over there, I was probably the first in the state of Georgia to play one of Elvis Presley's records on the radio.

"On TV, the Peach Blossom Special *was competing with me. My show was* Peanut Faircloth and the Hot-Roasted Hillbillies. *Brenda was first on the* Peach Blossom Special, *and then she came over to do some guest shots on my program."*

Sticking with his record-shop experience, my stepfather Jay Rainwater hooked up with an Augusta backer to open the Brenda Lee Record Shop on Broad Street. Peanut Faircloth was recruited for $10 a show to broadcast on WRDW radio from the store every Saturday with me.

Peanut was a natural for the job. He is just four feet eight inches tall. "I don't watch a lot of basketball—it's way over my head," he quips. As a little person himself, he was the perfect partner for somebody as small as I was.

"We might have been small in stature, but Brenda and I were a giant hit with the populace," recalls Peanut. "It was mobbed on the days we did shows. They had to have policemen directing traffic. Brenda, who was only ten years old, was in a trance when she saw those crowds for the first time. She was standing there with her mouth open. It was a mixture of everybody in town—she really drew a crowd. It amazed me."

I still remember my record-shop jingle. It went like this:

> *Brother if you want to get the lowdown*
> *Come on down and let's all have a hoedown*
> *At the Brenda Lee Record Shop Saturday at three*
> *With the Brenda Lee Jamboree!*

A man walked the sidewalk in front of the store wearing a sandwich board advertising my appearances there. Peanut was the emcee, the guitar player and basically the full band for us, not to mention the ad salesman for the show. He and I would alternate songs for three hours during our live broadcasts.

We were brave; we wouldn't try that now. Heck, even today I only do an hour and a half in concert! But we could do it. In fact, we'd run out of time before we'd run out of songs. We made it up as we went along.

"I remember selling radio ads to an Augusta appliance store," says Peanut with a chuckle. "They told me to say that anybody who brought in a washtub or bucket or anything like that to trade in, they'd get a big discount on a washing machine. So I did. I asked the store how it went. They said, 'Man, I'll tell

you, you have listeners. Within five minutes from the time you started plugging it, the store filled up. Didn't sell a single appliance. None of their credit was any good.' I said, 'Nobody listens to us but bums and deadbeats?' "

At the time, I was attending North Augusta Elementary School. Linda rejoined the family and started junior high in Augusta. Our family was living in an apartment on Lionel Street off Gordon Highway. On September 12, 1955, Jay and Mother became parents to a three months premature infant girl they named Robyn Renee. The baby was so small that she slept in a dresser drawer in the apartment and was outfitted in doll clothing.

Jay continued to book shows for me. In fact, it evidently became his full-time occupation.

Peanut Faircloth recalls, "I don't think he did anything else. Brenda was sort of the bread and butter. He didn't have any trouble getting her on shows. She told me then that she liked to sing, but that she liked to go to school, too. I don't think she got enough sleep. I remember her being tired all the time."

On February 23, 1956, Peanut was hired to emcee a big country show at Augusta's Bell Auditorium. It was a concert hall that I had played more than a dozen times before. The headliner on this occasion was Red Foley, one of the biggest superstars in country music. Mr. Foley had left the Grand Ole Opry in July 1954 to star on *The Ozark Jubilee* in Springfield, Missouri. This made history as country music's first major network variety program when it debuted on ABC-TV in January 1955.

"I was there as the emcee," recalls Peanut. "Grayce and Jay came backstage and asked me to take eleven-year-old Brenda to meet Red Foley. They wanted him to let her sing a song on the show that night. So I got with the promoter and said, 'Look, we've got this little girl. She and I are doing this radio program

together, and she's got the town by the tail. How about letting her sing a couple of songs?'"

I guess that Peanut Faircloth's showbiz clout and say-so were sufficient. Show organizers agreed to put me on the program.

Recalled Foley later, "I still get cold chills every time I think about the first time I heard that voice. About midway through the show we put her on, and she reared back and let go. One foot started patting rhythm like she was putting out a prairie fire, and not another fiber of her little body moved.

"And when she did that trick of breaking her voice, it jarred me enough to realize I'd forgotten to get off the stage after introducing her. There I stood, after twenty-six years of supposedly learning how to conduct myself on stage, with my mouth open and a glassy stare in my eyes."

Mr. Foley truly was a veteran professional. If you read about him in the Country Music Hall of Fame, you'll learn that Clyde Julian "Red" Foley was a Kentucky native. He'd initially come to fame in 1931 on Chicago's *National Barn Dance*, the earliest of all the country network-radio shows. He was a radio celebrity on both Kentucky's *Renfro Valley Barn Dance* and Tennessee's Grand Ole Opry before rising to national television renown at *The Ozark Jubilee*.

Disc stardom for Mr. Foley arrived in 1941 with the sentimental "Old Shep," but the honey-voiced baritone really hit his stride with 1950's "Chattanoogie Shoe Shine Boy," which was Nashville's first million-selling country hit. By the time the cameras of Springfield made him a household personality in 1955, he'd immortalized such tunes as "Goodnight Irene," "Peace in the Valley" and "Alabama Jubilee." He recorded with everyone from Kitty Wells to Lawrence Welk and even shared stages with silver-screen cowboy Gene Autry, so I guess he thought he had pretty much seen it all.

"The way I stood back and enjoyed watching her work," Foley reminisced, *"I felt guilty for not going out to the box office and buying a ticket."*

"She came out and sang 'Jambalaya,' " recalls Peanut Faircloth. *"After she finished, Red ran over and picked her up into his arms and hugged her. 'Sing it again for me, honey,' he said. She did about seven or eight encores."*

Another guy who was there that night was Lou Black. He was the program director at KWTO, the radio home of *The Ozark Jubilee* in Springfield. Coincidentally, Lou wore another hat as the talent booker of the show's new TV incarnation. He evidently wasted no time backstage after I sang. Peanut tells me that Lou quickly drew up a contract and presented it to Mother, right then and there. The document offered me cast membership on the national TV program and instantly made him my manager.

Our whole family celebrated by attending Elvis Presley's debut performance in Augusta a few weeks later. On March 20, 1956, Elvis performed at the same Bell Auditorium where I'd just sung with Mr. Foley. My fifteen-year-old sister Linda was particularly thrilled. "Heartbreak Hotel" had just been released as the King's first national hit.

Somebody took us backstage to meet him. You can't imagine how excited Linda was. He put his arm around her and kissed her cheek. I'm telling you what.

I was as mesmerized as Linda. Of course, you couldn't hear a word he sang all night, because all the girls were screaming and hollering and carrying on. What I remember is, he was driving a pink Cadillac. I'd never seen a car like that. Elvis and I would cross paths many times in the years to come, and we remained friends until his death in 1977.

A few days after the concert, Mother and I boarded a bus for the overland trip to Springfield, Missouri, the home of *The Ozark*

Jubilee. There were no interstates, and we changed buses at least three times. I think the trip took nearly twenty-four hours all told. But I didn't complain. I was excited. On March 29, 1956, I repeated my performance of the Hank Williams Cajun rave-up "Jambalaya" for the national television audience. Once again, Mr. Foley was beaming at me while I sang in my starched-petticoat Sunday best. During the coming weeks, he would become as dear to me as a member of my own family.

He was one of the sweetest, most gentle men I've ever met. The way he appeared on TV was exactly like he was in real life, completely warm and completely natural. I think that's the quality that people fell in love with when they saw him. He had the ability to make you feel right at home and at ease. I was only a child; he used to call me his "Little Bit." And I felt like I was real special in his life.

Without him, his kindness and his belief in me, I never would have had the career I've had. There's no question in my mind about that. He's the one who opened the door and unselfishly nurtured me during what I now realize was the most pivotal moment of my childhood career.

Mother thought he was a very classy guy, because he treated her with such respect. Everyone on the set seemed to love him as much as I did. He closed every show by waving his hand at the camera and saying, "G'night, Mama; G'night, Papa." And he always was like a father to me. But the adult cast members of the show now recall that live television sent him into a constant mental crisis. Those who knew him say he was a deeply troubled person with sharply contrasting mood swings. Apparently he would go from periods of dark depression to sunny optimism, perhaps the result of a lifelong struggle with alcohol. I never, ever saw that side of him. Singer-songwriter Mel Tillis, one of Mr. Foley's best friends, has more insight than I did.

"What I remember most is the guilt he felt [about drinking]," says superstar Mel Tillis. *"I met him at* The Ozark Jubilee *and later spent a lot of time with him when he'd come to Nashville to look for songs. We'd spend three or four days together drinking—he'd tell stories and sing those beautiful gospel songs. Then he'd talk about his parents and cry. He was a lovable guy."*

Looking at surviving tapes of the show, the camaraderie between Mr. Foley and me is pretty obvious. When I watch those old shows, he's smiling down at me like a doting father.

The Ozark Jubilee was broadcast from a 1910 vaudeville hall called the Jewell Theater built on a commercial strip in downtown Springfield. Pulsating neon surrounded its marquee. Inside, the auditorium's proscenium stage was wide and deep. After sets were built and painted during the week, Mr. Foley and the cast assembled each Friday for rehearsals.

By today's standards, the shows were pretty loose. Lines were flubbed, sets collapsed, camera shots were missed and boom mikes loomed into the nation's view. Part of the glue that held the whole thing together was a superbly adaptable band. Plus, Lou Black booked virtually every Nashville notable for the broadcasts, including Johnny Cash, Roy Acuff, Minnie Pearl, Eddy Arnold, Gene Autry, Tex Ritter and Bob Wills. Little noted at the time was guest singer Colleen Carroll, who would become the mother of '90s megastar Garth Brooks.

After the very first broadcast, more than 25,000 fan letters were reportedly received by the network. I remember that each week, cameras would pan across the sold-out live audience, whose members would merrily hold up signs boasting of their hometowns and states. During one broadcast alone, I counted people from thirty-four different states as being there. I've read that 20 million viewers tuned in weekly during *The Ozark Jubilee*'s 1955–60 run on network TV.

As a result, I believe I became one of the first singers to be launched via television exposure. I guess I was a new kind of musical stylist for a new kind of media.

I was only eleven years old, but like all the *Jubilee* regulars, I was expected to do comedy skits and read commercials, as well as sing. One surviving videotape contains one of my silliest moments on the show. I am introducing a group of child performers, and Mr. Foley asks me if they are talented. Reading the cue card, I reply that they are and add, "but of course, I'm prejuiced." "That's 'prejudiced,'" corrects Mr. Foley, laughing. I hold my hand to my mouth and bury my face in his coat muttering, "My teacher will kill me when I get back to school." But on another occasion, I was more on top of my game than the adults were. On this tape, Mr. Foley and guest star Snooky Lanson pick me up and begin swinging me between them on their arms while we sing, "You Are My Sunshine." "Pull out! Pull out!" I instruct the cameraman as the soles of my Mary Jane shoes veer closer and closer to the lens. What's even funnier is that the camera remains motionless.

With my national TV exposure, the adults around me thought the next logical step was a recording contract. My manager Lou Black, stepfather Jay Rainwater and others in my corner approached various companies, but they were turned down by RCA Victor and other labels. The feedback was that nobody wanted to fool with a child. I suppose the labels' reluctance was understandable—there just wasn't much precedent for a child recording artist. Even Shirley Temple had never had disc success. Jimmy Boyd was thirteen when he had one 1952 novelty hit, "I Saw Mommy Kissing Santa Claus." Judy Garland was a much older seventeen when "Somewhere Over the Rainbow" hit the popularity charts.

No offers were on the table, so Mr. Foley swung his considerable influence behind me. When the nation's country music disc jockeys gathered in Springfield for a conference in May 1956, he staged a Brenda Lee performance for them and pressured his label, Decca Records, into signing me. On May 21, 1956, Mother autographed the document that made me a national recording artist.

Weary of the long commute, Mother moved the family from Augusta to Springfield as soon as we were out of school for summer vacation. *Jubilee* executive Si Siman found us a big bungalow in the old part of Springfield on South Avenue. Unlike my daddy, my stepfather Jay always had a big fancy car, so traveling back and forth to the Jewell Theater for broadcasts was easy. For the time being, we gave up our gypsy lifestyle and settled down.

Robyn was eight months old now and was an adorably cute little baby. We all loved playing with her, because she was so teensy. Randall was a seven-year-old and finally old enough to fight back if I picked on him. He was a bright little guy, too.

Linda was fifteen and already had boyfriends. She developed early and had a great figure. She was real popular in school and a straight-A student. I got good grades, too, but I never thought I was as pretty as her. She was fifteen looking twenty, and I was eleven looking like I was five.

Decca Records wasted no time. They brought me to Nashville's Bradley Studio for my debut recording session on July 30, 1956. Studio owner Owen Bradley had supervised Buddy Holly's debut sessions there the previous January. In February, the Everly Brothers had staged their disc debut. Elvis had burst on the national scene with "Heartbreak Hotel" that spring. In May, Gene Vincent recorded his classic "Be-Bop-a-Lula" at the Bradley Studio. In June, Roy Orbison debuted on the charts with "Ooby Dooby." All of these records were peppy fusions of hillbilly heart and black rhythm patterns in the emerging style called rockabilly, and in my opinion that is the foundation of rock 'n' roll. Without really realizing it, I would somehow help shape this new style. With my energy and youthful spunk, I automatically took to rockabilly. It just felt natural to me.

"Brenda's first single from the session was a hepped-up version of her longtime showstopper 'Jambalaya,' complete with glottal vocal effects and forceful growling," recounts music historian Mary Bufwack. "On the flip side was a tune that is regarded as a cornerstone female rockabilly performance, the hiccuping, Elvis-like 'Bigelow 6-200.' The next day, she recorded the first of her jaunty novelty holiday tunes, 'I'm Gonna Lasso Santa Claus' and 'Christy Christmas.' These two ditties have a minor place in music history as the first rockabilly Christmas tunes ever recorded.

"Only a handful of female performers can be credited as rockabilly pioneers. Jean Chapel, Barbara Pittman and Janis Martin all emerged with rockabilly discs in 1956 alongside Brenda. But no one had the national impact that the eleven-year-old had. And no other female recording artist would embrace and refine the rockabilly style with as much gusto."

I was just doing what came naturally. The hiccuping little vocal trick I did was just automatically there. No one ever told me to do that. I didn't know it was part of the rockabilly style, because we didn't even call it that then.

I don't remember being scared at my first recording session. Even though I was only eleven, I felt pretty self-assured in the studio. And I refused to be treated like a child when it came to my music.

"She sort of blew my mind," recalled studio owner Owen Bradley, the piano player at that first session. "I mean, she would just stand there with her finger twirling her hair and just sing like that. She was putting all this phrasing and all this emotion in

there. She's always been like that. I never thought of her as a child.

 "She was very unconcerned about the whole thing. At one point, she stopped singing.

 " 'What's wrong?' I asked.

 " 'The bass player missed a note,' Brenda stated bluntly.

 "I never heard it, but the bass player admitted he had," Owen recalled. *"I also remember that after a 'take,' I'd think it was great and say so. Her mother would say, 'Do it again. She can do better. Brenda, do better.' And she would.*

 "Later in the session, [Decca producer] Paul Cohen began using baby talk to try and explain something to her. Suddenly, Brenda cocked her head back, looked him straight in the eyes and said, 'Well, "goo-goo" to you, too!' Everybody in the studio cracked up."

After the session, I continued to appear on *The Ozark Jubilee,* and that summer I also began to perform on country package tours with Mr. Foley and his *Jubilee* gang. On the road, the musicians in the band would get a kick out of teaching me dirty jokes, which I would merrily repeat to get a laugh without understanding the meaning behind any of them.

The *Jubilee* producers were giving me more and more airtime on the TV show, and it turned out that one of the *Jubilee*'s millions of viewers was influential *New York Journal-American* columnist Jack O'Brien. After seeing a show one August Saturday night he wrote, "Didn't catch the name of the 11-year-old singer on last night's *Ozark Jubilee,* but she belts out a song like a star." Mr. O'Brien told me later that he requested publicity materials. The staff mistakenly thought he meant ten-year-old Libby Horne, the host of the spin-off *Junior Jubilee* program. Mr. O'Brien said he took one look at her glossy publicity photo in heavy makeup and realized that she wasn't the plain little girl he'd praised, me. Once he got my name and likeness, he became my ardent champion.

In those days, the newspaper columnists had a lot more power than they do now. When they spoke, people listened.

Decca issued my debut single on September 17th, billing me as "Little Brenda Lee (9 years old)." Apparently, being eleven wasn't dramatic enough; and the ruse was easy—I didn't look that old, and the pinafores Mother was dressing me in only emphasized my kiddie appearance. The novelty of my youth, plus Jack O'Brien's New York write-ups, led to a booking on NBC's *The Perry Como Show* on October 27th.

"The Perry Como Show *was . . . pleasantly lazy . . . and pert little Brenda Lee, graduate of* Ozark Jubilee, *was a darling,"* raved O'Brien. *"Belted out a song with all the aplomb of the most proficient adult without losing her little-girl cuteness."*

Here's what Mr. Como had to say about me: "Never have I seen so much talent wrapped up in such a tiny package . . . As for the kind of performance she gives when she steps out in front of those cameras—well, I think we're all agreed that she's just about the greatest. I'm not trying to keep it a secret; this wee one has stolen my heart."

During my stay in Manhattan for the Como show, New York magazine writers gathered in my room at the St. Moritz Hotel. I was pretty blasé about it all. I informed them that my favorite singer was Fats Domino, who was then at the top of the hit parade with "Blueberry Hill." Then I also educated them on the relative merits of Hank Williams and Little Richard.

Going to New York City was the first time I'd ever flown, and that was just unbelievable. I adored the city, all the restaurants, all the shows, places open all night, everything. The hotel rooms seemed huge, better than any house I'd ever lived in. We learned how to order from room service; Mother would order up steaming pots of coffee, and I'd indulge in burgers and fries.

One night, Mother and I went to see Fats Domino at a show. He autographed a $20 bill for me, because I was his No. 1 fan. Mother and I spent hours and hours window-shopping and staring straight up at skyscrapers. We went to the Empire State Building. I loved Times Square, because there were so many colorful characters down there. Everybody seemed like they were in a rush to get somewhere; and that was new to me.

In those days, Mother was a constant in my professional life. Whether at a TV show, a concert or a recording session, she sat quietly in the background. Not wanting to appear uneducated, she seldom spoke up. But she was listening and learning all the while. Although musician Gary Walker and scriptwriter Bob Tubert remember Jay Rainwater constantly promoting my career at *The Ozark Jubilee,* the show's organizers evidently thought he was a pain in the neck. In later court documents, Mother testified that one producer offered her a salary of $100 a week if she'd divorce him. And although Jay might have had the gift of gab, it was Mother who remained firmly in control. All those years of sitting quietly and observing had given her much more showbiz savvy than I believe Jay had.

After New York, it was on to Chicago for an appearance on the popular ABC network radio show *Don McNeil's Breakfast Club.* Mr. McNeil used a folksy, conversational style that incorporated commercials into the flow of the broadcasts. And since it was a morning show, a major sponsor was a breakfast cereal.

"I bet little Brenda wishes she had some Grape Nuts right now, don't you?" he casually asked me.

"I don't like Grape Nuts," I replied on the air.

The audience howled and kept on roaring while Mr. McNeil attempted to repair the damage.

He said, "Well, that's alright, Brenda. You didn't say anything wrong. Because if you don't like 'em, I'm glad you told me about it. The thing is, if everybody liked them, they wouldn't have me advertising them, because then everybody would eat them and there would be no use trying to get people to try them."

Mr. McNeil's sidekick suggested, "I'd just let it go if I were you."

I piped up, "I knew you wouldn't want me to tell a lie, Mr. McNeil." I guess being that honest didn't hurt me any. I also got booked on the national radio shows of Martin Bloch and Robert Q. Lewis.

Although "Jambalaya" was a hit with TV viewers, the single failed to catch fire with country deejays. So my manager Lou Black figured it was in my best interest to curry favor with them. Since 1952, the radio men had been gathering every fall in Nashville for the Grand Ole Opry's annual birthday celebration. The idea was for them to discuss how they could promote country music, which was slipping in popularity by mid-decade due to the rise of rock 'n' roll. Record companies used the convention as an opportunity to promote their artists by wining and dining the radio tastemakers. So in reality, the Disc Jockey Convention was one big influence-peddling cocktail party set to music. What better place to publicize me as the nation's youngest recording star?

Lou Black brought Mother and me from Springfield to the Andrew Jackson Hotel in downtown Nashville in November 1956. That's where the action was during the Disc Jockey Convention. Bob Wills and the Texas Playboys—the kings of western swing, big-band music—were holding forth in the ballroom.

Lou somehow fast-talked his way through the din and got me on stage with them.

I hopped up there and did "Jambalaya." Bob Wills stood there on the sidelines with his chest puffed out, swaying back and forth to the beat and grinning from ear to ear. He yelled in this high voice, "Take it away, Leon!" And Leon McAuliffe did this fantastic steel guitar solo. I really didn't know how famous they were, but I could see right away that there was something magic about Bob Wills.

Everybody seemed to be amazed at me up there singing, and I was really happy to be there. But my elation was short-lived. The next night, Lou Black collapsed at the convention and died of a heart attack.

Charlie Lamb was at the Disc Jockey Convention promoting his *Music Reporter*, Nashville's first music industry trade magazine. He tells me that he was certain he knew who the perfect replacement for Lou would be.

"I was immediately on top of it, that night," Charlie recalls. *"The evening Lou died, he'd had little Brenda up in the Decca hotel suite singing a cappella for Paul Cohen and a bunch of people. I was there, and I saw what she could do to a room full of music executives. Later that night, Red Foley's manager Dub Allbritten and I were at the Grand Ole Opry. Afterwards, we walked the block down Broadway from the Ryman Auditorium to the Ernest Tubb Record Shop. That was our tradition, to go down there.*

"I insisted, 'Dub, you've gotta sign this little girl.'

" 'My God, what will I do with her?' an incredulous Dub replied.

" 'Just sign her!' I exclaimed. 'She's going to be a great artist.'

" 'She's just a kid, a baby,' argued Dub.

"So I begged him, 'Dub, please! I'll help you draw up the contract right now.'

"We sat in the backseat of a Cadillac in front of the Ernest Tubb Record Shop, and I scratched out a contract right there," Charlie recalls. "Then I said, 'Now go sign her.'

"Dub Allbritten was already managing Red. Surely he must have been aware of how talented Brenda was, since he'd been watching her on The Ozark Jubilee for months. Besides, she was touring steadily, and he was doubtless aware that she was booked to play the Flamingo Hotel in Las Vegas within a matter of weeks.

"I don't know if it was my prodding or not, but Dub signed little Brenda."

♪

The Flamingo Hotel was a fabulous place, one of the first fancy casinos on the Vegas strip. I was billed there with the superstar pop quartet the Ink Spots in December 1956. Reviewer Ralph Pearl caught my act and here's what he wrote in his "Vegas Daze and Nites" column:

An 11-year-old moppet shall lead them for the next three weeks at The Flamingo. Her name is Brenda Lee, whose singing style is phenomenal and general show business attitude up on stage is cool and cocky. And as I itemed once before after catching her on the Perry Como Show via television, she could easily pass for a combination Teresa Brewer and Kay Starr with a dash of Elvis Presley thrown in for good measure.

Generally a youngster in show business relies on cuteness and whimsy to sell an act. But not this little gal with the strange and tantalizing tonsil technique . . . As

for being cool, calm and collected, the Lee lass makes
Perry Como look like a jittery jumper in comparison.

Las Vegas was the first time I'd been exposed to gambling. I
always had to have a security guard escort to walk through the
casino to get to the showroom, because children weren't allowed
in the gambling rooms. One of the main things that struck me was
that there were no clocks. I never knew what time it was. The
Flamingo was the biggest hotel on the strip, I think. There were
real flamingos there, walking in the gardens. I'd never seen anything like it, the palm trees, the desert.

But there wasn't anything to do in Vegas for a kid. The most
fun I had was on stage. I was kind of the cohost, and they had me
in this Christmas dream sequence where I'd sing these little
songs introducing the various acts. There was a Chinese acrobatic
group, a comic and the Ink Spots.

I especially liked the recitations that the Ink Spots did in the
middle of songs like "If I Didn't Care." That really made an impression on me. I'd never heard anybody talk in a song before.

They let me decide what songs I wanted to do, so I picked
"Tutti Frutti" and "Jambalaya," because I liked the upbeat,
rockin' stuff. The audience seemed to like those, too.

I made history as the youngest headliner ever in Las Vegas, a
record that still stands today. We saved all the clippings, and by
all accounts I was a big hit.

My record company, Decca, couldn't have been happier
about this turn of events. None of its regular hillbilly acts were
welcome in Vegas; even Elvis hadn't gone over well during his
engagement there the previous April. So my label gave me a
party. Evidently regretting their earlier exaggeration of my age,
the label bosses tossed a "catch-up" tenth, eleventh and twelfth

birthday bash for me at the Flamingo on December 11, 1956. The extravagant, layered cake was taller than I was.

During 1957–58, I was booked for two more Perry Como programs, plus five appearances on *The Steve Allen Show*. Steve's NBC variety series was a prime-time Sunday night staple of U.S. television from 1956 to 1961. The host became a beloved icon to millions as both a musician and a comic.

"Most little kids sound like little kids; she never did," Steve Allen recalled years later. *"She not only had a mature sound when she was twelve, but she also had a mature attitude. She never seems to have gone through a gangly, amateurish phase. She was very professional, right from the beginning.*

"A good indication of the fun that Brenda and I had working together—and the ease with which we worked together—came when we were doing an old song called 'I Love You.' She was known at that time for that funny 'uh-oh' break in her voice. So at one point in the number, I imitated her. I made fun of her 'uh-oh.' She got the giggles momentarily, but being a real pro, she got control of herself immediately. If I had gotten the giggles, I probably would have laughed for five minutes, like an amateur."

With the continued appearances on *The Ozark Jubilee*, I was now being showcased on three national TV shows. My musical repertoire expanded quickly during this period. I had a modest country hit with a throaty hand-clapper called "One Step at a Time" and grazed the lower reaches of the pop chart with the rapid, raspy rocker "Dynamite." That's the song that led to my career-long nickname, "Little Miss Dynamite."

It's a hard moniker to live up to. You've got to be "on" and explosive all the time. You can't come out there like maple syrup. You can't come on stage as "Little Miss Dynamite" and sing "Am I Blue" as your opening number. You've gotta come out every time like gangbusters. But that nickname certainly has shown staying power. It's stuck with me all these years. They still bill me as "Little Miss Dynamite."

"That billing certainly fit her music at the time," believes *Holly George-Warren, the Grammy-nominated coproducer of* RESPECT: A Century of Women in Music. *"Brenda issued one rockabilly blaster after another in 1957–58. The precocious 'jail-bait' number 'Rock the Bop' was delivered in a sultry style that was supremely confident. She turned the Ray Charles blues tune 'Ain't That Love' into a soulful swinger. A raunchy sax punctuates the hiccuping 'stroll' song 'One Teenager to Another.' That one's lyric was a '50s take on the 'Men Are from Mars, Women Are from Venus' theme. The hot, frenetic wailer 'Little Jonah' and the sprightly, boppin' 'Ring-a-My Phone' are perfect examples of classic rockabilly."*

But none of these early discs made the popularity charts. My one glimmer of hope was a snappy little sizzler called "Let's Jump the Broomstick," which would later become a huge hit in England.

These happy tunes masked underlying tensions in the recording studio. Paul Cohen, the executive who'd signed me to Decca, was a controlling personality who rubbed Mother the wrong way. He felt he should make musical decisions for me; but Mother had more faith in my instincts.

"I hate to say it, but Paul acted like a know-it-all," Grayce *Tarpley recalls. "He was nice to Brenda, but he talked down to her.*

"There was one session where I took Brenda and walked out, because he wouldn't listen to Brenda's suggestions. She had a song she wanted to record, and he said no. That's the last time that ever happened. We walked out; and Paul Cohen wasn't her producer anymore."

Instead, I got one of the most wonderful men who's ever lived. Kind, fatherly and gifted pianist Owen Bradley was installed as my record man. For the next twenty years we worked side by side to create an extraordinary body of work.

"I know it sounds incredible, because she was only a child," Owen reflected in later years, *"but she really did know what she was doing musically. I always let her make decisions.*

"Red Foley called her a little girl with grown-up reactions, and I have to agree. He said that Brenda is the quickest study he'd seen in his twenty-five years in this business. Red thought it was fascinating to watch her sit alone in a corner and make changes in both words and music to suit her own style."

With all the Music Row studio work, Mother and I were spending more and more time in Nashville. So in July 1957, the whole family moved to the country music capital. We settled in a modest, one-story cottage on Brunswick Drive in a working-class neighborhood north of the city.

But what should have been a happy new beginning was clouded by marital difficulties. Mother and Jay were bickering openly. Toward the end of that year, she threw him out. They separated for the next year and a half before finalizing their divorce. Mother got full custody of Robyn, and never remarried. Jay Rainwater would marry five more times, twice to one of his brides. His subsequent career would include selling jewelry, doing a bit of music promotion and operating an antique store.

I was never close to Jay. He was never my "Daddy"; I was indifferent from the start. But I knew that Mother wasn't happy. Linda thought Jay was trying to replace Daddy, and I've always thought that's why she left home at such a young age.

Linda was just sixteen when she wed her childhood sweetheart from Lithonia, Ralph McFalls. She left school and began life as a military wife, moving from base to base with Ralph.

"Home life wasn't that stable," Linda recalls. "Mother was gone all the time on the road with Brenda. I had to grow up more quickly and was probably a lot more mature than most girls my age. Mother didn't want me to get married but gave me permission, because she knew that's what I wanted."

Says Grayce, "It was hard on the kids. They didn't have a father. And I was gone with Brenda all the time, so they didn't have a mama, either."

I used to think that Linda, Randall and Robyn had a lot of animosity toward me, because I took their mother away. They were always left with relatives when we were gone all the time. I carried that guilt around with me for years and years. It was only while writing this book that I finally got the courage to talk to them about it. I never had the relationships I should have had with them. But you can't control what happens to you as a child. When I found that they didn't resent me, it was like a weight had been lifted off me. I don't know why I waited so long. I guess I always felt like I'd messed their lives up so much—I assumed that they looked at me like somebody who'd lived in a dream world at their expense. But it turns out that they don't feel that way. They did miss Mother, but they don't blame me. I let that wound go unhealed for decades, and now, I feel so blessed to be an unapologetic part of their lives again.

At any rate, when Jay moved out of the picture, Mother was again the single parent of three. My income was more crucial than ever. But because of Tennessee laws protecting child performers, Mother was not allowed to touch any money I made.

That's why we appeared in Probate Court before Judge Beverly Briley in July 1957. My new manager, Dub Allbritten, had informed Mother of my legal situation as a minor and suggested that his friend Charlie Mosley would be a trustworthy legal guardian. Charlie was a prominent music business accountant and the co-owner of the Ernest Tubb Record Shop. So Judge Briley placed him in control of my finances. By law, my income had to be held in trust until I reached age twenty-one. The judge gave our family just $75 a week as an allowance. I've since found out that even a factory worker of the time averaged $83 per week.

By this time, my singing was earning pretty significant money. Each Steve Allen show paid $2,812.50. Perry Como paid $2,000. My Decca Records contract guaranteed several thousand more. For instance, the court records showed that singing on recording sessions had netted me $1,773 to this point. During the summer months, I earned about $1,000 per show. But all this income was directed straight into the trust fund, after management percentages and business expenses were siphoned off (probably 30 percent of the gross at that time). None of the profits came to me and my beleaguered family.

Further muddying the legal waters was a lawsuit brought against Dub Allbritten, Charlie Mosley and Grayce Rainwater by Crossroads Productions, the management arm of *The Ozark Jubilee*. The suit alleged that Mother had signed a five-year contract with Crossroads in 1956 on my behalf. From November 1956 through July 1957, my gross income had risen dramatically to $36,220, so I guess Crossroads wanted to hold her to its deal. Crossroads alleged that Dub had lured me from its contract with Mother.

I remember the day we went to court. I had no idea what to expect. Mother wanted me to look my best, so I wore a pink, sleeveless, polka-dot dress with a big squared collar, trimmed in lace. On the way in, somebody told me that the hearing might take hours. I said, "My goodness, I've got to eat sometime today!" Then as now, I'm always focused on the food!

During the legal proceedings, it came out that Crossroads had been taking an exorbitant 25 percent management commission, rather than the more customary 10 or 15 percent. Furthermore, this percentage was taken out of my gross income for personal appearances, rather than my net income after expenses. On top of everything else, I had been paid only $850 for six months' worth of weekly appearances on *The Ozark Jubilee*.

"Their contracts were just unconscionable," says Jubilee *scriptwriter Bob Tubert. "They had dual contracts on the acts, taking commissions for management and booking both."*

Mother testified that when the Crossroads management contract was presented to her, she asked, "How long will I have to look it over before signing?" The reply was, "Two minutes." She asked whether she could show it to a lawyer and the reply was, "Any attorney in Springfield will approve this contract."

Dub Allbritten and Charlie Mosley pointed out that under Missouri law, any contracts with minors had to be taken to court for approval and that a guardian should have been appointed. Crossroads' contracts with and payments to Mother were, in short, illegal. Dub and Charlie cross-sued, asking for a full accounting from Crossroads and $50,000 in damages.

Crossroads maintained that it had advanced money to Mother, bought me clothes, booked me on network TV, arranged for concert tours, arranged for my recording contract and, in short, made me a star. It claimed its booking division had arranged for more than thirty concert appearances across the United States, plus the three-week Las Vegas engagement and the Como and Allen TV shows. Mother countered that it was Decca Records who arranged for the network TV exposure, that Red Foley was responsible for my recording contract and that any advances to her had long since been repaid.

Davidson County Chancery Court Judge Ned Lentz denied the Crossroads lawsuit, saying, "If I grant this injunction it might injure this little girl who may be at the height of her career. I am not interested in the dollars and cents angle but in what is best for the little girl." He also dismissed Dub and Charlie's lawsuit. And that's how I came to leave the cast of *The Ozark Jubilee*.

♪

Then as now, music performers made the bulk of their living on the road. And since I was popular on TV but hitless on the charts, I was more dependent on concert income than most entertainers.

In retrospect, it looks like Dub Allbritten seized every opportunity that came his way on my behalf. He booked me on country package shows, at rock 'n' roll dances, in big-city nightclubs and anywhere else he could promote me. One of the earliest package tours he arranged billed me with up-and-coming vocalist Patsy Cline, among others. In 1957, Patsy was riding high with her first hit, "Walking After Midnight."

Patsy and Mother and I roomed together as the tour hopped through the western states. I was just twelve, but a reviewer in Denver, Colorado, took special note of my performance on the bill:

> The first half of the evening was dominated by the offerings of George Jones, a Grand Ole Opry favorite, and by Pat Kelly, a young rock 'n' roll exponent not unlike Elvis Presley in looks and song presentation. During the second half of the show, Patsy Cline, seen regularly on *The Arthur Godfrey Show,* offered . . . several country-music ballads and a gospel hymn. Jimmy C. Newman sang a couple of crowd-pleasers including "Jole Blon," the Cajun favorite of a few years back. But it was Brenda Lee, a veteran of three years in show business, that the audience came to see and hear. And it wasn't until her appearance that the audience really became enthusiastic.

Patsy and I became buddies as the tour of one-nighters rolled on. In fact, she literally took care of us. We were pretty green at this touring stuff, after all.

Back in the middle '50s when you were touring, sometimes you played places with promoters that were a little suspect. We always used to say that you needed to get a "first count," to get to the box office before the show went on and get paid; or perhaps the promoter would go out the back door with the money, and you wouldn't get paid at all. One time we had one of those dates where the promoter took the money, and Mother and I were left stranded in Texas. We had no money, and we had nobody to send us any money. We had no way to get back home.

Patsy was traveling in a big Cadillac limousine. She just took us under her wing—put us in the car, fed us, gave us money and took care of us for a week or so until we could work a few more dates and get enough money to get home.

Patsy was like a big sister to me. She sat me down and said, "You know, things are tough and hard, but you're gonna be all right. So hang in there. Because you're talented." And I appreciated that. We came to be very close. And I loved her dearly—she was wonderful.

She had a heart bigger than the world. She would just take you in and help you; and she did that for a lot of people. She was really, as I always say, the last of the "broads," in the nicest sense of the word.

This business has always been tough for a woman. Back then, it was practically unheard of for a woman to be the headliner of a show. Patsy was the first, at least in Nashville. I learned by her example—after I started having hits, I always headlined my own shows. That was just unheard of. Even today, this is still a male-dominated business.

Back home in Nashville, I'd often go over to Patsy's house to play dress-up in her clothes and shoes. That made her laugh, and then I'd get the giggles. Patsy wasn't a raving beauty, but she had a body to die for. I'd look at those clothes and wish I had a figure like that.

Mel Tillis was also a frequent touring partner whenever Dub booked me on country package shows. In 1958, Mel was still many years away from country music stardom. He was writing songs—such as my rockabilly single "Rock the Bop"—and was working as a guitar player in pickup bands backing Minnie Pearl and other Grand Ole Opry stars. Plus, Mel was designated as the "wheel man," driving the performers overnight to the next show.

In those days, entertainers traveled by car, sometimes pulling a trailer full of instruments and equipment. Luxurious tour buses were still years in the future. Mother and I rode with Mel. The tours were grueling, with frequent overnight jumps of 500 miles or so. In the spring of 1957, for instance, the route was Missouri, Pennsylvania, Illinois, Ontario, Oklahoma, Ohio, Iowa, New Mexico and Washington, D.C. I would sleep in the backseat of the car but had this uncanny ability to wake up just as we hit the city limits of the next town. "Are we there yet?" I would always ask.

"She'd keep me awake," Mel recalls. "It might be two or three in the morning, and I'd be nodding off. Brenda would stand up in the backseat, put her elbows on the back of the front seat, lean over and talk to me and tell me jokes."

Jim Reeves, Kitty Wells, Marty Robbins, Lonzo & Oscar, Ray Price, Minnie Pearl, Johnnie and Jack and Ken Marvin were among the other country celebrities I toured with in 1957 and 1958. But my country touring days were numbered. It was becoming pretty obvious that I really belonged to the new generation that was taking over the music world.

By the late summer of 1957, the teen music revolution was thundering loudly. Paul Anka ("Diana"), Sonny James ("Young

Love"), the Everly Brothers ("Bye Bye Love") and Jerry Lee Lewis ("Whole Lot of Shakin' Goin' On") were pouring gasoline on the rock 'n' roll flame. Jackie Wilson ("Reet Petite"), Sam Cooke ("You Send Me"), the Diamonds ("The Stroll") and Pat Boone ("April Love") would follow them to the top of the charts before the year was out.

I plunged right into the teen scene, headlining at the Illinois State Fair that August with Bill Haley & the Comets ("Rock Around the Clock"). In my scrapbook I have a clipping that says I set a record by putting 103,130 in the grandstands at the Minnesota State Fair on a bill with teen heartthrob Ricky Nelson. Dub Allbritten billed me as "TV's biggest little star," when I headlined in December at the State Theater in Hartford, Connecticut, at a rock 'n' roll revue with the Chantels ("Maybe"), Danny & the Juniors ("At the Hop"), Mickey & Sylvia ("Love Is Strange") and George Hamilton IV ("A Rose and a Baby Ruth"), among others.

I always loved those package rock 'n' roll shows. I loved working with all those other artists. I was just like the teenagers who came to see them. I was a fan—their music hit a chord in my life, too. We were all kids doing what we loved. We were having a ball together. I always stood in the wings and watched the other performers work while the audience screamed. I still do that today.

These singers weren't much older than me. Before then, I'd worked with entertainers who were way older. So I really felt at home. And performing live was much more exciting than doing television shows.

At home in Nashville, I appeared on WSM-TV's *Five O'Clock Hop,* guested on WKDA radio and starred in a summertime concert at the Centennial Park Bandshell. More than 7,500 kids attended, and after the show I signed autographs and answered their questions.

I spent part of 1958 on the road with Carl Perkins ("Blue Suede Shoes"). The two of us remained friends for decades to come.

I always thought that Carl could have been as big as Elvis or anybody. He was handsome; he could play guitar; he wrote; he sang well. But he'd had a horrible car accident in 1956 that nearly killed him. It seemed to me that his priorities changed after that. His heart was at home with his family, and the road was just a means to an end. We put on good shows, but Carl felt guilty about even being out there.

Later on, in 1963, Owen Bradley started producing Carl for Decca, and there was talk that we would do a duet album. It never came to be, and I've always regretted that.

During the 1958 touring season, I also ran through my fast-paced rockabilly set while co-billed with the Champs ("Tequila"), the Four Preps ("26 Miles") and the Nashville pop group the Crescendos ("Oh Julie"). I went down to Shreveport for an appearance on "The Louisiana Hayride." That's where I met rockabilly star Buddy Holly ("Peggy Sue"), who died the following year in the plane crash that was dubbed "The Day the Music Died."

I was a huge fan. Buddy was eight years older than me, and I really looked up to him. He was really the first complete artist we had in rock 'n' roll—a songwriter, guitarist, producer and singer all in one package. All my life I've been a record buyer. And you can bet I had a stack of Buddy Holly 45s.

Back at *The Ozark Jubilee* doing guest spots, I rubbed shoulders with Wanda Jackson. Today, the music historians have called both of us "founding mothers" of rock. Despite the glaring physical difference between the shapely Wanda and my childlike frame, fans often mistook Wanda's throbbing, propulsive "Let's Have a Party" as one of my tunes. Maybe that's because both of us performed our rocking material with a growling vocal attack.

One of the only other girls doing up-tempo material around that same time was Connie Francis. That's when she was coming on the scene with "Stupid Cupid" and her ballad hit "Who's Sorry Now." But she didn't have that same edge in her voice that we Southern girls did. For many years, Connie and I ran neck and neck with each other on the pop charts. But we never acted like competitors. We were friends.

My steadiest rockabilly touring partners in 1958 turned out to be Buddy Knox and Jimmy Bowen. The handsome Texans were both enjoying hits at the time. Buddy had gone all the way to No. 1 with his peppy, percolating "Party Doll" the previous year. Jimmy, the bass player in Buddy's band the Rhythm Orchids, made it into the top-20 with his more plodding "I'm Stickin' with You."

Billed as "Brenda Lee and Her Rock 'n' Roll Show," it was a pretty good package. We certainly drew the crowds. The Rhythm Orchids were great to me; they were just country kids like I was. We always traveled in separate cars but would get together before show time and talk about whatever was hot on the charts at the time. I was the only girl in the show and sang such up-tempo tunes as "Dynamite," "Ain't That Love," "One Step at a Time," "Tutti Frutti" and "Rock the Bop."

In those days, my enthusiasm and energy seemed boundless. Whenever anybody questioned them, both Dub and Mother insisted that they weren't working me any harder than I wished. And that's true. It was all new to me then, and I was loving every minute of it. Heck, I was twelve! Dub tried to amuse me by taking me to Coney Island when we were in New York. He let me run loose on the midway when we were at a state fair, allowed me to go to monster movies in the various towns we visited and bought me comic books to read backstage.

Mother was almost always along but wasn't able to go when I was booked to play the North Carolina State Fair in October 1957.

I wasn't feeling well, but I told Dub I wanted to perform anyway. I nearly fainted when I came off stage. My fever was 105.

Dub later told *The Augusta Chronicle,* "We got her back to the hotel and told her she couldn't go on that night; and she cried like a little puppy. She didn't want to disappoint the people."

Most of the time I was having fun. I was a pretty normal little girl, maybe a little on the devilish side. It must have been that rambunctious tomboy part of me, but that same newspaper portrayed me as "an incurable prankster."

Once on *The Steve Allen Show,* Marie "The Body" McDonald was wearing a white gown. I remember that I walked up to her carrying a glass of wine and pretended to trip. The glass of wine was one of those fake ones with a clear top. At *The Ozark Jubilee,* I reported for work one day with one arm and one leg in casts and with bandages on my head. Red Foley was preparing to make apologies to the crowd when I burst into laughter and ripped off the fake casts and bandages. At a benefit show in Nashville, Pat Boone and I were scheduled to come on stage in an electric car. I loosened the brakes to scare him, but Pat found out about it and fixed them.

I was a mischievous kid. They used to dare me to do things in school, and that's all it took. One time on a dare in the cafeteria, I put whipped cream off my dessert in the hair of the prettiest girl in my class. She went around half the day with a big glob of it on her while we snickered. Nobody ever told her.

But when it came to my job, I could be quite mature. Minnie Pearl once told me, "You were *never* a child." A lot of people I knew when I was a kid have told me that. Dub knew I could behave. He didn't hesitate to put me in sophisticated company. In addition to rock 'n' roll shindigs and country hay-bales shows, he booked me with the adult stars like Harry James, Duke Ellington, Howard Keel and Jane Russell.

In Chicago, I costarred at a 1957 Christmas charity show

alongside Tony Bennett, comedians Jack E. Leonard and Irwin Corey and the singing DeCastro Sisters. Backstage, Tony and Jack taught me to play poker.

Mother wasn't real thrilled about it, but I loved it. I forget if we played for pennies or toothpicks, but I got pretty good at it.

Two weeks later, I was back in Nashville for my debut performance at the Grand Ole Opry. Elvis Presley was visiting backstage; and the two of us danced together in the wings.

You can bet the cold December air in Nashville's Ryman Auditorium was thick with anticipation that night. Elvis was the hottest thing in the entertainment world and ruled the charts with such smoldering hits as "All Shook Up," "Hound Dog" and "Teddy Bear." I don't care how many other people were there—I swear to you that I was the most excited person in that hall. I looked my best in a crisp gingham dress, a pair of scuffed slip-on flats and a starched white pinafore, but I only had eyes for the King of Rock 'n' Roll. When I looked up at him, I grinned from ear to ear.

Elvis had just received his draft notice and was in Nashville to see his manager, Col. Tom Parker. I sang "Bill Bailey, Won't You Please Come Home" for my Opry debut. But I remember Elvis more vividly than my performance. When he danced with me backstage, I thought I had died and gone to heaven. His hair was dyed jet black; he was wearing dramatic-looking mascara; and when he smiled that curled-lip smile, I thought he was the sexiest thing I'd ever seen.

The record label, of course, took full advantage of the meeting. My Decca boss Paul Cohen called journalist Charlie Lamb on the spot, begging for coverage.

Charlie recalls, "Paul sputtered to me, 'I've got to have a photographer down here right now!'

"Well, my official photographer was Elmer Williams, who worked for an undertaking company. So I called him.

" 'I'm running real tight tonight,' the photographer apologized. 'I don't know if I can make it. I guess I can come by, but I'll have to just run in and out. I've got a body in the hearse.'

" 'Do what you've gotta do,' I pleaded. So Elmer dutifully showed up at the Ryman to snap Brenda with the King of Rock 'n' Roll.

"The next morning I called and said, 'How did you do?' He said, 'The pictures turned out great; the guy died.' And that's the famous picture of Brenda with Elvis."

Even though I didn't have a hit record yet, I must have been doing OK. The word came from Los Angeles that Brenda Lee was the winner of the Milky Way Gold Star Award for being an Outstanding Juvenile Performer of 1957. This resulted in my appearing on the long-lived *Art Linkletter's House Party* daytime TV show in Hollywood.

It was the first award I ever won. That's when I got to meet the other winners, the Lennon Sisters from *The Lawrence Welk Show,* Lauren Chapin from *Father Knows Best* and Tommy Rettig, the little kid on *Lassie.* I was thrilled: These were kids I watched on TV. What amazed me was that they knew who I was. It was a big catered dinner.

That was my first trip to Los Angeles. I saw everything that I could see. I was fascinated to be where all the movie stars lived. We stayed at the Hollywood Roosevelt Hotel, where they say Shirley Temple learned to tap dance with Bill "Bojangles" Robinson.

I was having a ball. But not everyone approved. Some country music fan magazines questioned the propriety of a child like me performing at all. *Country & Western Jamboree* wrote:

We cannot possibly understand why a nightclub would book a twelve-year-old girl, or why anyone in charge of the child's schedule would permit such a booking. We paused to wonder when we saw Brenda booked for eight straight days around Minneapolis during the first of May, right before normal school examinations.

True enough, schooling was difficult. But Mother made sure that my education remained a priority throughout my early career. If a concert date meant missing school, she arranged to get the lesson plan and took books on the road with me.

I was enrolled as a student at Maplewood Junior High in North Nashville. Dub's official line to newspapers and fan magazines pointed out my participation in the debate club, the cheerleading squad and the school newspaper staff.

But when I look back at his press releases to the music business I see that he painted a different portrait—Mobile, Alabama (6,200 in attendance); Rockford, Illinois (24,000); Pensacola, Florida (13,800); Evansville, Illinois (2,500); Augusta, Georgia (4,200); Chattanooga, Tennessee (3,700); Houston, Texas (27,000); Omaha, Nebraska (12,000). Dub was constantly trumpeting "TV's biggest little star" as a sold-out concert attraction.

At the Disc Jockey Convention in the waning weeks of 1958, Dub tethered a donkey outside the Andrew Jackson Hotel wearing fake antlers on its head and carrying a small billboard on its back. The stunt was to promote my new record, the effervescent "Rockin' around the Christmas Tree." The gimmick was a bust. My future holiday classic fared no better than my other rockabilly records during its first release. Nevertheless, I somehow knew that "Little Miss Dynamite" was here to stay.

THREE

Dub

What the manipulative Col. Tom Parker was to Elvis, what the smooth Ken Kragen later was to Kenny Rogers, and still later what the omnipotent Lou Pearlman was to the Backstreet Boys, Dub Allbritten was all that and more to me. He was the Professor Higgins to my Eliza Doolittle, the man who took a flower girl and made her into *My Fair Lady*. It might be a stretch to describe our relationship as a hypnotic Svengali in control of his doll-like Trilby. But not much.

If he said, "Jump," I said, "How high?" I never once questioned his authority. It would have never occurred to me to ask, "Why?" or to demand an explanation, because he had such good judgment. The only area where I'd put my foot down was in the music that I was performing. I had the final word on that.

In those days, a manager did it all. He made the decisions on contracts. He had full control over the act, on how they looked and were presented. He was the road manager. He set the price and collected the money. He did the publicity campaigns. He was the go-between to the record company and to the concert booking agency.

Despite the fact that Dub was in every nook and cranny of my life, I've been forever puzzled by his guarded personality. We spent so much time together—all those years, hours, days, weeks, months—but I never really figured him out. I've since come to find out that nobody else ever did, either. One musician from those days who I talked to called Dub Allbritten an enigma. All I know is, he was the manager who made me what I am. I was the focus of his life for fifteen years.

Dub Allbritten wasn't an easy man to get to know. He didn't give of himself, personally. Professionally, though, he gave 100 percent. There was nothing he wouldn't do if it meant helping my career.

It's funny what you remember about a person. Dub had these little half-moon glasses that were perched on the end of his nose whenever he was in the office. If he gave you one of his looks over the tops of the rims, you cowered in your shoes, because he was so intense.

I recall that he smoked unfiltered Pall Mall cigarettes like a chimney, sometimes using a cigarette holder. He'd take them out of a little silver case and flick open his solid gold Dunhill lighter. After the doctor told him to quit smoking, he switched to cigarillos and cigars, which he inhaled. He drank coffee that was as strong as mud. He brewed it in an espresso machine that he bought in France. He was so proud of that coffeemaker.

Dub was a dapper dresser. He wore silk shirts with monogrammed cuffs and suits custom-tailored in New York. He had beautiful jeweled cuff links and hand-tooled leather shoes. He had wavy reddish hair that he kept impeccably trimmed. Nobody in Nashville looked anything like him. And you should have seen his home. Dub always had beautiful furniture and artwork from around the world.

Other than that, he had no outside interests, as far as I could tell. Show business was his life. And I became his life, until the day that he died. He had no hobbies, didn't play golf. He wasn't athletic. He was a loner, an odd duck. Most of his friends were business associates. I never knew him to date any women. He told me that he'd fallen in love with a Mexican girl one time, but she broke his heart and wouldn't marry him. That was the only experience I knew of that involved the opposite sex.

On the road, he watched me like a hawk. There was no goofing off when show time came. Dub expected complete professionalism and discipline. He hardly ever smiled that I recall.

So I was always trying to please him. For instance, there used to be a part in my show where I sat on a stool. A band member was supposed to bring it out behind me in the dark and set it where I was supposed to go. One night as I got into the number and went to sit, I realized that he'd forgotten to bring it out. I knew Dub was absolutely going to have a fit after the show if it wasn't done just right. So for the whole number, I acted like I was sitting on the stool. The spotlight only showed me from the waist up, so the audience couldn't tell. By the time the song was over, my legs were cramping so bad I could hardly walk. Call it fright or call it wanting to please him, but we always did what he wanted. Needless to say, the band member got a severe tongue-lashing.

There'd be many times when I came off stage and knew I'd sung well, the band had played really well and everything really clicked. I'd say, "What do you think? How'd we do?" Dub would just say something curt like, "Oh it was OK; it's fine; not bad." I always thought he cared deeply for me and had my best interests at heart. But he never praised me, never hugged me, never told me I'd done a good job. I don't think he knew how to show affection. He might have wanted to, but it just came hard for him. Even though we were with each other almost twenty-four hours a day, seven days a week, he never once told me he loved me.

Where Dub Allbritten acquired his finesse and high-class tastes—not to mention his extraordinary entertainment smarts—remains a mystery to all of us who knew him. William Dumas

Allbritten was an orphan who was adopted by a middle-class couple in Paducah, Kentucky. When he was around ten, his parents opened a family-style restaurant in the heart of town. The family evidently had some showbiz flair. I remember that the Allbrittens had a fancy monkey house in their Paducah backyard, as well as two trained, circus-type dogs named Rusty and Candy.

As a teenager in the 1930s, Dub apparently began working at traveling carnivals in western Kentucky. After military service as a paratrooper, Dub launched his career as a talent promoter. I think he began by booking former Olympic track champion Jesse Owens as a vocalist with jazz bands in the 1940s.

"Dub told me he managed a series of professional wrestlers during World War II," recalls singer Bob Beckham. "He had one grow a little Hitler moustache and taught him to stiff-arm salute and yell, 'Heil, Hitler!' People would pack those small-town high school gyms to see that sonofabitch get killed in the ring.

"Dub was a real character. He used to keep me in stitches telling me stories about his carny days. I have no idea if they were true or not. One of them was about a bear that they tried to turn into a polar bear with a bunch of peroxide."

Dub told me that in his carnival days, he had a dancing duck. There was a hot plate under some sawdust in its pen, and the duck would lift its feet up and down when they heated it up. They'd play this little tune, and the duck would look like it was dancing. After a while, though, the duck's feet would get callused, and he wouldn't dance anymore and would have to be replaced. Any time I was sick or complaining or feeling bad, Dub would say to me, "Well, I guess I better get me a new duck."

No one's sure how he got the job, but in 1947 Dub Allbritten booked and promoted a series of Grand Ole Opry road shows in Texas. Around the same time, Dub became an advance man for Hank Williams. He'd travel to towns a few days ahead of performances to put up posters, buy newspaper ads for the show and sell advance tickets.

By 1950, two of the biggest Grand Ole Opry stars were Ernest Tubb and Hank Snow. Dub parlayed his concert-promotion savvy into signing both of them as management clients. He opened his first office in the back of the Ernest Tubb Record Shop in downtown Nashville. This is almost certainly where Dub met store co-owner Charlie Mosley, whom he later recommended as my legal guardian.

But Dub's time with Ernest Tubb was brief. When country superstar Red Foley left the Opry for *The Ozark Jubilee* TV show in Springfield, Missouri, Dub ditched both Tubb and Snow to sign Mr. Foley as his client. After that, he worked with acts as diverse as comedian Whitey Ford, "The Duke of Paducah," and whip-cracking movie cowboy Lash LaRue.

"He had a chain of jukeboxes, too," says Charlie Lamb. *"The jukeboxes were a prominent thing back then. The music magazines published a list of the top jukebox songs every week and that helped get those records played on the radio.*

"Dub and I had coffee together every morning for years. I was publishing the Music Reporter *trade magazine and he'd give me lots of inside scoops. I helped him, too, because I had all the contacts in New York and L.A.*

"We were both night owls. Dub was even more of a night person than I was. But Dub wasn't a drinker. He'd maybe have a glass of ale with me every once in a while. But mostly he just drank coffee and chain-smoked cigarettes. We'd sit in coffee shops and hotel lobbies and talk about show business all the time. Constantly—what this act needs is this, what so-and-so needs is that. We were always talking about how we could take that act and turn it around by doing this and that. We'd sit around and talk about how an act was being mishandled. Pop or country, it

didn't matter. Dub was just show business all the time. I thought he was kind of sad."

If anyone can lay claim to mentoring Dub Allbritten, it's probably Charlie Lamb, the man who talked him into signing me in the first place. I always thought they made quite a pair. Dub was tightly wound and tight-lipped. Charlie was relaxed and chatty.

Considering the friendship between the two men, it is no surprise that Charlie Lamb's *Music Reporter* chronicled every detail of my career. That publication is practically a Brenda Lee scrapbook. Every Dub Allbritten press release was dutifully printed and every new business deal he made was given prominent play in the trade publication. One typical story headlined him as a "Star Maker."

"People didn't think of him that way, but Dub did have a great sense of humor," says Charlie. "We had a lot of laughs together. But his friends were so few that not many of his contemporaries besides me remember this side of his personality."

"I liked him, I guess," recalls studio guitarist Harold Bradley. "He didn't have much of a personality, from what I remember. Zero. So there was no reason to dislike him."

"Dub wasn't affectionate with anybody," recalls songwriter and scriptwriter Bob Tubert. "I never saw him with a woman; I never saw him with a guy. I never saw him cast a glance at anyone. He might have been asexual."

"He was an old bachelor with Puritan ways of thinking," believes Bob Beckham. "For instance, he didn't think it was healthy for Brenda to shave her legs. She bought some hair remover, but he wouldn't let her use it until he was sure the product was OK. So here I am driving us to the next show date, and he's squirting a tube of this stuff on his arm, testing it to make sure it was safe for Brenda to try it, to see if it would burn her or anything.

"*Dub Allbritten worshipped that little girl; and I think he did everything in his power to take care of her. The most honest and honorable man I ever met.*"

"*I liked him, because he was a straight shooter,*" says Bob Tubert. "*I think he was as honest as the day is long. He protected Brenda from a lot of shady characters and bad deals.*

"*He was the most tunnel-visioned person I've ever known in my entire life. And that one vision was Brenda Lee.*"

"*Has anybody told you about the pills?*" asks Dub's longtime secretary Jackie Monaghan. "*Dub took them by the handful, pills to wake up, pills to fall asleep. In the morning, his hands would be shaking when he came into the office.*

"*Dub was a meticulous workaholic. He wouldn't tolerate anything less than perfection,*" Jackie reports. "*I remember him handing me Brenda Lee contracts to review into which he'd purposefully inserted unacceptable terms. These would be minute contract points, but I was expected to spot every one.*

"*Everything was a test,*" she recalls. "*Everything was definitely fraught with meaning.*

"*Every day I worked with him was like going to school. He was so very intense; he was not a laugher. The words 'I'm sorry' weren't in his vocabulary. But I was just absolutely crazy about him, because he had so much to teach. We usually worked until seven at night, sometimes eight.*"

Wheeling and dealing, he was pretty good at that. But Dub didn't really want to talk to anybody. His office manager, Sonya Worsham, wrote all the letters, drew up all the contracts, sent out all the publicity bios and promotional materials and made all the travel arrangements. Sonya says he always had sacks of cash around when he came home from a tour.

She told me that he'd praise me to the skies when we'd come in off the road, talking about what a "sensation" I was. But even though I know I was important to him, he never told me so. He told everyone else what a good job I did, but he never told me.

"That's true," says Jackie. *"He'd rave about Brenda in the office, but not necessarily to her face. Dub's affection for Brenda came out in the obsessive way he worked on her behalf.*

"If Brenda was coming in to the office that day, it was an occasion. You could tell that Dub was excited that she was coming. It was an event. He always had her office decorated beautifully. Things like that told you he cared."

Dub was stern; he wasn't charming. In the Nashville music industry, I think he was respected for his business sense, but I don't think he was particularly well liked. And if you talk with anybody who worked with Dub, they would tell you that they were just a bit afraid of him. But he was always very respectful toward women. I never heard him use profanity.

He was like a parent to all of us. Dub was only forty in 1958, but I thought of him as this ancient, wise old spirit. And it wasn't just me seeing through a child's eyes. We all felt that way. Jackie Monaghan says the same thing. So does everyone I've ever talked with about Dub Allbritten. He was our guiding light and our trusted maestro.

Dub's unerring sense of what was right for my career would take me, literally, around the world. He took a spunky child with raw talent and turned me into a chanteuse. He educated me and fashioned my every move.

He wanted me to be sophisticated. He wanted me to be his female counterpart—well dressed, well mannered, poised and polished. He bought records of Judy Garland, Billie Holiday, Dinah Washington and Edith Piaf and had me listen to them. He taught me a lot. I watched him to see how to eat, which utensil to use when. He would always say, "Don't slump. Sit up straight. You must have good posture. You're short; if you're slumped you're going to look shorter." Chewing gum, which I loved, was never allowed. He said, "You look like a cow chewing its cud!"

I wasn't allowed to wear much makeup. He didn't want me to shave my legs or wear hosiery. The first time I bought a padded bra, Dub had a fit. With me, he was very controlling. He would even ask me in the morning if I had taken my bath. If I said, "Yes," he'd go into the bathroom to see if the tub was wet.

I think a lot of that had to do with my youth. When Mother wouldn't be on the road with me, and we'd check into a hotel, he would take the key and lock my door and say, "OK, I'll see you in the morning." Those were some of my loneliest times. The hotel TV was my best friend. Later on I thought, "Shoot, what if the hotel had caught on fire? I'd have been trapped." I guess that was just his way of protecting me.

"Brenda's mother butted heads with Dub," recalls Bob Beckham. "I mean, head on. They didn't get along too well. But Grayce trusted Dub nevertheless. I think she realized she wasn't equipped to do his job."

Dub was taking over Mother's parental authority. He was deciding what I should wear, how I should act, when I could go places or when I could see my friends. He basically took over my discipline, and I think she saw herself being replaced.

Mother would speak her piece and have her opinion, but Dub was definitely in charge. If they argued, it was never in front of me. Dub was too professional for that. He never shared any business problems or any altercations with me, because he wanted me to stay focused on my music and my show.

In the beginning, he'd prepare me for interviews by giving me topics to talk about. But after a while, he wouldn't coach me. He would always say, "You know what to talk about and how to act and what to do."

He was right there with me, every step of the way. In the

1950s, he'd drive the car all night from show to show. Mother would sit up front with him while I'd sleep in the backseat. The air would be so thick with cigarette smoke that you could cut it with a knife. Maybe that was my training to perform in all those smoky nightclubs later. It's a wonder I can sing at all.

Half the time we didn't even check in to a hotel because it was "one-nighters" back in the '50s. You'd have to take off for the next show immediately, because it might be several hundred miles away. So often there was no time for a hotel stay. We'd clean up in a backstage bathroom when we got to the venue.

Dub would have to "do the count" at the box office, collect the money, do this and do that. Then we'd get back in the car and drive on to the next town. I don't know when the man slept.

After a few months, I complained about his car. It had a hump in the middle of the backseat. I said, "I don't care what you have to do, but we have to make some more money. We have to get a different car. I can't sleep in this one." Then we wound up getting a station wagon. I had a blow-up air mattress that we put in the back, so I would have a bed. That's how I slept; that's how we traveled.

Dub Allbritten and I traveled many a mile together. We went through so much side by side. So still in some tiny crevice in my heart, I have to think that in his own way he really loved me. Otherwise, that whole period of my life was a charade.

FOUR

Dynamite

Dub Allbritten had been working every angle on my behalf, but I could tell he was becoming frustrated. Dub was so intense. It was like he was obsessed with me. I can see him to this day, pacing the floor and smoking cigarettes while he was plotting his next move for my career. His brow was permanently furrowed, and his mood seemed constantly cranky. His nimble mind was doubtless going a mile a minute. By the time I reached fourteen, I'd had plenty of network television exposure, loads of touring experience, and was the "little darling" of the musicians in Nashville. But there was no denying the fact that I still lacked a solid hit record.

As a result, Dub had to be a tireless show promoter who refused to take "No" for an answer when it came to hyping my career. But by 1959 and still without a hit to promote, I think he was feverishly worried about how to take my career to the next level.

Whatever it was he wanted to get done, he'd move mountains. He'd convince whoever was in the way and make them a believer. Dub would always find a way.

When Dub learned that my rockabilly discs were receiving radio airplay in France, he sprang into action. My recording of the teen dance tune "The Stroll" was quickly pressed and marketed for release exclusively to the French market. Then Dub arranged for me to appear at the prestigious Olympia Theater in Paris.

In February 1959, Dub, Mother and I traveled to New York and boarded an intercontinental flight. The tickets were nearly $500 apiece, which was a lot of money then and a huge financial gamble for my hustling manager. After all, this was more than half the proceeds from an average Brenda Lee concert at the time. And there was no guarantee that there would be any return on the investment. There was no precedent for what he was attempting. No U.S. teen star had ever crossed the Atlantic to conquer Europe; certainly not one who'd never had a hit record. But Dub had a vision.

To generate excitement, he planted a story in the French press that I was actually a thirty-two-year-old midget. The press then embellished the tale by "leaking the news" that I was a divorcee with two children. I guess that my throaty alto voice, which did sound wise beyond its years, made the whole thing seem plausible.

Plus, my voice didn't match the Decca Records publicity photos anyway. They had heard me over there but had never seen me. So they said, "Send us some publicity pictures." We did. But they wrote back saying, "No. Send us some more recent ones."

Well, all we had were photos of me in my little crinoline dress. That was me. So the story broke in the French press before I even got there that I was a fraud. Nobody believed that a fourteen-year-old could sing like that. So it was printed that I was a midget posing as a child prodigy. It was great publicity.

I remember that I was initially booked for second billing behind French superstar Gilbert Becaud. When French fans realized I actually was a child, I suddenly became a sensation in the City of Light. My engagement was extended to five weeks, then more European appearances were tacked on to my schedule.

It lasted so long that I had to register for school there. Dub enrolled me in the American School in Paris and told me that I was going to have to learn the language. He was doing it to make me responsible, to educate me, but it scared the hell out of me.

He said, "You'll be going to school and taking buses and changing buses; and you can't do that unless you know the language. Plus, we're going to order food in restaurants and you're going to have to learn to read the menu. That's how it's going to be. You'll speak French. If you want to eat, you'll learn it." So I did.

He would make me eat things I thought were weird and exotic. I was a Southern girl used to Southern fare. I wasn't used to cuisine like they were having. He would make me try everything. And he tasted everything, too.

He'd go everywhere with me, but he would make me do the communicating. He wouldn't help me. I'd go to school during the days and work the show at night. On the weekends, we did afternoon matinees. One thing I'll never forget is that they had these male and female dancers. Every time I would come off stage they would be all naked and dressing together for the next number. Men and women, completely naked together. Of course, I'd never seen anything like that. That was also the first time I became aware of the gay lifestyle. There were lesbians and gays in the cast. It never shocked me, though. I figured that it was just their way. So I thought, "OK, it's fine with me."

Raved *Le Figaro* about my Olympia show, "Never before since Judy Garland has anyone caused as much clapping of hands and stamping of feet." The French wire service sent photos of me on stage at the Olympia around the world. The press there billed me as "the Shirley Temple of Rock 'n' Roll" and as "Baby Rock." I remember that I caused such a stir that I had to do twenty-five interviews in a single morning. They also hustled me in and out of Parisian record shops to autograph my records for clamoring fans. Superstar crooner Maurice Chevalier ("Thank Heaven for Little Girls") invited us to a Parisian party in my honor.

As soon as Dub heard that Maurice Chevalier wanted to throw me a party, he took me to see the movie *Gigi,* which I think had just come out. I always loved musicals, anyway, and Maurice was charming in that one. He was such a big idol over there that I couldn't believe he would want to meet a little girl singer from the United States. He invited all the famous actors and actresses and show people from all over Paris. At one point, I remember everyone standing with their glasses raised and toasting me. That's the first time I'd ever tasted wine. Over there, children were allowed to do that. It was champagne. It made my nose tingle.

I loved Paris. Mother and I took in all the sights. We went to Versailles, the Louvre, the Eiffel Tower, the Champs-Elysées, the Arc de Triomphe—I wanted to see it all. She even took me to Christian Dior; and we loved to eat at the little outdoor cafés. People brought their pets into restaurants, and I'd certainly never seen that before.

From Paris, Dub took me on promotional visits to Belgium, Italy and England. I sang on television in Milan but took time to sightsee and feed the pigeons on the palazzo in front of the La Scala opera house with Mother. They booked me on TV shows in Brussels and London, too, and I appeared on the popular pop music show *Oh Boy!* in the British capital.

Six months later, Dub had another "vision" and decided I could conquer Latin America as well. When my old recording of "Jambalaya" became a surprise hit in Brazil, he booked a concert tour of Rio de Janeiro, São Paulo and a number of other cities there.

When I arrived in Brazil, there was a tremendous amount of

excitement. The people there were very demonstrative and very hot-blooded. I loved it. They just love music so much, and they show their love by mobbing you. It's beautiful.

In Santos, fans were so enthusiastic that I was trapped for two hours inside the theater after my performance. A squad of policemen had to rescue me.

After an appearance in Pôrto Alegre, *Photoplay* magazine reported, "The fans were jammed sardine-tight at the front and rear doors. The police couldn't clear a path. As a last resort, they made a flying wedge and carried Brenda, hand to hand, over their heads to the waiting car."

That tour garnered me an amazing fifty-one front-page newspaper stories, nine major magazine features and the Brazilian billing "The Explosive Girl." Brazil's President Juscelino Kubitschek called me "the best goodwill ambassador the U.S. ever had." Kubitschek was then in the midst of massive loan negotiations with America. He was planning an ambitious economic development strategy for his nation as well as designing a modern new federal capital city to be named Brasília. He liked me so much that he invited me to his presidential palace for a state dinner.

I will never, ever forget that. His chief of staff called and invited me to dinner and asked what I would like to eat. I told him that I would love to have black beans and rice. It was my favorite dish there. But they wouldn't hear of it. That was peasant food, so apparently I shouldn't have requested that. When I got there, though, they had a small bowl of it at my place setting alongside a lavish steak banquet.

After sixteen sold-out concerts and a half dozen national radio and TV appearances in Brazil, Dub was elated. Against all odds, he was making an international star out of a singer he believed in. He was doing something that no other impresario had done before with any teen act, never mind one from Nashville.

"Dub was far-sighted," marvels singer Bob Beckham. "He had the vision. He opened up an international market for Brenda that nobody else was even thinking about."

Back in the States, my producer Owen Bradley thought it might be a clever idea to have me record a collection of standards for my album debut. My rockabilly tunes had made me a teen attraction, but Owen's strategy was to introduce me to an adult audience as well. The idea was to market Brenda Lee as a pint-sized, juvenile novelty act who was also a legitimate vocalist.

Reflects women's music historian Mary Bufwack: "The LP was titled Grandma What Great Songs You Sang *and featured little Brenda swinging confidently through Sophie Tucker's 'Some of These Days,' the Al Jolson classic, 'Toot Toot Tootsie Goodbye,' Bing Crosby's 'Pennies from Heaven,' the immortal Bessie Smith favorite, 'St. Louis Blues,' and other vintage tunes. Brenda is a revelation of self-assured phrasing and sheer joie de vivre on the LP. Listening today, it seems incredible that the polished vocal stylist was only fourteen years old at the time.*

"If there was even a shadow of a doubt that the pint-sized singer could handle far more than hillbilly ditties and rockabilly novelties, this album's recording sessions erased it completely. Owen Bradley was a former dance-band pianist who loved the old chestnuts. Brenda whipped through twelve of his favorites in just four short recording sessions. Throughout the rest of her career, it pleased him immensely to pepper her LPs with torchy supper-club material and evergreen standards."

Owen always told me I sang great. He was always bragging about my singing. I knew I was doing music to the best of my ability, and he accepted me. My confidence always came from Owen Bradley. Even when I was a kid, he always respected me as an artist. I was so comfortable with him, there was nothing I wouldn't try if he asked me.

Owen clearly guided me toward a more adult repertoire. But he kept his eye on the teen market, too. Recording sessions for my new singles were scheduled at his studio that summer in between my shows at county fairs, movie drive-ins, racetracks and sock hops. I costarred at these with folks like rockabilly star Carl Perkins, country comics Lonzo & Oscar, bluegrass greats Flatt & Scruggs and future teen idol Johnny Rivers. While I was home in August 1959, Owen took me into his Music Row studio to record a growling little bopper called "Sweet Nothin's." By the end of the year, I was finally en route to a national breakthrough in America with my first top-10 pop smash.

That was such a catchy song. Louis Nunley of the Anita Kerr Singers did that little whispering thing at the beginning. He's not whispering any actual words; it's just a sound effect. I'm pretty sure Owen thought of it. I remember thinking at the session that this song was a little more grown-up than a lot of the things I'd recorded up to then. I thought, "This might be the one; this could be a hit."

"It was all done on the spot," recalls Louis Nunley. "We were at Owen Bradley's Quonset Hut recording studio in Nashville. Brenda was at her microphone, and we were at ours. I was the one standing closest to her, on the end. Since I was the closest, I was picked to come over to do the whispering into her microphone. I wasn't saying anything, really. Just gibberish. Everyone was putting in their two cents' worth, acting silly."

I found out later that some disc jockeys thought my delivery was a little bit controversial. I was sounding sexy, and I wasn't even old enough to date!

We put it out in the fall of 1959, but it just laid around the radio stations for months. Finally, in December, the Decca promotion department in New York was able to get the big station in Cincinnati to play the single and that's what started it. A lot of the deejays thought that I was black, so I was played on the r&b stations, too. It was great to get that audience.

" 'Sweet Nothin's' is the kind of song that made me a Brenda Lee fan in the first place," says Holly George-Warren, who coedited The Rolling Stone Encyclopedia of Rock 'n' Roll. *"What's great is that it not only rose to No. 4 on the pop charts, it even went to No. 12 on the r&b charts. That little slip of a gal had such a bluesy voice that she actually crossed over to the black audience. And the record crossed the Atlantic Ocean, too, going gold in the U.K. Can you imagine people's surprise when they discovered it was this little white girl who had that raspy soulful voice? And that it was a fourteen-year-old who was responsible for that jaunty cha-cha beat booming incessantly out of radios in soda shops, department stores, drive-ins and teen bedrooms everywhere. How cool is that?"*

I've since read that during that time a certain lonely and blue GI in Germany was introduced to the teenage daughter of an Air Force captain when he was spinning his favorite platters. Priscilla Beaulieu says she remembers that Elvis Presley was playing "Sweet Nothin's" on his record player when she entered the room to meet him for the first time. Later, Elvis told me that my hit was one of his all-time favorites.

As soon as he got out of the Army in 1960, Elvis called me in Nashville to tell me how much he loved the song. He said it was his favorite and asked me if I would autograph a copy of "Sweet Nothin's" for him. He even sent a limousine over to pick it up at Dub's office. I couldn't believe it. The whole staff was excited.

"Sweet Nothin's" was written for me by rockabilly wild man Ronnie Self, who was another Dub Allbritten discovery. As a teenager, the Missouri native pestered *Ozark Jubilee* personnel for an audition until cast member Bobby Lord listened, liked what he heard and introduced him to Dub.

Ronnie Self seems to have always been a little unstable. One story has him chopping down a tree to block the school bus from getting to his house. Another has him attacking a teacher with a baseball bat in grade school.

At any rate, Dub saw promise in the erratic singer-songwriter. He sent some money to Ronnie for a trip to Nashville, arranged for a recording session and got the energetic bopper booked on some package tours. He also approached my label, Decca.

Owen Bradley liked Ronnie's songs but didn't sign the act that Dub was billing as "Mr. Frantic." Instead, Ronnie Self wound up on the Columbia label with the hoarse, frenetic 1957 rockabilly classic "Bop a Lena." Ronnie had the wildest stage show. He'd fall down on stage and sing lying on his back. He'd turn his back on an audience and just be jumping around everywhere.

But at the height of his rockabilly fame, "Mr. Frantic" abruptly quit touring. Still, Dub kept trying. They say that Ronnie was drinking heavily and shooting his mouth off to record executives all over Music Row. He'd listen to other artists' recordings of his tunes, then break the records in half. Maybe even mine. Ronnie was burning bridges left and right. But Dub kept loaning him money and arranging for song-publishing deals and recording sessions, eventually including some with Owen Bradley at Decca.

Dub wasn't a songwriter, but his name is listed as the cowriter on a lot of Ronnie's songs. I don't think he was trying to be dishonest. That was the only way Dub could hope to recoup all the money he'd invested in that crazy guy.

When he was in Nashville, Ronnie roomed with Roger Miller. They must have been a wild pair with all their partying. There was a rumor that Ronnie cowrote some of Roger's songs, but I don't know that I believe that. Even at his craziest, Ronnie always sent great songs to me. Besides "Sweet Nothin's," he also wrote "I'm Sorry," "Anybody but Me," "Eventually" and "Everybody Loves Me but You." All of them were hits for me, but I do remember that he was never allowed in the studio when I recorded them.

By the mid-1960s, "Mr. Frantic" was almost completely out of control. He'd added amphetamines and marijuana to his alcohol consumption. After Dub died, Ronnie reportedly became completely unhinged. The story goes that when he discovered that his Gold Record for "I'm Sorry" wouldn't play on his stereo, he burned all of his songwriter awards in front of his publisher's office on Music Row. Ronnie Self died dissipated in 1981 at age forty-three.

His roommate, my buddy Roger Miller, would go on to write and perform some of the most distinctive music in Nashville history. Between 1964 and 1968, he topped the pop charts with "Dang Me," "Chug-a-Lug," "England Swings" and "King of the Road." Roger had his own network TV series in 1966. In 1985, he scored multiple Tony Awards with his Broadway musical *Big River*.

Roger and I were friends from the time I was a little girl. I first met him when I was touring in country package shows in 1956. He was playing fiddle in Minnie Pearl's road band. Even then he had that one-of-a-kind, zany sense of humor. He was such a unique personality. I wanted to hang around him because he was so magnetic, so creative and so talented. You never knew what was going to come out of his mouth next.

Our friendship endured for years. In fact, one of the last shows Roger ever performed was when he and I costarred at a pair of weekend concerts at a fair in Ohio. He came on my tour bus after the show and told me he was having throat problems. I asked him what was wrong, and he said he was hoarse all the time. So I gave him the name of my voice doctor in Nashville. The next thing I knew he was diagnosed with throat cancer. Roger Miller died of the disease in 1992.

"Mr. Frantic," "The King of the Road" and me, "Little Miss Dynamite," were part of a thriving pop scene in Music City. Elvis, Conway Twitty, Tommy Sands, the Everly Brothers and lots of other teen acts were recording on Music Row, too.

By the late 1950s, record companies everywhere realized that rock 'n' roll was more than a passing fad and were churning out teen idols by the score. Riding high on the charts in 1959 were Frankie Avalon ("Venus"), Annette ("Tall Paul"), Freddie "Boom Boom" Cannon ("Tallahassee Lassie"), Dion & the Belmonts ("A Teenager in Love"), Bobby Rydell ("Kissin' Time"), Connie Stevens ("Kookie Kookie Lend Me Your Comb"), Dodie Stevens ("Tan Shoes and Pink Shoelaces") and Bobby Darin ("Mack the Knife"). Eventually, every one of them became a friend of mine.

By this time America's teen scene was in high gear. Rock 'n' roll was starting to replace the creamy-voiced crooners of the 1940s. Plastic transistor radios, portable phonographs and cheap 45 rpm singles were part of almost every teenager's life, including mine. Thanks largely to young consumers, record sales more than tripled during the 1950s. Jukeboxes played tunes for a nickel apiece; and 45s sold for as little as 69 cents. I've read that by the end of the 1950s, more than 70 percent of the records bought in the United States were purchased by teenagers. Teens accounted for an estimated $10 billion worth of consumer goods by 1959.

Critics labeled the new music "a menace to morals" and called it "a corrupting influence." Ministers railed from the pulpit against the sensuous sound with its "jungle" rhythms. But our sound was unstoppable.

On TV, Dick Clark's *American Bandstand* became a weekday staple on the ABC network. *The Adventures of Ozzie and Harriet* showcased heartthrob Ricky Nelson, who caused teen girls to swoon when he'd close his eyes to sing on the weekly broadcasts.

It was a time of drive-in movies, proms and going steady. Soda shops, hot rods and sock hops were the stuff of teen dreams. Angora sweaters buttoned down the back, circle pins, double bobby socks to make them look thicker, the class ring of your boyfriend on a chain around your neck. We called our saddle oxford shoes be-bops, and we wrote our boyfriends' names on them. We also wore penny loafers with shiny real pennies in them. Of course, we were never allowed to wear pants to school back then. You had to wear dresses or skirts. The hairdos of the day were ponytails, ducktails and crew cuts. Our biggest wish was just to kiss a boy during Spin the Bottle. It was a much more innocent time.

Nashville was a much smaller town in those days. Downtown was the heart of everything. There were no malls. Mama had a two-door white Corvair that she'd take us around in, to the skating rinks and the movies. I used to roller-skate all the time over at the Hippodrome and at an outdoor rink north of town. I can still dance on skates.

I was always pretty athletic and had lots of energy, but I was still strikingly tiny, and that was frustrating to me. Most adolescents experience a drastic growth spurt, but I never did. Mother says she doesn't recall my petite size being abnormal, even though all three of my siblings grew to average height. Even as an adult, I'm only four feet nine inches tall.

Kay Meadow was my best friend in junior high. They called us "Mutt and Jeff" at school, because I was so short and she was skinny and tall. We'd talk "girl talk" the way all teenagers do. Boys were always a favorite topic. We babysat a lot together for my little brother and sister. When I'd go on the road, I'd write Kay letters mooning over the boys at school and talking about our crushes. I called her my sister and collected autographs for her from the stars I worked with.

Kay saved all those letters. When I reread them now, what comes across unmistakably is my homesickness. In letter after letter, you can see I'm yearning for schoolgirl gossip and the intimacy of friendship. In the letters I ask about boys from school and talk about scheduling parties. It's obvious that I felt like I was missing out on my friends' social scene. Even when the postmark is Paris, New York or Rio, I rarely mention any show business adventures. It's like I thought the teen scene back home was the most important thing, not being a performer. Kay dutifully wrote back, sending her replies in care of hotels or nightclubs.

At Maplewood Junior High, I joined the debating club and the cheerleading squad. That's also where I became friends with Rita Coolidge. We'd ride on the bus together to basketball games—our school didn't have football—and cheer for the Maplewood Panthers. Our colors were maroon and white. I wore white bucks and bobby socks, a long flared skirt and a sweater vest with a big "M" on it. Rita matched me, but she was filling out her sweater, and I wasn't. We must have looked pretty funny shaking our pom-poms, because the whole squad was about a foot taller than I was, especially Rita.

Her dad was a minister, so whenever I'd go to her house we'd sit around the piano and sing gospel music. Rita was very vivacious, very outgoing and beautiful. She was always so pretty and popular. Even at age fifteen, she was a real looker with long black hair and dark eyes.

Rita and I would sometimes perform in the school auditorium, and all our classmates would be there. When we'd have sock hops, Rita was a great jitterbugger. We both were. We called it "the bop."

"When I moved with my family from Nashville to Memphis, Brenda gave me one of her huge, glossy show pictures," Rita recalls. "She had autographed it for me, saying, 'Rita: Don't forget about me.' As if I would.

"Brenda is phenomenal. She's as smart as a whip. When we went to school together, she never lifted a finger, and it was straight A's for her. Plus, she's so funny."

I lost contact with Rita when she went away to college at Florida State. Then we got back in touch and the next thing I knew, there she was in the '70s with hits like "Higher and Higher" and "We're All Alone." I went to see her in concert when she came back to Nashville, and I remember crying, because I was so proud of her. I knew how much she wanted to be in the music business.

With my Maplewood activities and social life with my girlfriends, I was still attempting to be a typical teenager. Dub and Mother wanted me to have a normal life. But in all actuality, it was never going to be normal.

At the turn of the decade, in 1960, "Brenda Lee" became a hit-making dynamo, a commodity. There would be no turning back—whatever youthful innocence I had ever enjoyed would vanish behind a velvet curtain of unending ovations on ceaseless concert tours. Because Dub Allbritten had a vision.

FIVE

The Nashville Sound

People are often surprised to learn that the record business isn't the biggest industry in Music City, U.S.A. Nashville is the state capital of Tennessee, the site of Vanderbilt University and the "Buckle of the Bible Belt" as a religious publishing center. In the middle of the twentieth century, it was also known as "The Wall Street of the South" because of its powerful, locally controlled investment banks.

In the 1950s and 1960s, it was a city controlled by a wealthy class who wintered in Palm Beach and lived in massive stone mansions along the broad manicured boulevards of their exclusive community, Belle Meade. They steadily built their community into a railway hub, an insurance center and a banking mecca. In those days, such people frolicked at weekend foxhunts, held cotillions and hosted glittering charity balls. They'd inherited an Old South culture of noblesse oblige to the lower classes. Jews, blacks and music stars were not represented in the city's most exclusive country clubs until the 1980s. To this day, debutante balls are a ritual of this elite.

"Remember, women didn't work in those days," says Freda Garrett, who was the daughter of a prominent Middle Tennessee land developer of the day. "And that was especially true of the money element. They maintained their off-season homes and sent

their children exclusively to private schools, Harpeth Hall for girls and Montgomery Bell Academy for boys. Those were the training grounds for Vanderbilt University admittance. It was really a closed society back then.

"I'll give you an example of how class-conscious Nashville was. You know how John Y. Brown wound up in Kentucky? Even though he was the head of Kentucky Fried Chicken, which was headquartered in Nashville, that wasn't good enough for admittance to the country club. So he left and eventually became the governor of Kentucky."

Local lore has it that Nashville had more millionaires per capita than any other Southern city. In 1958, Nashville also had more churches than other cities of its size. The city's religious conservatism meant you could not officially buy liquor by the drink in Nashville until 1967. So, of course, there was a lively bootlegging business, as well as a large number of private "gentlemen's clubs." You could tell where the city limits were on all the major arteries leading out of town, because just across the line there was invariably a nightclub, a dance hall or a honky-tonk.

According to my research, the total population of Nashville's metropolitan area in 1960 was just 399,743. Unlike most Southern cities—notably Memphis in cotton-growing west Tennessee—the number of African American residents in Nashville was a mere 19 percent. There were two Nashvilles. One was the downtown business figures and the rough-hewn cracker politicians who did their bidding. The other was the vast working-class populace, who lived in little cottages in the outlying communities of Woodbine, Madison, Inglewood, Germantown, Bordeaux and Richland Creek.

Although the elite might have preferred their fine arts and society orchestras, it was the taste of us everyday Southerners that shaped Nashville's international reputation. When WSM radio went on the air in 1925, it presented Uncle Jimmy Thompson, a seventy-seven-year-old rustic fiddler who became a huge listener favorite. Letters from blue-collar listeners poured in to the station, so thereafter, country music was featured every Saturday night on the Nashville airwaves. WSM was owned by the National Life & Casualty insurance company, which targeted its policies toward poor folks. Agents would arrive on doorsteps presenting themselves as emissaries of WSM's Grand Ole Opry country radio show. The station's call letters stood for the company's slogan, "We Shield Millions."

The sales strategy worked, and in 1932, the insurance giant pumped up the power of its station so that WSM's signal blanketed almost the entire continent. During the 1940s, the Grand Ole Opry embarked on a massive talent drive to attract the most popular country stars in the land to its cast—Eddy Arnold, Roy Acuff, Hank Williams, Red Foley and the rest of the cast I had listened to as a child in Georgia. Their presence in Nashville in turn lured record companies and song publishing companies to town.

The city recorded its first million seller in 1947. It was the pop tune "Near You" by the Frances Craig Orchestra. And, I'm proud to say, that record was produced by Owen Bradley, the same man who guided my recording career. Despite its reputation as a country music mecca, Nashville has always produced pop music as well. Dinah Shore, Snooky Lanson, Kitty Kallen and Phil Harris are among the pop vocalists who rose to fame from Nashville during its early evolution as an entertainment center. Even today, approximately half of the city's recording sessions are for noncountry projects.

In 1950, a WSM disc jockey named David Cobb ad-libbed an introduction to a Red Foley radio show, saying, "Coming to you from Music City, U.S.A.," and the name stuck. Between 1955 and 1965, all of America's major record labels set up offices in Nashville. Hundreds of aspiring singers and songwriters poured into the city during this era. They created a colorful and eccentric subcommunity, segregated from mainstream Nashville by the city's disdain.

The emerging entertainment scene was an embarrassment to Nashville's staid old guard. Rowdy, beer-drinking musicians, brash hillbilly honky-tonkers, hip-swiveling rockabillys, hayseed bluegrass bands and sideburned teen idols were not at all the images that the city wanted to project to the outside world. The ruling class preferred to call Nashville "The Athens of the South" because of the number of its colleges and universities.

The society people looked down their noses at the music people. They didn't have any interaction at all with them. Bankers wouldn't give them loans. Many landlords wouldn't rent apartments to them. If you wanted to buy a house, you dared not tell them what you did. The price would go up. It was hard for people in the music business to even get electricity without spending four times as much deposit money as somebody who walked in off the street.

"It wasn't until the music stars and executives began buying up land that things began to change," reports Freda Garrett. "They realized that the nouveau riche music people could buy fancy dresses at Lillie Rubin's, too."

I feel like I grew up with Nashville's music community. We banded together, because we had to. There was a small group of people who worked together so much that they became like family. And if I had to point to one personality who made it all happen, it would be Owen Bradley.

Owen was a staff piano player at WSM who moonlighted by performing in dance bands in the nightclubs beyond the city-limit signs. When record companies began recording the Opry's stars in Nashville, they initially used the radio station's studio. Owen thought it might be possible to make a living by building a free-standing recording facility. He aimed to rent studio time to the producers who worked for the record labels. In 1954, he took an army-surplus, domed "Quonset hut" and set it up behind an old boardinghouse in what was then a run-down area on the western edge of the city. It was the first music facility on what became world-famous as "Music Row." By 1960, a cluster of record company offices, song publishing houses and concert booking agencies had joined him in the neighborhood. Composers and studio musicians gathered to forge a tightly knit creative community. Their skills would distinguish Nashville as the most unique recording center in the world.

Owen was the first one to pull them together. What made Owen Bradley great is simply that no matter who he recorded, he believed in them, and he loved them. You weren't just another singer who came through the door. He cared. He knew what his artists could give and went the extra mile for all of us. From Patsy Cline, Loretta Lynn and Kitty Wells to Conway Twitty, Ernest Tubb, Bill Monroe and me, his sheer genius took us all to stardom. Owen Bradley was everything to me. He was like a father figure. Every musician in town respected him and loved him.

Something happened in Nashville that will never happen again. We were all in the studio together, making it up as we went along; and out came all those amazing records. Technology being what it was then, everything was done live, on the spot. If somebody messed up—even one note—you recorded the whole song over again. Today, they can fix each note electronically. A lot of times nowadays, you're singing when the musicians aren't there. Everyone can record their part separately.

But every hit record you hear from the 1950s and early 1960s is a live performance. Whether it's Roy Orbison singing "Oh

Pretty Woman" or Marty Robbins singing "El Paso" or Elvis singing "Are You Lonesome Tonight," those are live vocals with the Nashville musicians right there in the room with them.

When I started recording, I was introduced to a small group of players on Music Row who were so proficient at their craft that they could play everything from bluegrass to jazz. They came from all points on the compass, attracted by what was going on in this community. They became known as the "A-Team," which to me means that they were the best there was.

There was Bob Moore on bass, Buddy Harmon on drums and Ray Edenton on rhythm guitar. Hank Garland played lead electric guitar and so did Grady Martin, who also played acoustic. Floyd Cramer was the main piano player. Boots Randolph was on sax. You had either the Jordanaires, who backed Elvis, or the Anita Kerr Singers, who backed me, for background vocals. Harold Bradley, Owen's brother, was always there. He could do rhythm guitar or what was called "tick-tack" bass, which was a percussive technique to add more bottom to the sound. There were only a handful of players doing all the recording sessions. I know there are others who were called A-Team members, but these guys are the ones I usually had in the early days.

I credit my success and my sound to Owen and the musicians on those sessions. I don't think that magic could have happened anywhere but on Music Row. And it didn't. I've recorded in Europe and Japan; I've recorded in New York and L.A. The feeling was never the same. I felt so at ease with these musicians; they were my buddies.

I would get so excited about a session and look forward to one so much, because I knew I was going to get to be with these guys. I adored them; they were like my family. The camaraderie was just extraordinary. We were together so much it was almost like we could read each other's minds musically. I was never once treated like a "product" by them. Or a child.

There was no worrying about time schedules or how much we were going to make financially. It was just a pure love of what we were doing. Whatever that magic was, it became known as the Nashville Sound.

"They really should call it the Nashville Sounds," adds Harold Bradley. "If we could only play one sound, we'd have been out of a job. The key to the A-Team was how versatile you had to be. You might start out at ten in the morning playing honky-tonk music behind Webb Pierce, then go into an afternoon session for a bluegrass record for Bill Monroe and then wind up in the evening playing a pop song behind Brenda Lee.

"You had to be a real team. That's a really good way to describe it. And the favorite times for all of us were those evening recording sessions with Brenda. That's where you really got to stretch out and be really creative. It was like family when we went to a session with her. We looked forward to it. Owen and I felt like we raised her."

That isn't just talk. The Bradleys were so good to me. Once they even offered me the use of the Quonset Hut for a party I wanted to have for my classmates. Owen turned down paying customers and instructed the studio engineers to remove all the microphones and equipment so I could have a Friday night sock hop there. They even hung balloons and crepe paper streamers and ordered burgers, fries and soda pop for me and my gang.

"The hoopla was only natural," says Boots Randolph. "After all, all of us players agreed that it was always an 'event' when Brenda was in the Quonset Hut. She was a phenomenal talent. It was hard for me to believe that somebody that young could have

that much soul and that much presence. She could belt out a song that would just knock your socks off. She brought every musician there up a level or two."

"Yeah," Harold echoes, "if you couldn't get excited about a Brenda Lee session, you couldn't get excited about music at all. It's such a powerful feeling."

"When you'd hear that little ball of dynamite singing, she'd make you feel like playing, I guarantee you," says Buddy Harmon.

"She was a little kid, but we were young, too," says Louis Nunley of the Anita Kerr Singers. "She was hilariously funny. She'd come in off the road and tell the raunchiest jokes you ever heard. I don't think she even knew what she was saying. She'd always tell me first, because she knew it would embarrass the hell outta me."

What did I know? I'd hear jokes on the road from people like Mel Tillis and Faron Young. I thought, "Well, everybody else is laughing—they must be funny. I'll tell the jokes, and I'll get me a laugh, too."

"Brenda was like our little friend," comments bass player Bob Moore. "She was somebody enjoyable to be around. She'd joke with us and kid with us. And we'd kid with her. Normally, a bunch of grown men aren't going to kid around with a teenager, but we did with her.

"There'd be days when you'd do four sessions and you wouldn't be excited about any of them. But I can speak for all of the others when I say that whenever we'd go in to work with Brenda, we were excited. Because we knew it was going to be something special."

"We loved her from Day One," adds Harold Bradley. "It was like being on a football team. Brenda was running for a touchdown and we were blocking like crazy—everybody was strumming like crazy. That's how great it felt when she sang."

"Brenda Lee came to Music City at a great moment in history," says John Lomax III, the author of Nashville: Music City U.S.A. *"Owen Bradley took his skills as a pianist, arranger and studio innovator and applied them to a string of records that reached young buyers worldwide. Brenda's powerfully emotional voice was the canvas for the masterpieces of his career."*

On March 28, 1960, the Decca log books show that I was with my musician buddies in Owen's studio. At the time, that rollicking breakthrough "Sweet Nothin's" single was in the top-10 on the pop charts, and I remember that everyone was excited about recording a follow-up hit.

We usually recorded four songs during a three-hour session. On that date we'd already done five, which was a lot, and there was just a little bit of time left. Ronnie Self had given Dub Allbritten a sad little ballad that Dub and I had been dying to record for months. Owen thought it was too short and awfully repetitive, but agreed to give it a try.

"I thought it kind of monotonous," Owen recalled later in life. *"It was just 'I'm sorry, I'm sorry, I'm sorry,' over and over."*

We didn't have an arrangement. We just played Ronnie's tape for the musicians, and they quickly worked up an arrangement on the spot. Owen came up with the idea of having the violins he'd hired for the date answer my vocal with a little string embellishment. It was only an eight-bar song; it was still too short. It needed to be sixteen bars. That's when I remembered the recitations I'd heard the Ink Spots doing when I'd appeared with them in Vegas. We all agreed that I should do a spoken verse in the middle of the song.

"I'm sorry, so sorry; please accept my apology," I recited solemnly. "But love was blind and I was too blind to see." Then I tossed in a slowed-down version of that hiccuping effect I'd been using on my rockabilly discs. It just came naturally. It wasn't in the song as it was written. It just seemed like that "Oh-oh-oh-oh, oh-oh, oh yes" belonged in there.

We did it in two tries. I don't think we spent more than fifteen minutes on it, all told. When we finished, I was thrilled, because I'd fought for "I'm Sorry" and believed in it for so long. The musicians all thought it was an interesting sound; and it had been truly a collective effort.

But the record company had its reservations. That single sat on the shelf for two months before Decca decided to release it. Executives felt that the dark, romantic regret in the lyric of "I'm Sorry" seemed too mature for me as a fifteen-year-old. Besides, "Sweet Nothin's" had been an up-tempo hit and it seemed more logical for the follow-up record to be in that vein. So "I'm Sorry" was released as the B-side of the thumping bopper "That's All You Gotta Do." In retrospect it's easy to see why the decision was made. My vocal on "That's All You Gotta Do" had that same rasping, rocking quality and the A-Team players kicked up a lot more dust than they did on "Sweet Nothin's."

"Much to Decca's surprise, deejays around the country began playing the ballad side first instead of 'That's All You Gotta Do,'" reports Diana Reid Haig, annotator of The Brenda Lee Anthology *career-overview CDs. "By the summer of 1960, Decca 45 #31093 was a genuine double-sided smash. Both songs were top-10 in the U.S. 'That's All You Gotta Do' climbed to No. 6. 'I'm Sorry' soared to No. 1, leaping past Roy Orbison's 'Only the Lonely,' Connie Francis's 'Everybody's Somebody's Fool' and Duane Eddy's 'Because They're Young.' It remained on the charts for an impressive twenty-three consecutive weeks and was a huge international success as well.*

"It was very unusual for both sides of a single to become a hit. Brenda Lee was one of the few singers who could perform

ballads and up-tempo numbers equally well. And, from this point forward, she would pair torch songs and rockers. Today, Brenda has had more double-sided hits than any other female artist in any musical genre. In fact, the double-sided hit single became a Brenda Lee trademark."

Decca quickly rushed a *Brenda Lee* album into production. My collection included "Sweet Nothin's," "I'm Sorry," "That's All You Gotta Do," "Dynamite" and "Jambalaya." The LP's jaunty "Weep No More My Baby," written by Marijohn Wilkin and John D. Loudermilk, became a favorite in Europe. My rock-abilly tune "Let's Jump the Broomstick" bounded up the British charts. The album sailed into the top-10 in America, reaching No. 5 in the fall of 1960. It remained on the popularity charts for an astonishing fifty-seven weeks.

To say that "I'm Sorry" changed my life is an understate-ment. It changed the lives of everybody around me. Suddenly we weren't begging for concert bookings anymore. Instead of Dub calling, everyone was calling him.

The Ed Sullivan Show wanted me. *American Bandstand* wanted me. Decca Records offered me a new contract.

After all those years of hoping for a big breakthrough, here it was. And it was poetic justice that it was with a song that nobody but me wanted to record.

My hits had far-reaching consequences for others, too. Jerry Reed was one of them. My first remembrance of Jerry was when I was changing planes in Atlanta. He was in his Army uniform and introduced himself to me. Jerry said he was a writer and told me he had a song that he thought I could really sing well. I said, "Well, great. Send it to me." He did; and that's how I came to record "That's All You Gotta Do." Upon his discharge he moved directly to Nashville to embark on his own hit-making career.

East Tennessee's Dolly Parton, then fourteen, heard me

singing and says she immediately identified with me. That fall, Dolly recorded her first single. Titled "Puppy Love," it was similar to the peppy rockabilly style that I was doing at the time.

Floyd Cramer, who played piano on the "I'm Sorry" recording session, was given his own recording contract in the wake of the ballad's success. By the end of the year he was at the top of the hit parade with his plaintive instrumental "Last Date."

Six months later, "I'm Sorry" bassist Bob Moore recorded the staccato trumpet instrumental "Mexico." It became a top-10 pop hit and inspired Herb Alpert to create the Tijuana Brass.

Meanwhile, "I'm Sorry" and "That's All You Gotta Do" catapulted me to those heights of pop stardom that Dub Allbritten had long envisioned. Fan letters from teens were coming in to Dub's office by the sackful. Magazines and newspapers were clamoring for interviews. Concert dates were being offered daily.

I should have been on top of the world. But incredible as this sounds, my family and I were living in a run-down trailer park while I had the No. 1 record on earth. Mother's divorce from Jay Rainwater had forced us out of our modest cottage and into one of the most depressing and spirit-crushing addresses in Music City. Even today, visiting this location on Dickerson Road brings tears to my eyes.

I was so humiliated that I'd walk down the street to catch the school bus in the morning so no one would see where I lived. The pitiful trailer that we rented is still there, and it's hard for me to believe that we had to live like that.

My mother was trying everything she could to hold it together. She was a resourceful woman. I remember one time we only had potatoes to eat. This was for several weeks. She must have cooked the potato every way known to man—baked, fried, hash browns, boiled, mashed, soup, scalloped. You name it, we had it.

Royalties from a hit record aren't paid immediately to the artist. Record companies generally send out checks semiannually. So there was no instant wealth as a result of "I'm Sorry." And even if there had been, my family and I had no access to my income because of laws enacted to protect child performers. In this case, however, the "protection" was rather extreme—even our most basic needs weren't being met.

I was only fifteen, but since I was the breadwinner, I figured I ought to shoulder the responsibility. With my family still subsisting on the meager, court-ordered $75 a week allowance, my guardian Charlie Mosley and I approached the court. We went to ask for funds to be released from my trust, so I could buy my family a home. I'd already picked out a split-level ranch house on Anchorage Drive in the new Haileywood Estates subdivision south of town.

Charlie Mosley said to the judge, "Brenda is very popular and enjoys entertaining her friends, but has been much embarrassed by having no place where they could visit with her." He also asked the court to okay the renewal of my Decca contract with its advance of $10,000. The judge agreed to both requests.

So we bought the new house. Finally, we had a decent place to live, someplace I could be proud of. On moving day, I felt like I had died and gone to heaven. We bought furniture from the nicest store in Nashville and left behind all the debris of Conyers, Lithonia, Augusta, Springfield, the trailer park and all the rest.

A month later I was back in the studio with Owen Bradley and my beloved A-Team. "I'm Sorry" was still at No. 1, and everyone was excited about creating a follow-up hit for me. Actually, we created two.

Thanks to Owen, I was always getting songs with great substance. "I Want to Be Wanted" was an Italian ballad called "Per Tutta la Vita." We had to translate it. The song had the most gorgeous melody with a great big range, from my lowest alto almost to the top of my voice. Owen had Bill McElhiney do this exquisite string arrangement with the violins soaring way up high. It was like they were sighing, answering the vocal. I still think it's one of the most hauntingly beautiful songs I've ever sung.

On that same day, we also recorded "Emotions," which was cowritten by my old touring buddy Mel Tillis. That one had kind of a bluesy quality. The strings answered me like before, but there was more angst and drive in the sound.

"I Want to Be Wanted" was paired with the teen toe-tapper "Just a Little" and released as my follow-up to "I'm Sorry." In October 1960, that Italian ballad of aching loneliness became my second No. 1 smash. "Just a Little" also made the top-40 on the pop hit parade.

As the year drew to a close, Decca then delivered a one-two punch. "Rockin' around the Christmas Tree" was reissued, and this time it became a smash. Then "Emotions" hit the charts on New Year's Eve. It became a top-10 hit in the early weeks of 1961. The up-tempo, saxophone-punctuated jitterbugger "I'm Learning about Love" was on the flip. Just like its predecessors, it made the top-40 as well.

It was the greatest time to be making records in Nashville. It was just magical how it all came together.

I remember we recorded "Rockin' around the Christmas Tree" on a really warm day in the fall. Owen had put up Christmas decorations in the studio, a tree and everything. We turned the lights down low to get in the mood. And everybody just jammed—Hank Garland's guitar and Boots Randolph's sax riffing back and forth really made that record.

Decca Records kept pushing the future holiday evergreen every year throughout the '60s. After that, the song took on a life of its own. Throughout the '70s, '80s and '90s it became a staple of Christmas radio programming. "Rockin' around the Christmas Tree" eventually reached the status of a standard, I'm proud to say. It now ranks right behind "White Christmas," "Rudolph the Red-Nosed Reindeer" and the like as one of the top-10 holiday hits of all time. That little song has sold an estimated eight million records for me.

To have a standard that lasts forever is almost impossible. I never dreamed that more than forty years later it would be played everywhere, every Christmas. People tell me they've raised their children with that song and that it wouldn't be Christmas for them without it.

There was a Hallmark tree ornament, a little light-up jukebox, that played it. There's a battery-operated Santa who does the twist to "Rockin' around the Christmas Tree." There's even a snowman doll named Willie Winter who dances to the song when you turn him on. And I got the surprise of my life when I went to see *Home Alone* in 1990 and heard myself singing on its soundtrack. I'm told that was the biggest movie comedy in history, so it brought a whole new generation of fans to me and that tune.

You never know when you record something the impact that it will have. You don't know what's going to touch the public's emotions. The only thing you can do is give every song your best shot.

For example, the recording session for "I'm Sorry" was one of the first ones in Nashville that had a string section. We were making history, and we didn't even know it.

What's amazing to me is how good those records still sound to me today. They were just simple little three-track recording sessions, but they've stood the test of time. And that's a true testament to Owen Bradley's genius and the talent of the old A-Team. I owe it all to the Nashville Sound.

SIX

Nashville's First Rock 'n' Roll Band

One of the most intriguing things about the rock 'n' roll wild-fire was how quickly it spread. It seemed within a matter of weeks after the opening drumbeat of Bill Haley's "Rock around the Clock" that teenage bands were everywhere. And it turned out that I joined forces with the first one ever formed in Music City.

Keyboardist Richard Williams and drummer Billy Smith were students at Nashville's East High in 1955 when Haley's hit exploded on the nation's radio airwaves. Like hundreds of teens across the country, the untrained adolescents were in-spired to pick up instruments and form a band. They met Litton High School junior Buzz Cason on the local Nashville teen TV show *Saturday Showcase* and invited him to become their lead singer.

"We weren't very good musically at all—we even had B-flat marked with a piece of tape on the neck of the bass, so we'd know where it was," says Buzz. "But we hopped around a lot; and that's how we became popular around Nashville. We jumped and shook and got down on the floor and thrashed around. It was just natural—that's what rock 'n' roll was."

Poking fun at their frenetic performance style, they named themselves the Casuals. In addition to Billy, Richard and Buzz, the group eventually included saxophonist Joe Watkins and guitarist John McCreery, who was soon followed by Wayne Moss, then Larry Bushnell, plus a succession of bass players including Bobby Watts and John Orr. The Casuals began barnstorming the mid-South and became hugely popular on the fraternity party circuit.

"We'd open with Buddy Holly's 'That'll Be the Day,' and then I would come out and do an Elvis imitation, a medley," Buzz reports. *"We'd do our little record that was out, 'My Love Song for You.' And then we would just do whatever the current hits were—'Be-Bop-a-Lula,' 'Crazy Little Mama,' 'Shake Rattle and Roll.'"*

"We wore 'early tacky' matching suits," says Richard with a laugh. *"We had Mohair, every kind of hair. Yellow jackets. Red jackets. Almost every color of jacket. I particularly remember an ugly striped set of sport coats, yellow and white, that we used a lot. Little skinny ties. Peg-leg pants. White buck shoes. We had it all."*

"We were showmen," says Billy Smith.

"We stacked six guys in the station wagon, two on the backseat, two lying down in what we called 'the cage' in back, plus the driver and one guy to keep him awake with slaps on the back of the neck, screaming, loud music, black coffee and the wind through the window."

Nashville's first rock 'n' roll band was the talk of the town. The local notoriety of their hit disc "My Love Song for You" led to the Casuals' first headlining tour in 1957. And that's how I came to meet them.

In November, the Casuals were booked on a tour with musical comics Lonzo & Oscar, cowgirl singer Judy Lynn and others. As a twelve-year-old with my first records on the market, I was on that tour, too. All of the Casuals tell me that I was a real rockabilly belter on those shows. Buzz and Richard both think that the first time they saw me was at a show in Rockford, Illinois.

My manager Dub Allbritten and I came up to the group after the show and Dub said, "We don't have a band of our own. Would you guys like to back us up?"

"Yeah, we'd be glad to," responded Richard Williams, as I recall.

"After we get back to Nashville, we'd like to sign you on as our regular band," replied Dub.

Richard told me later that he thought nothing of the comment, because Opry stars had made such offers to the Casuals before. All of them had turned out to be empty promises.

"So I was really surprised when the phone rang a couple of months later and it was Dub, just as he'd promised," Richard confirms. "We became Brenda's band in early 1958. That's how it started.

"What did I think of Brenda Lee? Well, I never thought of her as a child, because we weren't much older ourselves. We were all kids doing what we liked. I was only seventeen when I joined her; and she was thirteen. She was younger, but she was dynamite. On stage, the guys in the band would jump all over the place, but all she needed was her voice and the snap of her fingers to bring the house down.

"Dub Allbritten was like a father to all of us. He was stern and he was rough. But it was just like he was a father—we hated not to please him."

"We knew he wanted perfection and wouldn't settle for anything less," adds Buzz. "He was all business. We had very strict

*rules on the road. No drinking. No foul language. No girls in the
room. He was our leader, and we were all very young and very
pliable. When you get somebody with a strong personality like
Dub and he tells you, 'This is the way it's going to be; you will
like it; and you will do it,' you do it. Behind his back, we called
him the Allbritten Cat. But under all that hard shell, Dub was a
compassionate, loving guy."*

The moderate successes I'd had with "Dynamite" and "One
Step at a Time" in 1957 kept the group and me working steadily
that following year. So steadily, in fact, that my schooling was
apparently becoming an issue. After all, I was only thirteen
years old.

*"The state of Tennessee was really strict about atten-
dance," relates Odell Braswell, Brenda's science teacher at
Maplewood Junior High. "That's what shook us up with
Brenda. She's the first student we ever had that said right up
front, 'I'm in a career and cannot be in school living up to the
state's standards.'*

*"Our principal, Morris Estes, went to the Board of Educa-
tion to arrange for special permission for Brenda to have nonex-
cused absences from classes. We had to fight a battle to get the
teachers to go along with this thing. They'd never done it before."*

The Nashville school board took the progressive and un-
precedented step of allowing me to miss school days as long as
Mother hired an approved, full-time instructor. A young tutor
named Jerri Crawford was chosen to accompany me on the road.

*"I'd be responsible for overseeing and grading the work and
giving Brenda her needed credits as far as the state was concerned," says Braswell. "She was really a forerunner, paving the
way for excused absences for career work.*

"Brenda was sharp as a tack. No problem whatsoever. I even believe she progressed faster than most students did.

"When she'd come back to school after touring, she was just one of the kids. Everyone loved her. None of the other kids seemed jealous. In fact, they were always interested in where she'd been. I'd always give Brenda a chance to tell her classmates about things like this. She was nothing but a pleasure in class."

I loved school. I loved my teachers, and I still see Mr. Braswell and several of the others around Nashville. I thought one of the coolest things about school was getting to ride the school bus. Because that's where us kids really socialized. Many times I yearned to be with my friends rather than be out there on the road. I was a cheerleader, and I hated it when I'd have to miss basketball games on the weekends. But I knew I had a family to support and that was the way it was going to be.

On the road, the Casuals and I were a good little package. We didn't just stand up there and sing. We were energetic, and we'd try new things. Even though the Casuals weren't that adept as musicians, we'd always pull it off. Richard would play that piano like Jerry Lee Lewis. Billy would pound away on those drums. Buzz would be jumping all over the stage with a tambourine. The audience ate it up; they didn't care if the band was good or not. Here were these handsome young guys and this big-voiced little girl.

I've kept a review of our show in Savannah, Georgia, in my scrapbook all these years. In his article titled "Survival from Rock-n-Roll," Joe Lambright gushed about the Casuals and me after he saw us at the City Auditorium in 1958:

It isn't often that a mossback such as myself, from the dark ages, has an opportunity to escort three teen-agers to an evening's entertainment. They tolerated my presence because someone had to drive the car and permitted me, with some reluctance, to go with them into the auditorium . . . Let me tell you, it was quite an experience.

The fare opened with seven young men equipped with striped coats, a saxophone, a couple of electric guitars, drums, and a P.A. system on which the volume control was obviously broken. They called themselves the Casuals, but were about as uncasual as any group I've ever seen—in fact, I was afraid some of the Casuals would become casualties before they finished their stint.

By this test, at least, the showmanship couldn't have been better. The audience, most of which could qualify collectively as the younger generation, took part in every number. They clapped their hands, stomped their feet, screamed, shrieked, and appeared, all the while, to be in a hypnotic state of divine ecstasy.

But the star of them all came last—a 13-year-old moppet by the name of Brenda Lee . . . and I still can't understand how such a little girl can possess such a mature voice.

From my experience, am I worried about the effect that rock-n-roll might have on today's youth? Not in the least.

I remember that first tour with the Casuals as being a total blast. The band members would always look after me like I was their little sister. Whenever we were working at a county fair, they'd always take me to the midway. If I wanted to ride the roller coaster twenty times in a row, which I sometimes did, one of the boys would have to ride it with me, per Dub's instructions.

Looking back, I guess it was a good thing that we were all so young, because the pace was pretty grueling.

"We were playing armories and car shows," recalls Billy Smith. "Sometimes we'd play small halls with no air-conditioning in the heat of July. Brenda would get so hot, she'd pass out. But she'd get up and go back on again. We were doing three shows a day at each stop. Then we'd travel all night and do it again. It was nothing to have a 500 or 600 mile overnight jump."

"It was physically pretty challenging to all of us," adds Buzz Cason. "We were all sick or exhausted half the time."

"We'd put 100,000 miles a year on the band car. Brenda and Dub would ride separately in his car. I remember we had an old, blue 1959 Plymouth wagon. Then we got the wise idea to get a Cadillac, a used 1956 beautiful, black, four-door, hardtop Caddy. If we had it today, it would be worth a fortune. But we burned it up."

Burned-up car or not, we had a show to do. We were booked. Constantly. The boys were always having trouble with their cars. But popping pills and downing strong coffee, Dub never had a major accident. He also never seemed to get sick. But he was no more an automotive expert than the teenage Casuals. The reason Dub always had a nice new car was because he'd drive them without any attention to even the simplest maintenance. Because his vehicles never even got an oil change, they would break down and be replaced annually.

On the road, Dub was always the proper taskmaster. Like me, the Casuals were a little frightened of him but also loved and respected him.

We were pretty good kids. Dub trusted us. We were a pretty straight bunch, especially compared with rock bands nowadays.

Besides, we worked so much, we just didn't have a lot of leisure time.

You talk about innocent, we personified that. I wasn't allowed to date. And I had six Casuals plus Dub watching me. That's just the way it was.

Still, I was reaching that awkward age. Suddenly, Dub was shepherding a girl going into puberty, plus six teenage rockers. It can't have been easy for the lifelong bachelor.

To the *Minneapolis Morning Tribune* Dub complained, "We never know how to dress her. She looks nine, is 14, and sings like 30 . . . if we dress her to fit the way she sings, people say we're pushing her. If we dress her according to her age, people say we're trying to make her look like a child. We can do no right."

With the gigantic successes of "Sweet Nothin's," "I'm Sorry," "That's All You Gotta Do," "I Want to Be Wanted" and "Rockin' around the Christmas Tree" in 1960, I became the centerpiece of my own road show. Although female headliners were rare, Dub Allbritten made me the leading attraction of a package.

For Dub's new touring production, the spirited Casuals switched from Mohair suits to tuxedos. And I finally earned the right to wear junior-miss dresses on stage instead of little-girl crinolines. They finally let me dress my age. I was now a bona fide "teen queen." Because I was so small, a seamstress in Nashville sewed my stage clothes. They were like teen party dresses, and I began to wear stockings and high heels. On album jackets they let me pose in Angora sweaters and brocade peg-leg pants. And for the first time, Dub gave me permission to use makeup. Not much. Just a little.

All outfitted and coiffed, we hit the road harder than ever. For the first time since the beginning of my career, I had my own repertoire of hits to perform. The Casuals had "My Love Song for You." Then Buzz got a hit on his own.

The pop music world was a lot more freewheeling in those days. A British singer named Garry Mills started up the charts in the summer of 1960 with a ballad called "Look for a Star" from the soundtrack of the movie *Circus of Horrors*. Liberty Records rushed Buzz Cason into the studio in Nashville to record a competing version immediately.

Said Buzz, "We've got the record done now. What name am I gonna put on it?"

"What's the other kid's name?" asked producer Snuff Garrett.

"Garry Mills."

"Good. We'll call you Gary Miles."

"Can you imagine?" exclaims Buzz. "We not only took the guy's song, we pretty much stole his name, too. There'd be a huge lawsuit if you did that nowadays.

"We recorded it on a Saturday, and it hit the streets on Monday. Liberty Records could pull some stunts."

Buzz's version of "Look for a Star" passed the original disc on the charts and sailed into the top-20. As if that weren't enough, Buzz and Richard teamed up with Hugh Jarrett of the Jordanaires to record as the Statues. That same summer of 1960, the Statues scored a minor hit with "Blue Velvet." So we were like the ultimate self-contained show. Buzz was a Casual and a Statue and was also Gary Miles. And he had to perform as all of those on the show. Sometimes even he got confused.

In our 1960 touring show, Buzz would come out as "Gary Miles" in a gold lamé jacket with his hair slicked back, not wearing his glasses. He'd do his bit, then he'd exit. He would put his glasses back on, take off the gold lamé jacket, put a tux jacket on, kind of ruffle his hair and go back out as a Casual. Believe it or not, no one ever knew.

To complete the touring package Dub added handsome pop singer Bob Beckham. The thirty-three-year-old Oklahoma native had joined his first touring road show at age eight. While still a boy, Bob went to Hollywood and appeared in the 1939 Bing Crosby film *The Star Maker* and in 1940's *Junior G-Men,* which starred the Dead End Kids. After service in World War II, Bob went to work as an electrician and entered *Arthur Godfrey's Talent Scouts* as a singer.

A 1958 recording contract with Decca Records brought Bob Beckham to Nashville and into the orbit of Dub Allbritten. My producer Owen Bradley introduced the two, and Dub instantly saw Beckham's potential and hired him as the opening act in the Brenda Lee road show.

As soon as school let out for the summer of 1960, Dub's package headlining me with "Gary Miles," Bob Beckham and the Casuals began its sweep through the South and West. Tour costars Johnny Preston and the Hollywood Argyles were hot with their hits "Running Bear" and "Alley Oop," respectively, and kids packed auditoriums wherever we stopped. Three shows had to be staged to meet the demand for tickets in Tampa. More than 33,000 attended a trio of shows at the Gator Bowl in Jacksonville, Florida. Some 5,000 screaming teens packed the house in Rome, Georgia, and the same was true in Atlanta (4,500), Lubbock (8,000) and Savannah (4,500).

Our troupe bounced from Birmingham to San Antonio, Beaumont and Fort Worth in early August. But we hit a bump in Shreveport, Louisiana.

"Our usual routine was that 'Gary Miles' would do his thing, the Casuals would do their thing and then I would do mine," re-

members Bob Beckham. "We'd have a little intermission and then Brenda would come out. In Shreveport, Buzz found out that Jerry Lee Lewis was in the audience. Right after I got through he said, 'Jerry Lee, do you want to come up on stage?'

"Well, here comes Lewis; and he's a riot act. He got up there and just tore those people up. They had to close the curtain.

"Allbritten was so damn mad! When they closed the curtain Dub was stomping around backstage. Buzz and the boys would go over to one side of the stage, trying to avoid him. Dub would go over there, and they'd go to the other side of the stage.

"He told Jerry Lee, 'You cradle-robbing sonofabitch! If you ever come on one of my shows again, I'll kill you!' And that was so funny, because Dub couldn't hurt a flea. But he was just furious. Because Brenda had to follow that shit.

"It didn't faze Brenda. She just went out there and did her show. I just think the world of that little gal. She's one of the finest people I've ever met.

"With her, there was never a dull moment. There were some pretty funny things that went on. Brenda had a bad habit of standing in one place on stage. Then she'd slowly but surely work her way backward into the band. We were doing a matinee some-place. I forget where. And Dub decided to teach her a lesson.

"Dub said to Billy, 'Next time she backs up to the band, you take a drumstick and goose her right in the ass.'

"Billy protested.

"Dub said, 'Do it!'

"Sure enough, here she came, going back and back and back," Bob says, laughing loudly at the memory. "Billy did what he was told and, boy, did she jump! From that point on, son, Brenda Lee worked the front of that stage and never went back!"

As summer became fall, our package show hit the state fair circuit. At the Minnesota State Fair, I was billed with Johnny

Cash. In Indiana, I costarred with the Dakota Cloggers. The West Texas Fair in Abilene featured me with a juggling brother act from Argentina and an acrobatic troupe called the Flying Valentinos. At the Allentown Fair in Pennsylvania, it was ice skater Dick Button and an Indian billed as Cochise.

But more often than not, I shared stages with my rock 'n' roll peers. That winter, I was booked at deejay Murray the K's fabled three-day Christmas extravaganza at the Brooklyn Paramount Theater.

It was the most incredible bill. I can't imagine attending a show today and seeing so many top names all in one place. The Shirelles were there, and I'd just bought their record "Will You Still Love Me Tomorrow." I was a huge fan of theirs, and later on, I recorded the song myself. I loved watching Dion work. He'd just gone solo from the Belmonts, and he had that crowd in the palm of his hand. I wasn't a bit surprised when he exploded with "Runaround Sue" a few months later.

The Drifters had great moves. They were on the charts right then with "Save the Last Dance for Me," which had that great Latin groove. The Coasters were hilarious. I just loved Cornelius Gunter, who was just as funny off stage as he was on. They'd already had "Yakety Yak," "Charlie Brown" and "Poison Ivy" by then and had one of the top stage shows in the business.

One of my best friends on that show was Chubby Checker. He's the one who taught me how to do the twist, and he did it just a little bit differently than anyone else. He'd lift that leg up and just go to town. So that's the way I did it.

The bill was packed with such names as Neil Sedaka, Johnny Burnette, Kathy Young, Bo Diddley, the Bluenotes, Bobby Vee and Jimmy Charles, all for the low price of $2 a ticket. More than 17,500 attended. It broke all house records.

Bobby Vee tossed beach balls into the crowd when he sang

"Rubber Ball," and the audience went crazy for that. Backstage, Little Anthony was chasing me all around the theater. I guess he wanted to do the "Shimmy Shimmy Ko-Ko-Bop" with me. He was "Little" and I was too—he must have thought we'd make the perfect couple.

I'd say, "Dub! He's chasing me again!" Dub would say, "Oh, he's just being nice. Don't be so nervous." I wasn't so sure.

California natives Dante and the Evergreens were one of the minor acts on the Brooklyn Paramount bill. Like Buzz Cason, they'd come to prominence by copying someone else's record. "Alley Oop" originally belonged to the Hollywood Argyles, who'd toured with me. But the Evergreens were rushing up behind them on the charts with their own version of the novelty tune. Evergreens guitarist Tony Moon shared a dressing room with the Casuals. The boys loved Tony's guitar playing and invited him to join their group.

The band made $200–$250 a night for performances on the road with me, $1,400 a week if it was a stint in Las Vegas. Band members could also pick up an extra twenty-five bucks a night by selling glossy Brenda Lee photos to my fans during intermissions.

Whenever I was home in Nashville or overseas on tour, the Casuals pulled in plenty of extra cash at appearances on their own. Nashville's first rock 'n' roll group continued to be a top show band throughout the 1960s.

"We used to say that the Casuals would play any place you could plug in," chuckles Buzz.

Almost everyone in my road show went on to have a successful show business career. Bob Beckham became one of Nashville's top song publishers. Guitarist Wayne Moss became one of Nashville's most in-demand studio musicians and founded the critically acclaimed fusion band Area Code 615.

Buzz Cason became a studio owner, hit songwriter, publisher

and ad jingle vocalist. After careers as a songwriter, publisher and talent agent, Tony Moon opened Jack Russell's, which is a suburban Nashville restaurant. Drummer Billy Smith quit the road to become a booking agent at Dub Allbritten's company One Niters. After Dub's death, Billy inherited the agency. He still books show bands that are in many ways descendants of the Casuals.

The Casuals' band name was retired when our longest tenured member, keyboardist Richard Williams, departed in 1975. Since then, Richard has been a solo entertainer.

I was a very lucky girl. I didn't know it at the time, but I couldn't have been surrounded by a sweeter group of boys.

What happened to all of us could never happen again. I feel kind of sorry for the rock 'n' rollers of today. I'll bet they're not having nearly as much fun as we did.

SEVEN

American Bandstand

The early rock 'n' roll era wouldn't have been the same without *American Bandstand*. After debuting on network TV in the summer of 1957, Dick Clark's durable institution entertained generations of teenagers. And for those of us teens who were making records in the '60s, his stage was Mecca.

Watching *American Bandstand*'s broadcasts from Philadelphia after school was a daily ritual for millions of teens like me throughout the country. Rock 'n' roll culture was woven into a national phenomenon as kids tuned in to catch the latest dance steps and fashion trends. New records were rated by *Bandstand* attendees and countless hits were born thanks to exposure on the program. The show's dancers became celebrities. Affable host Dick Clark became known as "the world's oldest teenager" in the mass media as he guided the show through five decades of glory.

Dick was a real hustler, an entrepreneur with his fingers in a zillion pies—record labels, publishing companies, TV, radio and concert booking. Every year, he'd round up the top teen talents of the day and put them on the road for a cross-country marathon dubbed the Caravan of Stars.

The entertainers were packed together on a bus and routed from city to city, day after day. Each performed only a couple of numbers at each stop. It wasn't the stage work that got to you, it was the traveling.

I was fifteen years old when I was booked on the Caravan of 1960. Also on the bus were Fabian, "Twisting" Chubby Checker, guitarist Duane Eddy, Jimmy Clanton ("Just a Dream"), the Bill Black Combo ("White Silver Sands"), Freddy "Boom Boom" Cannon ("Tallahassee Lassie") and Jimmy Charles ("A Million to One"), plus the Casuals, "Gary Miles" and Bob Beckham. Leading the backup band was future star Bobby Vinton ("Roses Are Red").

It was incredibly grueling—we were in a different city every night. But I thought it was so exciting getting to be the only girl on the road with all those guys. I was at that age when you really start noticing the opposite sex, and those guys were the fantasy of millions of young girls at that time.

We had a great camaraderie on that tour; we all got pretty close to one another. So it was like a slap in the face when we encountered segregation. I distinctly remember that when we got down South the black acts weren't allowed to stay in the same places we were and weren't allowed to use the same dressing rooms as the white guys. I had never been taught to be prejudiced like that.

I just hated it. Chubby Checker was my friend, my buddy. We spent a lot of time together in those days. We were even tour mates in Hawaii together in the winter of 1960. So I couldn't stand to see him treated with prejudice. It wasn't the kids. Rock 'n' roll was all about bringing the races together. I remember that the audiences at the shows were racially mixed. But there were these weird laws—the whites were seated on one side and the blacks were on the other. There wasn't any trouble with the two races being there, because all the kids were loving the music. I just remember the kids loving the entertainer, no matter what their color.

I had firsthand exposure to the problems of segregation, because it was my new hometown, Nashville, that launched the civil rights movement. Students at Fisk University were outraged at the hypocrisy in downtown Nashville. Blacks were free to spend money in any of the city department stores but were not allowed to eat at the whites-only lunch counters in them. In November 1959, a group of students bought items at the retailers Harvey's and Cain-Sloan and defied the status quo by sitting down to eat there as well. They were refused service.

During the next five months, hundreds of students protested the policy. They brought a song with them to downtown Nashville, "We Shall Overcome." By the end of that period, sit-ins were erupting in towns throughout the South, and the movement had a new musical anthem. As racial tensions mounted in Music City, arrests were made. A black leader's house was bombed in April 1960, leading Mayor Ben West to speak out.

On April 19th, *The Tennessean*'s headline read, "INTEGRATE COUNTERS—MAYOR." Martin Luther King Jr. arrived in Nashville the day after that. By May, Nashville was on its way to becoming the first peacefully integrated city in the South.

It was a pretty tense time. Mother wouldn't take any of us kids downtown to go shopping for spring clothes. Remember, there were no suburban malls back then. Downtown was the heart of Nashville's shopping district. If we asked her why we couldn't go or what was happening, she wouldn't give much explanation. She was pretty closed mouth about that sort of thing. Maybe she just didn't want to subject us to it. She was probably scared.

It was typical of Mother and Dub Allbritten to shelter me. Indeed, Dub seemed to be watching my every move. I remember that about a year after the sit-ins, I went downtown shopping with some of my sixteen-year-old girlfriends. I got a stern phone call from Dub afterward.

"I heard you were downtown without makeup!" he barked at me. "You know better than that. You're never supposed to be seen in public not looking your best! Don't let it happen again."

To this day, I have no idea how he found out. He must have had spies. The band and I used to say, "Dub Knew All." He also monitored me constantly on the road. Needless to say, a rock 'n' roll troupe of unchaperoned young guys with raging hormones made Dub more than a little nervous.

Because I was the only girl on the Caravan of Stars, I usually traveled separately. On short hops, I'd ride with the guys. I was doing a lot of other dates at the time, so I'd often fly to the cities and meet the Caravan. Looking back, I think the reason Mom and Dub didn't want me on that bus too much was because it was so gross—like a football locker room—not to mention the possibility of hanky-panky.

Despite being sheltered, despite the travel schedules, I did develop a serious crush on one of my Caravan costars, the handsome "twangy guitar" man, Duane Eddy.

Oh, he was *it*. I thought he was the man I was going to marry. I just thought he was so handsome. He was kind of a loner, and that drew me to him. He was shy and kept to himself. He seemed so romantic. If we took a flight together, I'd always try to sit by him. If it was on the bus, I'd try to get a seat near his. Of course, he was six years older than me, which seemed like a lot at the time. So even though I had stars in my eyes, I don't think he ever felt as strongly about me as I did about him. But he was always very sweet to me. I think he just didn't want to hurt my feelings.

"I did think she was just a kid," says Duane. "You know how

*it is when you're young. Six years seems like a lifetime. I always
knew she had a crush on me. We kid around about it even today."*

Duane's teen hits included "Rebel Rouser," the movie theme
"Because They're Young" and TV's "Peter Gunn" theme. He
was a soft-spoken Southwesterner who became the most successful instrumentalist in rock history. He saluted me on his *Girls
Girls Girls* album. I still remember what a thrill it was posing for
the cover shot, but I should point out that the two years older and
more, um, "developed" Annette was on the album jacket as well.

One thing that kept my teenage crush alive was what he
wrote about me in that album's liner notes:

Scene: Onstage . . . A dynamic bundle of talent . . . One
minute exploding—the next, caressing a song . . . All
heart . . . All feeling . . . Giving everything. Scene:
Backstage . . . Alone in a crowd . . . Reporters, stage-
hands, friends, fans . . . All love her, but don't quite understand the special needs of a young girl who wants to
be wanted—just for herself. Scene: The show is on!
From the wings she hears her band start her music . . .
The audience roars . . . She tosses her head, squares her
shoulders . . . And buries her loneliness in a smile . . .
Here she is—Miss Dynamite!

Wasn't that sweet? Can you blame me for carrying a torch for
Duane? He gave me a little stuffed animal, a seal. What was I supposed to think? I carried it around in my pocketbook for months
and called it "Big D." I think I've still got it up in my attic.

I know it all sounds silly now, but I was trying my darnedest
to grow up. I styled my brunette hair into a classic '60s hair-
sprayed bouffant. Dub was aghast when I started having bra cups
sewn into the bodices of my dresses. And he practically pitched a

fit when Rose, the wife of Casuals band member Buzz Cason, bought me my first brassiere.

Eventually, Dub had to go along with my growing up. In fact, he started to capitalize on it. In late 1960, he put me on the road visiting department stores and modeling teen fashions. The promotion was a cooperative venture with *Seventeen* magazine, which predictably chronicled my progress; with Decca Records, which promptly issued the LP *This Is Brenda Lee* as a tie-in; and with the Celanese Corporation, the makers of the dress fabric that I modeled at these "Datesetter USA" fashion shows.

"You've got to get both boys and girls to like your singer," Dub explained to one reporter. "Boys throw eggs at Fabian, because their girlfriends are the ones screaming and falling all over themselves for him. If we had the boys wild about Brenda, rather than their girlfriends, we would have a problem. I felt this was a good way to get her before the teenage girls and win their admiration."

Further testing the marketability of "Brenda Lee" as a brand name, Dub negotiated with Sears to sell a line of Brenda Lee costume jewelry. I still have one of the necklaces that was manufactured as a result.

Dub was one of the first pop entrepreneurs to fully exploit the emerging teen media of the day. When I went to New York to appear on the *Big Beat* TV show and to pick up my Gold Record for "I'm Sorry," Dub made sure that *Hit Parader* covered my every move.

The magazine's cover story was "The Little Country Girl Visits the Big City," with photos of me clutching a suitcase while standing with a traffic cop in the middle of Park Avenue. "The Little Doll from Nashville, Tennessee, 'hit' New York and impressed all the 'city slickers' with her charm, wit, sincerity and talent," read the article.

In *Teenagers Weekly,* writer Robert Feldman began with "Move over, Elvis," in his coverage of the Manhattan visit. "I wish she'd get spoiled," he quoted "an exasperated" Dub Allbritten as saying. "This girl is so completely unaffected that she'll stand for hours in the rain signing autographs or talking to complete strangers." Feldman wrote of police escorts and wildly enthusiastic crowds at my concerts, then continued:

> Even in blase New York, Brenda created a stir when she got off a bus from Nashville—fancy any other celebrity traveling by bus!—and was instantly recognized.
>
> Not far away, mobs were booing [Russian leader Nikita] Khrushchev at the U.N., but a small crowd collected around Brenda at the bus depot, causing the harassed New York police some concern.
>
> When a special detail was dispatched to break up the "riot," it ended by escorting Brenda, sirens screaming, up Park Avenue to the Decca Records office.
>
> There the president of the company, Milton Rackmil, was waiting to give her a Gold Record, representing a sale of one million copies of "I'm Sorry." Rackmil, the story went, wanted her to fly back to Nashville, first class.
>
> "No thank you," Brenda said politely. "I have my return ticket on the bus, and the driver is expecting me."

Dub concocted all kinds of publicity to keep my name in the news. He sold *16 Magazine* on the idea of having me "review" my Caravan of Stars experience with all those male rock 'n' rollers. The publication's March 1961 issue contained "Brenda Lee Gives You the Secret Scoop on the Boys":

Boy, am I a lucky girl! I just came back from a tour with some of the top boy stars in show business. Fabian, Jimmy Clanton, Freddie Cannon, Duane Eddy . . . I'm a normal teenage girl just like the rest of you, and I have my idols and "crushes"—just as you do . . .

Fabian—is a doll! Can you imagine what it is like to be introduced to Fabe, and to be suddenly swept off your feet (literally) and whirled about in the air? That's what happened. Of course, I'm so tiny (not quite 5 feet tall) that a lot of fellows try this—but that Fabe! He really took me for a ride.

Fabian . . . has a deep attachment for his "fans" (he calls them his "girls") and spends as many hours as possible with them when on the road.

. . . Last of all (and you'll be glad to hear this), Fabe is an incurable romantic. After every show, he'd tell me how he saw this or that girl's face in the audience, and how sweet, interesting, or pretty she looked—and how awful it was that he couldn't stay behind and meet and get to know some of these girls. Then he'd sigh and look sad, and say, "Someday, Brenda, someday."

. . . Duane Eddy is sort of an "enigma" to many people. But that is because he is so quiet and withdrawn. Actually, that's a part of Duane's appeal.

Duane is probably one of the most honest and sincere people I've ever known. He's completely honest and basic—and in the same moment that he constantly seeks the truth, you know he could never tell a lie . . . Of course, he—and The Rebel Rousers—have a zany side, too, and we all had plenty of laughs together.

Well, there you have my "bird's eye" view . . . of

your Prince Charmings. But this is just the beginning. Someday, I'm going to tell you the scoop on some of the other boys I've met—like Johnny Tillotson, Gary Miles, Bob Beckham and many, many more—including the dreamiest guy of all (and my idol) the great Elvis Presley.

Till then, be good and think of me—like I always think of you.

Love,
Brenda

Dub regarded my every move as a photo opportunity for the teen press. He even sent a camera crew to a sock hop party I threw for my friends in the pine-paneled den of my family's suburban home. Needless to say, Brenda Lee's sixteenth birthday could not go unpromoted.

While I was on the West Coast for a tour, Dub arranged for *Wyatt Earp* TV actor Hugh O'Brian to take me sight-seeing one afternoon. As we were cruising down the Sunset Strip in Hollywood, Hugh pointed out to me that the marquee on the Crescendo nightclub read, "Happy Birthday Brenda Lee."

He suggested that we stop so I could go in and thank the management. When I walked in, there was this giant cake decorated with replicas of my million-selling records. All these celebrities were yelling, "Surprise!" Dub had arranged for *Photoplay* magazine to run a two-page spread on the gala, so there were reporters there, too.

Among the Tinsel Town stars who congratulated me on becoming Sweet 16 were *Leave It to Beaver* teen TV heartthrob Tony Dow, Shelley Fabares of the *Donna Reed Show,* blonde beauty Tuesday Weld, Edd "Kookie" Byrnes of TV's *77 Sunset Strip,* durable movie yokel comic Judy Canova and rising young thespian Dennis Hopper. Among the pop chart idols waiting with gifts and hugs were r&b superstar Sam Cooke, Connie Stevens, Bobby Vee, Jan & Dean, Dodie Stevens, Frankie Avalon and my "dreamboats" Fabian and Duane Eddy.

For yet another photo op, Dub drove me to the film set of *Wild in the Country* the next day. My friend Elvis Presley was in rehearsals for his role as a backwoods boy with dreams of literary acclaim. I chatted with Elvis on the lot and posed for publicity photos with him and Tuesday Weld, leaning up against a black Lincoln Continental coupe on the 20th Century Fox parking lot.

Wild in the Country turned out to be one of Elvis's best movies, in my opinion. Tuesday Weld was in it with him, and I thought she was so pretty and sexy. Millie Perkins was there, too, and I'd loved her in *The Diary of Anne Frank* the year before. You know who else was in the cast? Christina Crawford. Who knew she had a book in her as juicy as *Mommie Dearest*? I wish I'd been nosy enough to ask her about being Joan Crawford's daughter. Think of the stories I'd have heard.

Dub aimed for press coverage outside the fan-magazine world as well. My L.A. visit included interviews with wire services, newspapers and radio news shows. "I get an average of 300 fan letters a month—almost twice that number after a TV appearance," I told columnist Charles Deaton in *The Los Angeles Herald Examiner*. "The writers are about equally divided between girls and boys, but only the boys ever enclose snapshots of themselves."

As nonchalant as I may have seemed about my male fans' amorous attentions, I yearned to be part of the dating scene with my Nashville girlfriends. Instead, my "dates" were usually staged publicity "romances" concocted by Dub.

Teen Life magazine printed a four-page photo spread of me "dating" handsome Tony Dow, who played Wally, the older brother on TV's *Leave It to Beaver*. Our cavorting in Disneyland was actually little more than a publicity gimmick.

In *Movie Life,* I was purportedly seeing teen idol Bobby Vee. "I think he's the most with a capital M," they quoted me as saying. *TV and Movie Screen* magazine's Marilyn Beck headlined, "Brenda Lee—Bobby Vee—Puppy Love or the Real Thing?" She reported that our date consisted of attending a recording session by "A Hundred Pounds of Clay" r&b hit maker Gene McDaniels and of going out for Mexican food.

TV Life reported on a photo op dinner date with the then-new TV star, thirty-six-year-old Andy Griffith. *Hit Parader,* on the other hand, pictured me dancing with Johnny Tillotson, who was at the top of the charts in 1960 with "Poetry in Motion."

Earl Lloyd fretted over my love life in *Teen* magazine: "Everybody loves Brenda Lee and Brenda loves everybody—but is that enough? Every woman needs one guy to drive her out of her cotton-pickin' mind. What Brenda needs is just one lover boy to dream about, fuss over, fight and make up with, and spoil silly with sweet talk, kisses and stuff like that. Stupid Cupid has goofed off."

Real romance was, of course, out of the question. Dub wouldn't hear of it. Nor Mother.

I wished I had a red-hot love life. Lord knows, I wanted one. But I was traveling with a lot of adults; and I was extremely insulated because I had my mother with me. I mean, I wanted to "get in trouble," but there was no way. All the other acts were in their twenties and were having a lot more fun than I was.

I did have a terrible crush on Duane Eddy, and he broke my heart. When he married Jessi Colter—of "I'm Not Lisa" fame—I thought I was gonna die!

I wasn't even allowed to date until I was sixteen. And even then I could only double-date. I remember when I was on tour with Fabian, he asked me for a real date, and I was so thrilled. We were in San Antonio, and we were going to go walking down by the RiverWalk. Oh, I was so excited. I got all dressed up. It was our night off; we didn't have to do a show.

So, we're walking along, and he kept looking back. I thought, "What is wrong with him? Am I boring? What is this? What is he looking at?" Well, behind every bush or every building, there was one of my band members or my mother or my manager all peeking to make sure of what Fabian and I were doing.

Needless to say, it ruined my night. I don't think he even kissed me. He did seem fond of me, however. Fabian gave me a solid gold St. Christopher medal at my Sweet 16 party in Hollywood. He told the press he wanted me to costar with him in the movie *Voyage to the Bottom of the Sea.* But his role went to Frankie Avalon instead.

Born Fabian Forte, the pompadoured dreamboat was an Italian street kid from Philadelphia who was picked for teen stardom because of his dark good looks. One of the first of the "manufactured" teen idols, Fabian had succeeded on the charts with "Turn Me Loose" and "Tiger" in 1959.

Fabe was the original "Italian stallion." He was a really hot-looking guy. He knew he wasn't the greatest in the vocal department, but he didn't care. On the bus, he'd make jokes about himself. The girls didn't care, either. All he had to do was just stand there.

Fabian's hometown was the headquarters of *American Bandstand*, and Philadelphia was producing other hit youth acts aplenty—Bobby Rydell (1960's "Volare"), Dee Dee Sharp (1962's "Mashed Potato Time"), the Orlons (1962's "The Wah Watusi"), Chubby Checker (1960's "The Twist") and Frankie Avalon (1959's "Venus"). The City of Brotherly Love was a rock 'n' roll heaven.

I remember debuting on *Bandstand* on October 27, 1959, singing "Sweet Nothin's." Then, on February 12, 1962, Dick

Clark devoted his entire ninety-minute broadcast to me. I was on top of the world.

Being that I was one of those teens around the country who watched *Bandstand* every day after school, I was thrilled when I got to do the show. I wanted to meet Bob and Justine, Kenny and Arlene, Pat, Frani and the other kids who danced on *Bandstand*. I wanted to get to know them even more than I wanted to chat with Dick Clark. I was a complete fan. And I knew how important the show was, because I knew what it could do for a record and for an artist.

Back when I did the show in 1959, I hadn't even had a big hit yet. But before the year was out, "Sweet Nothin's" was on the charts, and I had my first big record. I think it's safe to say that my appearance on the show really boosted my popularity.

By the time of my second appearance on *Bandstand,* my career was really roaring. "Emotions," cowritten by country music's Mel Tillis, became my third consecutive Gold Record in early 1961. Then my torchy revival of Louis Armstrong's "You Can Depend on Me" stormed the charts.

"You Can Depend on Me" was cowritten by black songwriting great Charles Carpenter in 1932. By the time I met him, Charles had already enjoyed an illustrious career working with such legends as Earl Hines, Fletcher Henderson, Ella Fitzgerald, Duke Ellington and Nat King Cole. Charles was the road manager for my buddy Chubby Checker. He invited me to dinner in New York, and in gratitude for my repopularizing his ballad, he gave me a toy silver-haired poodle. Using his initials, I named the puppy CeeCee. It was the first pet I ever owned, and CeeCee became my constant companion.

I returned to rock 'n' roll—and another Gold Record—with Jackie DeShannon's soul-drenched, thumping "Dum Dum" in the summer of '61.

Jackie was a great singer herself. I always loved getting her demo tapes, because they were just like hit records. Jackie wrote six of my singles—everything she pitched me, I did. They used to complain about me showing so much favoritism to one writer. She told me she wrote some of her songs specifically with me in mind. The only one I wished she'd sent me was "When You Walk in the Room." I'd have sung that in a heartbeat, but the Searchers got it instead. Later on, Jackie had hits of her own, like "What the World Needs Now" and "Put a Little Love in Your Heart," and I was so proud for her. I always knew she should be a star in her own right.

In late 1961, the lilting ballad "Fool #1" became yet another Decca Gold Record for me. The song inadvertently gave a start to another lady who became legendary in the music world. The Grand Ole Opry duo the Wilburn Brothers brought a tape of a song called "The Biggest Fool of All" to producer Owen Bradley. They wanted him to sign the woman who'd taped the tune to a recording contract. But Owen wanted the song for me, not its demonstration vocalist. The Wilburns insisted that if he took the song, he'd have to sign their singer to Decca Records. So I got "Fool #1" as another smash hit and Decca, and the world, got Loretta Lynn.

This was the era when women were just beginning to make a few breakthroughs in the music world. In r&b there were people like Dionne Warwick, Dinah Washington, Ruth Brown, Etta James and LaVern Baker. In country, my buddy Patsy Cline was breaking down all kinds of prejudices against female performers, and singers like Loretta, Dottie West and Jan Howard were right behind her.

Like Patsy in country, I ended up being one of the break-through women artists in rock. Carole King wrote songs for me before hitting the charts in 1962 with "It Might as Well Rain

Until September." New York's Lesley Gore ("It's My Party"), Nashville's Sue Thompson ("Sad Movies") and Britain's Petula Clark ("Downtown"), as well as California's Jackie DeShannon, were still several years away from stardom in those days.

In the beginning, the only other female hit maker for teens was Connie Francis. We ran neck and neck on the charts, and Connie often recorded in Nashville as well. Her hit era roughly paralleled mine, beginning with "Who's Sorry Now," "My Happiness" and "Lipstick on Your Collar" in 1958–59. When I was hitting with "I'm Sorry," "I Want to Be Wanted" and "That's All You Gotta Do" in 1960, Connie was clicking with "My Heart Has a Mind of Its Own," "Everybody's Somebody's Fool" and "Many Tears Ago."

Connie and I were friends even though she was my closest "competitor." We'd call each other, just to see how the other one was doing. We did a few big benefit shows together. One of the first telegrams I received when my first daughter was born was from Connie. See, one of her big dreams was to get married and have children like I did. She always talked about the big love of her life—Bobby Darin—who she'd wanted to marry, but her dad didn't like him. I think that still haunts her to this day. If I was jealous at all of her, it was because she always looked so beautiful and dressed so wonderfully.

I never worked or toured with other female singers, because I almost always headlined my own shows. But I never felt threatened by any other girl singers. I wasn't jealous. Besides, we were all doing different kinds of material. I did get to know Petula Clark and Lesley Gore when we'd cross paths on the road in the '60s.

"If imitation is the sincerest form of flattery, then teenage Brenda Lee should have felt highly complimented," observes women's studies authority Mary Bufwack. "Taking her cue from

Brenda, Connie Francis started to insert recitations into her ballads, beginning with 1961's 'Together.' Music City recording artist Skeeter Davis scored big on the pop charts with 1963's 'The End of the World,' which also featured a Brenda-like spoken passage. West Coast vocalist Timi Yuro scored a double-sided hit with 'Hurt' / 'I Apologize,' both of which lifted Brenda's distinctive style, from her torch-song phrasing to her husky recitations. Many fans in fact assumed discs like 'Hurt' and 'The End of the World' were Brenda's, and she later incorporated both into her show.

"In 1963, RCA Records aped its rival Decca by issuing the smash 'I Will Follow Him' by fifteen-year-old flame-thrower vocalist Little Peggy March. Cash Box magazine billed Noeleen Batley as 'The Mighty Atom' in answer to Brenda's billing as 'Little Miss Dynamite.' Patsy Ann Noble was promoted as 'Australia's Brenda Lee.' "

♪

My fan letters were mostly from girls. Some of them wanted to sing and would ask me how to get started. They said I was their role model.

But most of the letter writers kind of looked at me like a sister. The fans would tell me their troubles. They said they could relate to "I Want to Be Wanted" and my other songs because they were lonely, too. I think they sometimes told me things they might not even tell their parents, because they felt like I would understand. I really think my fan letters were more personal than a lot of other entertainers'. After all, I was their age and was going through a lot of the same feelings. I really did understand.

Just about every state in the country had a chapter of the Brenda Lee Fan Club. There were dozens of them. Whenever I'd be in their town, I'd go have dinner at the homes of the fan club members. They'd come to the shows, and I'd meet with them there, too. Even today, several of the former presidents of the fan clubs are my best friends.

Jackie Monaghan has the most remarkable saga of any of the Brenda Lee fans. She turned her love of my singing into a career in the music business.

"When I was twelve, I heard Brenda sing," recalls Jackie, a native of Rochester, New York. "All of a sudden it struck me that I would love to go to Nashville and work for Brenda Lee. Honey, did I join the fan club? I not only joined it, I wormed my way into the upper strata of the fan club. In those days, Brenda had dozens and dozens of chapters of these clubs. I joined the one that was in Westchester County.

"I would get 16 Magazine *and cut out her pictures. It was always with the idea that this was my destiny, this was my future. By the time I was fifteen, I'd gotten to be the head of Brenda's New York fan club and was writing a newsletter that mailed internationally. I contacted Dub's office to send me publicity material, so I could write these magnificent newsletters. After I turned sixteen, I'd go to Brenda's shows wherever they were—Toronto, Atlantic City, Syracuse, it didn't matter.*

"I was determined. I enrolled in Rochester Business Institute and studied everything from law to accounting to typing. I figured by the time I got to Nashville I better damn well know how to type. So that's what I did."

Upon graduation, Jackie asked Dub Allbritten for a job, moved to Nashville and became his receptionist. Eventually, Jackie Monaghan became my publicist and, later, my booking agent. She now has her own public relations firm.

There are lots of other fans who ended up working professionally with me. There was a guy who introduced himself to me in Florida. His name was Andy Courtenay, and he wound up being my road manager for eight years. We're still dear friends. I met Bob Borum in Nevada, and it was the same story. He came to work for me, too.

I don't know about other entertainers, but my fans have always become my friends. You ought to see the gifts they give me. There are several who have even moved to Nashville. Because I've always felt so close to the fans, I always answered all my own fan mail and signed all my own pictures. I never had a rubber stamp with my signature or had anybody else do it. I still do it myself.

My persona was always "the girl next door" that all the mothers and grannies loved. The girls loved me, because I was someone they could talk to. The boys liked me—not as a girlfriend—but as someone they could confide in about the girl they did like. I hated that.

There wasn't much point in promoting me as a sexpot. I was too young looking for that. And at four feet nine inches I was much too short to be played up as a glamour queen. So in the media, as in life, I was the best friend, the buddy, someone who other teen girls could identify with. Some of the resulting press was unintentionally humorous. *Teen World* magazine, for instance, claimed that its article "Brenda, Surrender!" was compiled from quotes from "hundreds of fan letters" to me in 1961:

> Some of your fans are pleading with you, Brenda. What they're begging you to do might surprise you . . .
>
> Brenda we love you! But please for goodness sake, here are some changes you've just gotta make!
>
> Brenda, it's only because we love you and care about you so much that we're going to tell you this—so please listen and don't get mad . . . Brenda, a lot of your appeal is based on the fact that you're so natural. And that's fine—up to a point!

Why do you take your success so casually? Here you are, 16 years old, and the singing idol of all us teens. Now that's quite an achievement—yet you're always trying to play it so "cool." Why, the only time you really live up to your name, Miss Dynamite, is when you're singing!

And Brenda, why no make-up? Everyone knows that one of the greatest things about being a girl is the fun we have making-up. So how come you hardly ever even wear lipstick? Brenda, you're in the world of fashion and glamor now—an exciting dreamy world. But you're missing all the fun!

. . . And your clothes! Don't you realize you're a young lady now—in the "public eye"? Loafers are okay for loafing—but aren't high heels more fun to wear? Why can't you surrender to the marvelous, sparkling world that surrounds you—and try on some of its glamor? Being natural and true to yourself is nice . . . but wouldn't it be more natural to be fascinated by the color and dazzle? Wouldn't it be more natural to want to experiment with new hairdos, make-up, fashions, the way all girls love to do?

Brenda, why do you date so seldom?

. . . Brenda, the thing that has won you the name of "Miss Dynamite" is your terrific vitality . . . To us, you're as exciting as dynamite—only, don't fizzle out on us, Brenda!

Brenda, surrender! Surrender to all the fantastic, the make-believe, the phony, the real—keep your wonderful natural touch, but don't go overboard! Surrender to it all, be fascinated by it all—and then, "Miss Dynamite," you'll really explode! Explode! Explode!

Isn't that silly? An article in *Motion Picture* magazine was even funnier. In its May 1961 issue, the publication contrasted the romantic woes of leggy, six-foot actress Paula Prentiss with those of little ol' me. "The Tall of It—the Short of It" depicted a highly fanciful "date" between me and a fictitious Nashville boy named "Jimmy." The story went that I burst into "hot, burning tears" because he treated me like a buddy instead of a girlfriend. Of course, none of that ever happened. But the pathetic thing is, the story was pretty much the truth about the way my love life was.

In the spring of 1961, Dub arranged for *Teen Life* to publish a monthly column written by me called "Brenda in Teensville." My debut journalistic attempt was characterized as "Strictly Inside Stuff about Fads, Parties, Fun and Other Delicious Data from Our Singing Doll." I guess it was inevitable that I'd kick off my narratives by describing my gala Sweet 16 party.

"I'm looking forward to telling about so much in the months to come—fashion news, dating tips, makeup ideas, travel hints and so much else," I wrote to the readers. "And since I'm writing this first column from Hollywood, I must tell you about the funny and strange and different and unusual things here that make this magic land one of my most favorite places in the whole world."

Later that year, "Brenda in Teensville" featured "girl talk" about a topic that I think still has universal appeal:

I've lost 18 pounds! Don't you think I have reason to be proud? It's taken me awhile for I decided to go on a diet where I would eat sensibly and lose slowly so I would be able to keep the weight off. I ate lots of protein—eggs, meat and cheese—and naturally, being a Southern gal, loads of greens. . . . My whole outlook on life has changed, along with my new figure. It's even easier talk-

ing to boys, having the self-confidence that comes with
knowing you look well.

I really did write those "first-person" columns, but I have no
idea how I found the time. Anyway, it was good publicity. That's
what teens, including me, liked to read in those days.

I got to know all of those teen magazine writers. The most
legendary name among them was Georgia Winters. I met her in
New York and instantly took a liking to her. She seemed so
worldly and smart.

Georgia Winters—her real name was Gloria Stavers—was a
very attractive woman and a really colorful character. She had an
affair with Lenny Bruce, the controversial, confrontational comic
who died of a heroin overdose. She was older than me, of course,
and kind of sassy; but we became really good friends. I'm telling
you, she was a fascinating woman. You're not supposed to show
favoritism when you have a magazine, but every chance she got,
there was an article on me in *16 Magazine* that she would write.
But more than that, she was a real mentor to me. I looked up to
her. She was a Southern girl, like me. One who'd made her way
in the big city.

Authors Danny Fields and Randi Reisfeld depicted Gloria in
glowing terms in *Who's Your Fave Rave,* their affectionate recollection of the glory days of *16 Magazine*. Gloria Stavers was born
in North Carolina in 1926. By the time I met her, she'd already
ditched a husband and learned to survive on her wits in Manhattan. In the early 1950s Gloria was a high-fashion model who par-
tied with the jet set at nightclubs like El Morocco. She reportedly
had an affair with New York Yankees slugger Mickey Mantle
during this era.

Gloria became the editor of *16 Magazine* in 1958. She aimed
the publication directly at girls aged ten to fifteen, and understood

what they cared most deeply about. Gloria dished out romantic fantasy to the girls in huge dollops, and the response was volcanic. At its peak in the 1960s, *16 Magazine* was read by 4 million teens a month. This massive readership brought its editor to a position of enormous influence. The raven-haired thirty-two-year-old provided the teen singing stars with their images, became their career advisor, developed powerful friendships with them and was often their most trusted confidante.

The Saturday Evening Post once wrote of her, "Gloria Stavers's power today is truly awesome. The teenagers she influences pour about nine billion dollars a year into the economy and record companies, cosmetics manufacturers and clothing firms are all scrambling eagerly for a share of the loot. Talent agencies count the number of pages in *16* devoted to their clients as an indication of the act's popularity. Record companies seek Gloria's approval before launching publicity campaigns for their artists."

Remember, there was no such thing as *Rolling Stone* at that time. Most magazines were condescending to teens. Gloria didn't dismiss us. She presented us as we were. I mean, the stories were written for kids, but the images she gave us were true to who we were. Gloria took all the photographs herself. That's what gave the magazine that up-close and personal touch.

She really taught everyone how to write for teens. She just about invented the teen magazine genre. She was the first to give out awards—she'd do readership polls and rank the kids' favorites. I've got several *16 Magazine* plaques.

Annette of the Mouseketeers and I were among the few females who became Gloria's pets. The magazine's real bread and butter was the teenage male pinup—the "fave rave" boys in *16 Magazine* were often photographed shirtless on their beds. Yet *16* was a clean magazine. Teen fantasy was OK, but sex was taboo.

Stars were never shown drinking or smoking. Gloria took her responsibility toward her impressionable young audience seriously.

Her behavior behind the scenes was another matter. Despite a dramatic age difference, I hear that Gloria had an affair with nineteen-year-old Dion and tried to lure him away from drugs. Danny and Randi's book says that she also became the paramour of Mamas and Papas lead singer Denny Doherty and of Jim Morrison of the Doors, among others. Gloria gilded the teen-dream stardom of everyone from Fabian and Ricky Nelson to Donny Osmond and Michael Jackson before leaving *16* in 1975. She died of lung cancer eight years later.

Gloria knew everyone. She was a queen in New York, hanging out with everyone from Andy Warhol to Marilyn Monroe. All of us teen stars communicated directly with Gloria. She had our home phone numbers. I talked to her long distance all the time. We all did, so that she could keep the readers up to date. Whenever I was in New York, I would always, always visit with her. We'd have lunch or she'd meet me at my hotel.

You might think that Gloria's fluffy articles were all fabricated. But the image she gave me was based on the truth. I really did think of myself as the typical girl next door.

In the April 1962 issue of *16*, "Georgia Winters" headlined her column "Watch Out Brenda, There's Danger Ahead!" Directly addressing me, she lectured, "You've got to realize that learning to care for your health is a part of growing up, too."

I must say, Gloria was as perceptive as she was affectionate. The pace of my career was taking its toll. In July 1960, I passed out from the heat at a concert in Georgia. In the winter of 1961, my whole troupe fell ill—I developed cellulitis from a roller-skating accident, Bob Beckham burst a blood vessel in his throat and Buzz Cason developed pneumonia. Our tour was canceled, losing $50,000 in business. Later that year, I developed throat problems.

In 1962, I dislocated a vertebra in my neck during a rocking stage show and was hospitalized. Colds and flu were chronic.

Bizarrely, Dub made news events out of my maladies. My manager even issued press releases about my health problems, capitalizing the spelling of my name at every mention, I might add. Said one:

> Doll-sized BRENDA LEE is a giant-sized star who has taken too many curtain calls from a hospital bed, all because of a fierce determination to go on with the show . . . even when it meant going out on a stretcher . . .
>
> BRENDA's dedication to "the show must go on" spirit has often come at a mighty price. . . . In Philadelphia, Pennsylvania, early in the show, BRENDA slipped and her head snapped wickedly. She smiled, she danced, she sang her heart out . . . inside she wanted to cry from the pain. In the wings, with the crowd shouting for an encore, BRENDA told her manager, "I think my neck is broken!"
>
> In Manchester, England, BRENDA insisted on doing the show despite the fact that she could barely stand up. There were no encores that night for BRENDA. The British fans shouted, stamped and whistled for a curtain call . . . but BRENDA did not hear them . . . she had collapsed from sheer exhaustion.

"She can't stand the thought of letting an audience down," Dub stated in his press release's conclusion.

Touring acts today have no idea how rigorous the road was back then. There were no interstates, no tour buses, no private jets and few decent accommodations. The pace was grueling, and I was pretty much exhausted all the time. But the show had to go on. You weren't allowed to be tired. There were times when I was so hoarse before I'd go on stage that I couldn't even talk. I'd wonder, "How in the world am I going to do this show?" Dub would give me a form of codeine to coat my throat. I don't even think you can buy that anymore. It made your voice better. I had to sing. You couldn't say no.

I have an awful lot of sympathy for entertainers who get hooked on drugs. I know they don't mean to—they have to keep up the pace. And a lot of times the people around them ignore any problems as long as the money keeps coming in.

I never became a druggie, thank goodness. But the opportunity was there. A physician in East Nashville named Dr. Snap was famous for prescribing amphetamines to entertainers. When I was fifteen, I was going through a "fat" period. I did have "diet pills." Dub didn't object when I got them prescribed. He never told me, "You can't be fat or you won't be popular." But I knew he wanted me to look as good as I could.

I took those things, and it almost drove me crazy. I did lose weight, but I also lost my memory. I couldn't remember the lyrics to my songs on stage sometimes. It had a real adverse effect on me. I didn't like it. I said, "I'd rather be fat than feel this way." I'm not sure what the pills were. I was just a kid.

If you got throat trouble in New York, there was the man we called the Miracle Doctor. He'd come and give you a shot and all of a sudden it would be like a miracle. You'd feel just wonderful. Later you found out it was all amphetamines.

Needless to say, none of this made its way into the pages of *Brenda Lee's Life Story*. This was a 15-cent biographical Dell comic book that appeared in 1962. Also omitted in the publication were any mentions of Peanut Faircloth, Red Foley, *The Ozark Jubilee,* Paul Cohen, Owen Bradley or Jay Rainwater, among others. In this version of my life, Dub Allbritten appears magically on "Mrs. Lee's" doorstep in Georgia, saying, "I'd like to talk to you and Brenda about something very important, her future." Stardom, of course, was instantaneous.

The comic book cited Cary Grant and Ingrid Bergman as my favorite movie stars, *Little Women* as my favorite book and water skiing and horseback riding as my favorite sports. The dramatic high point comes when I take off on a runaway dogsled while on tour in Alaska and fall in an accident. Dub rushes to my aid, but I am unhurt.

The most hilarious thing about that comic book is that I have a va-voom figure and long legs in the drawings. It was the same deal with the Brenda Lee paper dolls that were sold. Where they got those figures that they put my head on I'll never know. But for once in my life, I was stacked and tall.

The story about the dogsled was partly true. We were supposed to be posing for photographs. I was sitting in the sled, and the Casuals were on the back. I had heard that if you said, "Mush!" the dogs would go. I thought that was so funny—I didn't believe it. So when the guy was taking pictures I yelled, "Mush! Mush!" And those darn dogs took off like lightning and gave us the ride of our lives. We just hung on for dear life. We finally wound up back where we started. There was no crash or rescue attempt by Dub. He was chomping on that cigar when we got back, and he was mad. Smokin,' shakin' and mad!

The comic book singled out "Brenda Lee Day" in Baltimore as one of my career highlights. This really did occur, too, on July 13, 1962. Buddy Deane was the Baltimore version of Dick Clark. Deane's TV dance party aired on WJZ. En route to the show, Dub and I missed a flight. Decca executives were so eager to promote me that they chartered a private plane to Washington, where a standing-by helicopter flew me right to Deane's waiting mob of teens, 4,000 strong.

"It's the largest turnout for a musical celebrity I've seen," Deane stated. The copter then whisked me back to D.C. to appear on *The Milton Grant Show,* yet another *American Bandstand* imitator. Decca Records also sent me on a ten-day tour to visit radio stations in Hartford, Boston, Rochester, Buffalo, Syracuse, Cleveland and Detroit.

In addition to flying us from interview to interview, Decca pulled out the stops in promoting my albums. In 1961, the label declared March 29th as "Brenda Lee Day" and ordered its promotion staff nationwide to go all out in marketing my *Emotions* LP released on that date. Maximum exposure was ordered for coast-to-coast sales. The state of Georgia went along with the hype when Governor Ernest Vandivar declared its own Brenda Lee Day. Steve Allen sent me a congratulatory telegram. Trade reports declared that the promotion resulted in one-day sales of 125,000 copies of the record.

Whenever I look at the cover of that *Emotions* album, what I remember is that ring I've got on in the photo. It was the first fine piece of jewelry I ever owned, and it was a gift from Dub. It's a star sapphire with diamonds surrounding it. I cherish it, because he gave it to me years before I was ever popular, as if he believed in me.

He also gave me a diamond pendant necklace that I wore all the time. Later on, he made me a gift of a beautiful diamond watch. Each time, it touched me. The presents made me think that he really did care, even if he was never able to say so.

The record company gave me a gorgeous, solid gold charm bracelet when I turned sixteen. It was designed by David Webb, who was a famous jewelry designer in New York. The charms depicted all the achievements that I'd had up until that point. My first house, my first Gold Record, my first trip to Europe, my first trip to South America and things like that.

"Decca's enthusiasm was understandable," comments veteran music journalist John Lomax III. "Brenda was basically carrying the label as its primary hit maker. The company's roster was top heavy with adult legends like Bing Crosby, the Mills Brothers, the Ink Spots, the McGuire Sisters, Teresa Brewer and Ella Fitzgerald, all of whom had long since vanished from the hit parade. Jackie Wilson, on Decca's subsidiary Brunswick, was a force in r&b. But after Bill Haley and the Comets faded in 1956 and Buddy Holly died in 1959, only Brenda remained as a consistent Decca chart-topper. Executives at the company's office in Nashville called their building 'The House That Brenda Built.' "

"By 1962, Brenda had come into full command of her vocal powers, and everything she sang turned to gold," concurs longtime Brenda Lee observer Diana Reid Haig. " 'Break It to Me Gently,' which featured one of Brenda's most memorable performances, topped the charts in the beginning of the year. 'Speak to Me Pretty' became a smash in the U.K. 'Everybody Loves Me but You' hit No. 6 in the U.S. that summer. Pop singer-songwriter Jackie DeShannon's soulful 'Heart in Hand' was another summertime hit, followed by 'All Alone Am I,' with its unusual harpsichord arrangement.

"In my opinion, Brenda's soaring vocal and expressive phrasing on 'All Alone Am I' make it one of her finest performances. The single hit No. 1 in the U.S., entered the top-10 in England and also became a huge Continental success. In Germany, 50,000 copies were sold in just three days alone! Back at home, Brenda's LPs All the Way, Sincerely and Brenda, That's All glided to the top of the charts in 1961–62."

Lomax recounts the singer's award-winning streak: "In 1960, Brenda won the National Association of Record Merchandisers (NARM) award as its Most Promising Female Vocalist. 'I'm Sorry' was nominated for a Grammy Award. In 1961 she de-

throned Connie Francis as Britain's No. 1 female vocalist. State-
side, Music Vendor *named her its Top Female Singles Artist of
the Year.*

*"Hit Parader named her its Star of the Year for 1962. The
trade publications* Music Reporter *and* Cash Box *both named her
Top Female Vocalist of the Year. NARM gave her its honor as the
best-selling female vocalist of '62, and she repeated her win as
England's top warbler."*

Show offers were pouring in for me, and Dub was saying yes
to everything that could physically be done. A string of one-
nighters in the summer of 1961 was capped by my appearance at
the Alan Freed Spectacular at the Hollywood Bowl. I headlined a
bill that included bluesman B. B. King, soul queen Etta James,
electric guitarists the Ventures ("Walk Don't Run"), the creamy-
voiced trio the Fleetwoods ("Mr. Blue"), r&b veteran Clarence
"Frogman" Henry ("I Don't Know Why I Love You but I Do")
and my L.A. recording-session buddy Gene McDaniels (who'd
followed "A Hundred Pounds of Clay" with the top-10 smash
"Tower of Strength"). The roster also included my 1960 Brooklyn Paramount costars the Shirelles (now at the top of the charts
with "Dedicated to the One I Love") and Bobby Vee (headed for
No. 1 with "Take Good Care of My Baby"), plus rock 'n' roll
wildman Jerry Lee Lewis. The show was a sellout and kicked off
a cross-country rock 'n' roll tour featuring most of the partici-
pants. But that was impresario Freed's last hurrah.

Alan Freed was the epitome of what a rock 'n' roll disc jockey
was at that time. I don't care what anybody says, he was a great
man. He cared about us artists, and he cared about the music. His
was a terribly sad story—he didn't deserve what became of him.

Alan Freed was the deejay who'd coined the term "rock 'n'
roll" and was the music's most ardent early champion. But by the
time of my Hollywood Bowl appearance, Freed was a nearly bro-

ken man. Both he and Dick Clark had been subpoenaed in the federal payola investigation of 1959–60. This was when the government held hearings to uncover alleged corruption in the rock 'n' roll record business. Disc jockeys, it was said, were being bribed to play records.

Dick Clark walked away unscathed. But Alan Freed became what many believe to be the music industry's fall guy to payola, a martyr to the rock 'n' roll cause. After the scandal ruined his East Coast reputation, he moved to Los Angeles to continue show promotions and radio broadcasts. But his heyday was over. His drinking was reportedly spiraling out of control, and he was beset by tax-evasion charges and still mounting legal fees. His payola case dragged on into 1962. Freed became destitute and died on January 20, 1965. How could everyone turn their back on the man who had laid the foundation for the rock 'n' roll industry? It still makes me mad to think about it.

The only thing I knew about payola was what I saw on TV. It did put a blight on our music, and that is what upset me. As far as I know, nobody ever paid anybody anything to put any of my records on the air. Mostly it was the small, independent labels who had to play the game that way.

Despite Dub's dislike of Jerry Lee Lewis, the Hollywood Bowl appearance sparked a reunion between the piano-pounding rocker and me. We were billed together on a swing through the Northeast. But Jerry Lee's reputation preceded him. The show was banned in Rochester, New York. That wasn't the tour's undoing, however. Attitude was. Jerry Lee hadn't had a hit in three years, but he was too proud to be an opening act.

At the next show, Jerry Lee just completely disrupted everything with his onstage antics. He got the crowd in a frenzy, tearing apart the piano and busting up the piano bench. They were even ripping the seats out of the auditorium floor. I was the headliner and couldn't even go on after that. I told Dub, "If this tour continues, he's going to close and I'm going to open." No matter how good you were, you couldn't follow something like that. After Jerry Lee went off, the crowd was practically bloodthirsty. Needless to say, Dub had that tour end prematurely.

Conservatives branded rock 'n' roll as the downfall of Western Civilization. It was blamed for juvenile delinquency, school truancy, teen drinking and smoking and all sorts of social problems. I was asked to comment in the pages of *The Music Journal* in 1961, so I wrote:

> Americans have constantly criticized the current trend in popular music, claiming that is it responsible for low morality. I, being both a teenager and a pop singer, naturally disagree. I feel the musical taste of the young people in this country is a healthy one. We can dance to the music, sing it, tap our feet to the rhythm and identify with the lyrics.
>
> If radio stations would be listened to fairly, our critics would find that many current hits are ballads, and some very lovely ones, too.

"It was her powerful, torn-from-the-chest delivery of those gorgeous ballads that would pave the way to Brenda's future," says Nashville author John Lomax III. "In those days, the ultimate mainstream show biz accomplishments were headlining in Las Vegas showrooms, appearing on The Ed Sullivan Show, *starring in musical comedy and becoming a movie star in Hollywood. Between 1961 and 1963, teen queen Brenda Lee would do all four."*

EIGHT

Hollywood and Beyond

Sometimes I wonder where it all went. Whatever happened to the tomboy I used to be, the mischievous prankster, the lovelorn junior high girl and the slightly rebellious rocker I aspired to be? They were all taken away from me. I was forced to grow up and become something that other people wanted me to be.

I went along willingly, but I lost part of myself in the process. I was forced to become one-dimensional, an icon named "Brenda Lee." I was no longer somebody's girlfriend, daughter or sister. I was a Star, and I was expected to devote myself to that, twenty-four hours a day. When I was seventeen, it became clear to me that I really wasn't in charge of my own life. That's an age when most kids are starting to assert their independence. Instead, I was shoehorned into being a "diva."

I was assaulted from all sides to forsake my rock 'n' roll past and advance into "legitimate," adult showbiz. My label, my manager, my tutor and my choreographer presented a united front—I was to become a lady.

My manager Dub Allbritten was increasingly aiming for press coverage in the non-teen media. Publications like *Woman's Day* and *The Hollywood Reporter* were covering my career now. In July 1962, I was profiled in *Esquire*. Despite the piece's condescending tone about my youth, it pointed out that I was making

$300,000 a year and quoted Decca's New York promotion executive Lenny Salidor as saying that the label was eager to disassociate me "from the stigma of rock 'n' roll."

Taking the first step toward a potential new audience for me, Decca issued the album *Sincerely* that year. It contained no teen hits, nor was it aimed at my young fan base. Instead, the collection presented me performing such standard fare as "You Always Hurt the One You Love," "I'll Be Seeing You" and "How Deep Is the Ocean." On the jacket, I sport glamorous, bouffant brunette tresses. And I look wistfully upward through mascaraed lashes over darkly lined eyelids. All in all, the image was much more sophisticated than my pert portraits as a juvenile pop star had been.

In addition, Decca repackaged the album of standards that I had recorded when I was fourteen. The kiddie photo of me was removed from the jacket, and the original *Grandma What Great Songs You Sang* LP was retitled *Brenda Lee Sings Songs Everybody Knows*.

Dub did his part for the career transition by stirring up interest in Hollywood. My name was floated in the gossip columns as being connected with films such as *Blue Hawaii, Learning About Love, State Fair* and *The Shirley Temple Story*. None of these came to fruition for me. But Dub kept fanning the flame. That's why Mother and I moved to Los Angeles in January 1961. Mother left five-year-old Robyn and eleven-year-old Randall behind with relatives.

"The kids didn't cry or complain about us leaving," comments Grayce. "By this time, they were used to it. I felt a little bad about it, but that's what we'd always had to do, ever since Brenda started singing. Of course we missed them, but at least I knew they were being well cared for, because they were always with close relatives, primarily my sister Irene."

For the eleventh grade, Mother and Dub enrolled me in the Hollywood Professional School. That's a place where they sent children who were performers—dancers, singers, actors or whatever. Plus, there were a bunch of rich kids and "problem" kids, the children of Hollywood studio executives. It wasn't your normal school by any means. It sat right on Hollywood Boulevard, at the corner of Serrano Avenue. I don't remember there being a school yard, a lunchroom or a gymnasium. It used to be a mortuary.

It was an accredited high school, but it was pretty surreal. You'd be sitting in class, maybe having an English test, and the principal would come in with a casting agent, saying, "We need a five-foot-two blonde for a commercial," and someone would get up and leave. Imagine a classroom full of child stars and how dysfunctional that would be. Some of those spoiled little monsters would even sock the teachers. Poor Miss Anderssen, our red-headed English teacher, was especially tortured.

I took classes with other young performers of the day, on a schedule that allowed us to attend school for half a day and then leave for work. My schoolmates included the children of singers Peggy Lee and Dinah Washington, as well as such up-and-coming young acts as Tuesday Weld, Peggy Lipton, Sue Lyon, Mickey Rooney Jr., Connie Stevens, Kathy Young and Tony Butala.

Life at my new school was nothing like it had been at Maplewood Junior High. There were no extracurricular activities at the Hollywood Professional School. But there was a peculiar kind of camaraderie of sorts among the self-absorbed showbiz students. The classmates even came up with their own school song: "Let's all cheer for Hollywood Pro! You get the grades, if you got the dough."

Impromptu performances were encouraged. During one school morning, I was asked to put on a show for my fellow students. So I quickly got together with guitar hotshot Larry Collins of the teen duo the Collins Kids and former Walt Disney Mouseketeer Cubby O'Brien, a frenetic drummer. My classmates said the Hollywood Professional School had never been so rocked.

The school held an annual dinner at the Sportsman's Lodge in Studio City where the yearbooks were handed out. When I was a junior, I unintentionally shocked both teachers and parents by belting out "What'd I Say," the Ray Charles wailer. When I rocked out with "She knows how to shake that thing!" my classmates were delighted, but the elders were dismayed. I'll never forget that Mrs. Mann, the school director, gave me a tart tongue-lashing for my rambunctious choice of material.

It seemed like I was always causing some fuss there. When singer Paul Anka came calling on me at the school one day, I was delighted. I remember bursting into Mrs. Mann's office breathlessly. "He came to see me! He came to see me!" I squealed excitedly. Paul was a major idol with such hits as "Puppy Love" and "Put Your Head on My Shoulder." And I wasn't the only one excited. He provided tickets for a group of my classmates and me to attend his show at the Coconut Grove.

Here's what's hilarious. We all thought we were there as guests of Paul Anka. We were eating and having a merry old time. Just ordering away and thinking, "Isn't this grand?" Then the bill came. None of us had any money except surprised and unlucky Larry Collins. He got stuck with the whole tab.

I knew hardly anyone in L.A. when we moved there. But I gradually made contacts. My album *Let Me Sing* included the standard "Where Are You," which was cowritten by Jimmy McHugh. And that connection forged one of my most beneficial Hollywood alliances. Jimmy McHugh was the boyfriend of the power-mad gossip queen Louella Parsons. She could make or break anyone's career in those days and was universally feared and loathed.

But she loved me; she was like a surrogate mother to me out there. I know everyone hated her, but she really took me under her wing. I did wind up recording Jimmy McHugh's "On the Sunny Side of the Street" and "I'm in the Mood for Love." Maybe that's why she kept being so nice to me in her column all the time. She continually informed her millions of readers about my career.

One event Louella didn't cover was my Sweet 16 party at the Crescendo. In deference to my age, the nightclub did not serve alcohol that day. "Where's the booze?" the columnist demanded upon entering. When informed that there wasn't any, she stomped out.

I'm certainly glad she liked me. She spared no one, and there were plenty of people in Hollywood who'd have been glad to drive a stake through her heart. Maybe it was because of Jimmy McHugh. Maybe it was because I was such an innocent young girl. Whatever the reason, Louella Parsons was always in my corner.

Louella wrote liner notes for my LP *The Versatile Brenda Lee*. She dropped my name whenever she could and lobbied on my behalf in the silver screen community.

After all, doesn't every kid dream of being a movie star? I didn't. In the early 1960s, teen singers left and right were invading the silver screen. Fabian, Annette, Frankie Avalon and Connie Francis all made the transition from music to movies. And so did Elvis.

My manager was an acquaintance of Col. Tom Parker's, and I think the Colonel might have been instrumental in getting me into the movies. I really was not interested—it wasn't something that I wanted to pursue. I was interested in my singing. And at the time, I was sort of a little, short, chubby girl, nothing to really set the world on fire, looks-wise.

They'd tried to keep me from being a sex symbol, but I don't think they had to try too hard. I mean, that's never been one of my problems.

But glamorous or not, I was being groomed for films. In March 1961, I took a dramatic role on TV's *The Danny Thomas Show*. I played a young girl with a promising voice who was counseled by Thomas to continue on her singing path. This was somewhat ironic in that Dub was steering me toward acting at the time.

Scripts kept coming. I was too busy or not interested. Finally I accepted a part in *The Two Little Bears,* a light comedy starring Eddie Albert, Jane Wyatt, Soupy Sales, Nancy Kulp and Jimmy Boyd. I enjoyed my first movie experience but found it difficult to emote for the camera and to do scenes out of context. And without an audience to play to, I felt like a fish out of water.

Nevertheless, I loved Jane Wyatt and Eddie Albert. I was not an actress by any stretch of the imagination. That's obvious when you see it. But the foray was never intended for me to be a serious actress. It was just another of Dub's vehicles to promote Brenda Lee.

Believe me, you haven't lived until you've seen *The Two Little Bears*. In it, a gypsy puts a magical spell on my two brothers and they keep turning into bears, then boys, then bears again. Film critic Leonard Maltin calls it "harmless." I call it a bomb. The film completely tanked at the box office.

One of the only good things that came out of this cinematic flop for me was its music. I sang two songs in the film—"Honey Bear," and "Speak to Me Pretty," the latter of which hopped up to No. 4 on the British popularity charts.

Good movie or bad, I was having a ball in Los Angeles. My best friend was Sandy Ferra, who was a dancer in several of the Elvis movies. She was a beautiful Italian girl with a bubbly personality.

When I met Sandy at the Hollywood Professional School, she wasn't impressed with my credentials. I think she saw a little Southern girl in the big city and decided to take me under her wing. The other kids seemed distant. They dressed differently than I did. They wore more makeup than I did. They were more sophisticated in every way. I didn't feel all that welcomed. I guess I would have survived, but her friendship sure made it easier. She told me the do's and don'ts and welcomed me into her circle of friends and her family.

By the time I met her in 1961, Sandy was already dating the world's most famous entertainer. The previous year, Elvis Presley had attended a show at the Crossbow nightclub in L.A. and was attracted to a photo on the owner's desk. It was a winsome portrait of Tony Ferra's fourteen-year-old daughter. That was Sandy. Elvis, then twenty-five, asked to meet her, and they were soon dating steadily. The couple danced and necked together for hours at a time. So at school, Sandy started sharing confidences with me.

Sandy and I talked about Elvis a lot. The day he married Priscilla in 1967, the two of us sat down and cried.

Actually, it was because of her ties to Elvis that Sandy was allowed into my inner circle in the first place. Dub Allbritten guarded my social life zealously.

Here's how it happened. By this time, Lamar Fike was working as my road manager. Lamar was a member of Elvis Presley's "Memphis Mafia" collection of intimates. But he bounced back and forth between the two camps in those days—when he was on the outs with Elvis, Lamar would work for me. And it was his OK that made Sandy my buddy.

I asked Dub if Sandy could travel with us to shows. He said OK, because he knew she wouldn't be any trouble.

"When I went to shows with her, I'd help her with her makeup and clothes," Sandy reports. *"Elvis loved makeup, so I'd always worn a lot of eye makeup. But I didn't put as much on Brenda as I did on me.*

"Today you see these acts with fancy sound and lights. Brenda didn't have all that. She'd just walk out there on stage with that God-given voice. She didn't need anything else. Her talent was just amazing, and still is. There is nobody like her."

We were typical teens when we were at home. We were good kids; we didn't get into trouble at all. Sandy and I would drive down Hollywood Boulevard, cruising to spot other teens at burger joints. Eating was one of our great joys in life. We loved tacos—I think she introduced me to Mexican food. She'd buy a dozen tacos, and we'd eat them all at one sitting. Sometimes when we were out riding around, my hit "Dum Dum" would come on the radio, and we'd turn it up real loud, rock to the beat in our seats, snap our fingers and sing along.

We used to go over to Eddie Hodges's house a lot. He's the child actor who sang "High Hopes" with Frank Sinatra in *A Hole in the Head* and starred in *The Adventures of Huckleberry Finn*. His mom would make us these great Southern dinners. One night the Hodges family took us out with Hayley Mills. She was a big movie star right then with *The Parent Trap* and *Pollyanna*. She was very sweet, very unaffected. I loved her English accent.

Sandy and I drew even closer outside the Hollywood social scene. She became my confidante on the road. For despite my Tinsel Town explorations, my concerts continued to be the major source of income.

When we were in San Francisco, we ran into our classmate Tony Butala and his partners in the Lettermen. They asked us out for dinner after my show. The problem was, Dub would always make us lock ourselves in the hotel room at the end of the night. So here we were sneaking through the lobby of the Fairmont Hotel to meet the Lettermen. From behind a palm tree we see these smoke signals. It was Dub's cigar.

"Where do you girls think you're going?" Dub fumed.

"Um, we were just going to have something to eat," I stammered.

"OK, but you be back in exactly one hour," he decreed.

He kept a really close eye on us. We didn't get away with much.

Later on, I was the maid of honor at Sandy's 1967 wedding to handsome actor Robert Blair. But their marriage was annulled a few months later. Since 1975, Sandy Ferra has been happily married to TV game-show host, radio deejay and recording artist Wink Martindale.

While on tour and absent from the Hollywood Professional School's classrooms, I completed my remaining high school credits through correspondence courses. I was tutored by a striking and polished Vanderbilt University senior named Freda Garrett.

"I had enough credits for my teacher's certificate, but I think the reason I was hired was that Dub wanted her exposed to a higher class of people, a little more sophistication," says the forthright Freda. "I traveled quite a bit showing horses all my life. So the very first thing I did when I met her was teach her to horseback ride out at our farm."

Freda was the daughter of Ray Garrett, a prosperous retailer and land developer. Through one of her family's horse show friends, Freda was contacted by Charlie Mosley, my guardian. He made Freda an offer to accompany me on the road. Freda's older brother Mark was a noted Nashville interior decorator who was styling Dub Allbritten's fancy new penthouse office at the time. So that might have been another factor in her hiring.

Although I was only three years younger than Freda, she was much more mature than me. She was poised, yet relaxed and natural around entertainers. Her droll sense of humor was a plus as well. Looking back, Freda couldn't have been more perfect for the position of my high school tutor.

We were like a family; we had a good time. Freda and I looked at schoolwork like we had a job to do. We'd do it together. After I got done with my lessons, we were more like girlfriends.

When Freda was with me, I was singing in a lot of clubs at night. There'd be two performances. Then in the mornings, we'd usually get up early and have to go to radio and TV stations, doing publicity all during the day. By the time we got back to the hotel, took a bath and ate, it was time for the two dinner shows again. If we didn't have to do work promoting the shows, we'd spend all day catching up on my studies.

"After the very first concert when I went on the road with her, I realized that Brenda had no appropriate clothes to wear to interviews and such. I told Charlie Mosley and Dub, 'She needs some clothes!' They gave me $500. I took her to my dressmaker and had her measured. She made twenty-one outfits. I just didn't think it was right that the tutor had better clothes than the star.

"I also bought her luggage. She was a big star by 1962, and I thought she should get off a plane looking like one. Dub and them were a bunch of men. What did they know?

"When we got to Boston, I got in a cab while they were rehearsing. I said, 'Take me to the best department store in Boston.' I went in and bought $300 worth of lingerie, nice bubble bath and stuff like that. Went to the hotel, took all of her things out of the bureau and threw them away. Put all this new stuff in her drawers. I was so proud of myself. When I came back from

the club with her, I threw open the drawers and said, 'Look, Brenda!' She got mad at me."

Well, I didn't see anything wrong with the underwear I had. Heck, no one ever saw it anyway. I thought I had the latest thing—each pair was labeled with a day of the week. I thought they were so cool. But Freda thought I should have satin and lace. Whatever.

Freda was so meticulous with her appearance. Her clothes were tailored and expensive. Her makeup had to be perfect, and she wouldn't let anybody see her without it on. To this day, she has this gorgeous, thick, copper-colored hair. She is so striking.

I told the band, "I've never seen anybody take so many baths. Freda's gonna wash her hide off!" Like most of the people who have worked for me, Freda became my dear friend. She was far more than a tutor; I depended on her for so many things.

"My job soon expanded into being wardrobe mistress and chaperone," Freda explains. "I would be backstage. Her show had two quick changes. I'd have her dresses ready behind stage. She'd come off, and I'd unzip her. She'd step out of that dress and into the other and go back out within two minutes. That was a time when girls wore lots of crinolines.

"I remember one show when Brenda had on a red dress with all these starchy petticoats. She had this number where she'd go down on one knee. When she came up, these petticoats just started falling out of the dress. Brenda stood up, and the petticoats just stayed there on the ground. She was so cool about it. She stepped out of the petticoats very ladylike, picked them up and threw them to me. Everybody thought it was part of the act. She never missed a note.

"Another one of her outfits was a party dress—white, frilly organza with hand-painted red flowers all over it. Brenda cut her hand on the mike, and it bled all over the dress. When she came

off stage, I handed her a hanky. She handled it so coolly—the au-dience never knew the dress was ruined.

"I didn't work for the money—I only made $200 a week—I did it for the experience. I look back on those days as some of the best of my life. There was so much funny stuff that went on. When Dub wasn't on the road with us, he'd call me, and I'd go down to see if Lamar Fike was doing things properly. He'd call Lamar and find out if my story backed up his. I knew that's what he was doing. He knew every day what was going on."

Freda and I played a gag on Lamar one night. After the show, he'd left his briefcase sitting in the middle of the dance floor. Freda got it, and it had about $20,000 in it. In those days you carried around cash from the shows with you until you got home. When Lamar came back to get the briefcase, we pretended for a long time that it was lost. He was about to have a heart attack. Freda and I finally told him we had it.

There was this one club where the bathrooms were on the other side of the audience. Once the show started, you couldn't get across from the dressing rooms to use them. I'll never forget, Freda and I both had to "go." We couldn't get across. So we found some cups and there we went. That was certainly an unla-dylike thing to do, but when you gotta go, you gotta go.

Freda and I shared a wacky sense of humor. But there were times when we needed sheer guts to survive. I was used to it, but this was Freda's first experience up close with showbiz. And she thought things were pretty crazy.

"Brenda was hot as a firecracker and selling millions of records," Freda remarks. "She was great at interviews and could handle hecklers from the stage like nobody's business.

"And she put on such a great show. One night, she got the crowd so worked up that people rushed the stage after the show. We were all running around trying to get out of there. Lamar was

sitting in the car at the backstage entrance. I was collecting her clothes and shoes. Somebody in all the confusion crashed into me, and I dropped the shoes. That's when I got cut off from Brenda and the rest of them. Out in the alley, the crowd started rocking the car. That was scary. I finally pushed my way to the car, fought my way in and Lamar started rolling us slowly out of there.

"Brenda was just a plain little girl. But when she walked out from behind those curtains and the spotlight hit her, she was totally transformed."

NINE

"The New Judy Garland"

The mastermind behind my transformation into a supper-club chanteuse was Dick Barstow. Decca had pushed for my new musical sophistication. Dub had worked on multimedia exposure. Freda had provided the polish. But it was Dick who got me off the county fair stages, out of the rock 'n' roll arenas and into the elite showrooms and elegant supper clubs of America.

Everybody should have a Dick Barstow in their life. He was one of the most colorful and talented people I've ever met. He taught me so much about show business. He connected me with my emotions and taught me truly how to relate a lyric. I learned how to gauge the feelings of an audience and how to play to them. He taught me everything from staging to lighting to dress to dialogue. The things he taught me about the pacing of a show are still with me today. I think that's one of the most important things he taught me.

"Others could deliver hits; others could stand and sing; others could attract crowds; but by late 1961, Brenda had a top-flight stage show," reports journalist Charlie Lamb, who witnessed the transformation. "None of her Nashville peers, and few teen performers elsewhere, could entertain the way Brenda did. And that was Dick's contribution. He took a naive, small-town girl and transformed her into a diva in full command of her

*stage. Brenda learned dramatic skits, impersonations, costum-
ing, stage moves, entrances and exits, production, sets and a million tricks of the trade from him."*

Dick Barstow would remain a part of my life as an advisor
and friend until his death in 1982. Dick was quite a character. He
showed you love while he taught you. He would scream and yell
and holler, but if you did it well, he would be the first to compli-
ment you. He was a choreographer, producer, director, stage designer and all-around showman. If you ever met him, you never
forgot it.

He was a different breed altogether for me. I'd never seen the
likes of him before. He wore an ascot and lived in a Manhattan
penthouse. He was an incredibly accomplished dancer. He was
regal and theatrical. He was openly gay. He was fascinating.

Dick told me that he was raised in a brothel and came of age
during the Roaring Twenties. The story goes that legendary mob-
ster Al Capone took the boy's struggling family under his wing
and became his benefactor. Dick had been born with a clubfoot.
Capone reportedly paid for corrective surgery to help the boy realize his dream to dance.

Capone also paid for the private tutors that coached Dick and
his sister into becoming a childhood dancing team. Throughout
his life, Dick's pinky finger sported a heavy gold signet ring en-
graved with the initials A. C.—a gift from Mr. Capone.

After becoming a solo act in the 1930s, Dick toured in musicals and was billed as the World's Greatest Toe Dancer. In the
1940s, he headed for Hollywood to become a choreographer in
movie musicals starring the likes of Jack Benny, Dan Dailey,
Dennis Day and Lena Horne.

His most famous movie moment is unquestionably the tour
de force, fifteen-minute "Born in a Trunk" production number by
Judy Garland in 1954's Oscar-nominated *A Star Is Born*. Dick

not only choreographed this famous sequence, he was its director as well.

If you watch that medley, you can see a lot of Dick's genius. I notice many of the things he later taught me. There's the tensing of Judy's hand gestures, especially at the ending of songs. He had me do that. There's that stance she takes with her legs spread apart and her arms out, palms lifted. He coached me to take that same posture in the spotlight, as if to say, "Here I am; I love you; now love me back." The "Born in a Trunk" sequence ends with a pin light moving tighter and tighter in on Judy's face. Dick used that in my show, too. And overall, that whole theatrical, storytelling concept was something he incorporated into my repertoire.

The Oscar for Best Picture in 1952 went to Cecil B. DeMille's *The Greatest Show on Earth*, which starred Charlton Heston, Betty Hutton, Dorothy Lamour and James Stewart. This was another of Dick Barstow's credits as a choreographer. And I don't think there has ever been a more fabulous, more musical, more glittering circus parade in history than the one he created for that film.

He certainly knew how to deliver "The Greatest Show on Earth." That's because Dick Barstow was the director, stager and choreographer for the Ringling Brothers, Barnum & Bailey Circus for nearly thirty years, 1949–78. He also choreographed touring ice-skating extravaganzas.

When television arrived, Dick developed flashy productions for the new medium. In 1952–54, he served as a writer, choreographer and stager of NBC's *The Colgate Comedy Hour*. This weekly production featured the likes of Dean Martin, Jerry Lewis, Eddie Cantor, Abbott & Costello, Jimmy Durante, Sammy Davis Jr. and Bob Hope. In 1953, it became the first network color telecast.

By the 1950s, Dick Barstow was also creating nightclub acts and stage productions for such top-drawer celebrities as Jane Morgan, Phyllis McGuire, Martha Raye, Gertrude Lawrence and, of course, my idol, Judy Garland. His special touch helped revive Judy's flagging concert career in 1959 and brought her acclaim as a legendary theatrical performer.

I met Dick through Harry Kalcheim of the William Morris Agency. As soon as I got a hit record, Dub Allbritten took my booking out of Nashville and straight to New York. Harry was my agent; he believed he could get me booked into the supper clubs and expensive nightclubs if I had a classier show. And Harry thought that Dick Barstow would be just the guy for me.

Harry Kalcheim was the William Morris agent who made Milton Berle into a television superstar. He brought Andy Griffith, Eddy Arnold, Carl Reiner, Elvis Presley and dozens of others to William Morris. According to Frank Rose in his book *The Agency,* Harry had also begged the firm to sign Barbra Streisand, who was virtually unknown in 1961–62. To its everlasting regret, the company didn't listen to him. "Kalcheim could spot talent wherever he found it, from a Socialist summer camp in the Poconos to a hillbilly roadhouse in Tennessee," wrote author Frank Rose. And I agree.

I think Harry Kalcheim had seen some kind of potential greatness in me as a teenage singer, and I know he'd witnessed the talents of Dick Barstow on *The Colgate Comedy Hour,* which was a William Morris property. The combination, the wily agent figured, could be dynamite.

There was just one hitch. Dick Barstow wouldn't work with just anyone. He had to really like you. The money didn't matter. Before he'd work with me, I had to send him all my albums. Then he came to see my show.

He must have seen something he liked. All I know is one day Dick showed up at rehearsals in New York. And, boy, did he start putting us through our paces.

"I hate those 'cafeteria arms'!" he yelled at me.

"What does that mean?" I asked.

"It looks like you're holding a tray! I want to see those arms fully extended!"

"Raise those hands out to the sides, *never* in front of you! That gesture you're doing with your palm toward the audience means 'stop.' Turn your palm inward and stretched up toward the sky. *That* is a move of love."

"Remember, boys, Brenda is the diamond, you're only the setting!" he instructed the Casuals. "The setting looks like hell without that stone. Always remember that. Think of Brenda as a precious stone. If you threw that diamond down on the floor, people would think, 'That can't be a diamond; it's on the floor.' But if you put that diamond in a box with black velvet, that's altogether different. *You* are the velvet."

"When I say take five steps, I mean take exactly five steps. Not four, not six."

"But Dick," complained Richard Williams of the Casuals, "we're doing a song in four-four time. That's out of tempo with what we're playing. Besides, I'm behind a piano!"

"Do it!"

"I don't like the way you walk," Dick spat at one band member. "By the end of the day you'll know how to walk differently."

He was trying to teach us presentation and staging. And you could never say, "Dick, it can't be done." Anything could be done if he wanted it to be.

"You did it his way," says Casuals member Buzz Cason. *"There was no compromising. He wouldn't take 'no' for an answer.*

"We were a bunch of musicians with two left feet apiece. He terrorized us. One afternoon he got so frustrated with me he just got on the floor on his back and started kicking."

"He single-handedly created these theatrical set pieces for us," recalls Casuals guitarist Tony Moon. *"We were doing 'Trouble in River City' from* The Music Man *and carrying protest signs. He'd make you do things that were almost physically impossible."*

"Dick, I can't hold a sign and play guitar at the same time," Tony protested.

"Oh sure you can," Dick snapped back flippantly.

Freda Garrett had the best wisecrack about that experience. She said, "Dick Barstow got circus elephants to do the twist. I figured if he could do that, he could train the Casuals."

"Barstow was trying to make Brenda palatable to the older, non-rock generation people who were paying the big bucks for tickets," Tony continues. *"He really had to change us around a lot. With Barstow, our rehearsals became a whole new, butt-kicking deal. We became stage professionals because of him. He was very influential in all of our lives.*

"Brenda had great, great natural ability. She just needed to be taught how to get the most out of what she had. It's like a great athlete. They might have great natural talent, but they still need a coach."

My new show was all Dick Barstow's doing. We had this big opening where the boys would be singing, "Brenda, Brenda, here comes Brenda Lee" while the accompanying orchestra kept building up in intensity. Finally, I'd come on and do something like "Fools Rush In." We also did specialty bits that Dick would write, comedy schtick between the Casuals and me, my impersonation of Jimmy Durante and tributes to some of the great female vocalists.

The set list included all my hits, but they were woven in and out of the show like a tapestry. We also did a lot of standards and big-band numbers. It was really classy. Every year Dick would come out on the road with us to tweak things up and embellish the show. I'd call him several times a year for him to come up with new ideas. Each year—usually early in the summer—we would go into rehearsals for six weeks or so and incorporate new pieces that Dick would devise.

In the 1968 show, for instance, Dick had me walk out into the crowd singing "When You're Smiling," "Smile," "Put on a Happy Face" and "Baby Face." While I'd be doing this medley, I'd pose for Polaroid snapshots with various audience members. I kept that bit in my show for years and years. People still ask me about it.

We started carrying stage sets that he'd design. The set for "Bye Bye Blackbird" was a hotel room. I'd sit at an antique table and talk on the telephone. It was a soliloquy about a girl named Molly who found that life in the big city was not what she'd dreamed of. She's telling her mother to leave the light on, because she's coming home. It was quite moving.

We started carrying our own lighting, especially for the outdoor shows. In the supper clubs, Dick knew how to tailor their lighting grid especially for me. You practically had to be a college graduate to read Dick's lighting charts. He specifically said, "No amber! It makes you look yellow!" He loved to create pools of lighting and dramatic effects.

He insisted that I start performing with a full orchestra. The Casuals would be joined by an eighteen-piece group. He had elaborate musical arrangements created by the top composers of the day. He put me in heavy beaded evening gowns, brocade wraps trimmed in mink and long satin evening jackets.

The "new" Brenda Lee debuted in November 1961 at Blinstrub's supper club in Boston. That venue was a big barn of a place that seated nearly 1,000. The balcony swept all the way around the hall. The stage was cavernous. But I wasn't intimidated. I couldn't wait to try out all the new stuff. Outfits. Lighting. Arrangements. I was ready. We hadn't tried this out with an audience, and we were all anxious to see if it was going to work.

It did. My week-long engagement was completely sold out. My tireless booster Louella Parsons reported breathlessly that Prince Thaimar Ibn Saud of Arabia occupied a front-row seat at Blinstrub's for the show. The evidently smitten prince asked for an autographed photo of me and brought his private photographer backstage to immortalize the moment of our meeting.

Blinstrub's led to the Coconut Grove in Los Angeles, the Shoreham Hotel in Washington, D.C., and the Palmer House in Chicago. Then Pittsburgh's Holiday House, Detroit's Roostertail, Windsor's Top Hat, New Orleans' Roosevelt Hotel, Baltimore's Venus Club and Miami's Deauville Hotel all opened their doors to this new show of mine.

The Latin Quarter in New York was owned by Lou Walters, who was Barbara Walters's father. That's where they had the trained chimpanzees as my opening act. The trainer was so mean to the chimps—he beat them viciously backstage. The poor things were so frightened of him when they were doing their tricks that they would poop and pee and mess all over the stage. They had to clean it completely before I could go on.

Years later, Barbara Walters and I reminisced about her dad's club at a big party at the Pierre Hotel in Manhattan. The Latin Quarter was one of *the* places to be back then.

It was a beautiful club. All those supper clubs were—dripping in chandeliers, with red velvet covers on the chairs or booths. Plush carpets. Martinis and champagne. People came dressed. Sometimes the men came in tuxedoes, always a suit.

Women would come in ball gowns or short cocktail dresses. They were all just dressed to the nines. Very elegant. Kind of like a magical world. There is nothing like it today. It's an entertainment scene that has just about vanished, but what a time that was.

The only thing I didn't like about the clubs was the cigarette smoking. That was considered very glamorous, and everybody did it. There was no such thing as a "no smoking" clause in your contract. I would come off hoarse every night.

A lot of those clubs were controlled by the Mob. I wasn't aware of it at the time, but apparently, I was a big favorite with the Mafia.

"It seemed like every club we worked was Mafia," recalls Tony Moon. "Once a week at the Copacabana, they'd have what they called 'Big Nose Night.' That was when all the mobsters would bring their babes to the show and sit there and smoke cigars. A lot of times those guys could be hecklers. But how could you be ugly to Brenda Lee? There was this diminutive young girl up there who was just singing her ass off. No one could sit there and deride her. No one."

If there had been any problems, Dub Allbritten could have held his own. My manager was a guy with "connections."

"We were at the Deauville Hotel in Miami, and the comedian who was opening for Brenda was being an asshole," Tony remembers. "Brenda had a dressing room with a star on it; and his dressing room only had his name on it. So he told the management of the Deauville that he wanted that room with the star."

"This little bitch from Tennessee is not going to have that room," railed the arrogant humorist. "I'm also not going to open for her. If anything, she is going to open for me. I'm the star and not that little hillbilly shrimp."

Tony says, "Dub got wind of all the b.s. that was going down, and he was clever. He told everybody, 'OK, we'll open. No prob-

lem.' Of course, he knew damn well that no one, certainly not a stand-up comic, could follow Brenda Lee.

"Naturally, Brenda wore those people out. So the guy gets up there and starts saying things like, 'What did you think of that midget?' and other derogatory comments about her and her show. This started to piss Dub off. He called Nashville's biggest bootlegger and gambling kingpin and told him the story."

The next night, there were big guys in shiny suits with slick black hair visiting backstage. All of a sudden, the comedian was very sweet and nice. And he opened for me like he was supposed to do. No yelling, no screaming, no nothing. There was evidently a phone call and a visit, and from then on, there was no problem.

He also gave me back my cabana at the swimming pool. He'd taken it away from me because he didn't have one.

In New Orleans at the Blue Room in the Roosevelt Hotel, the club owner came backstage before the show and said, "There's a gentleman here that is a real big fan of yours who wants to meet you after the show."

"I'm not able," I protested. "When there's two shows a night, I'm exhausted, and I go right back to my hotel room and to bed."

"You really ought to meet this guy."

"I'm telling you, I don't do that."

"You should for this guy."

"Well, who is he?"

"Joe Marcello."

"Oh."

I knew he was from a famous Mafia family. And you can bet I stayed after the show and met him. And you know what? I really liked Mr. Marcello. Every time I came to New Orleans after that, I called him. One time when I was hospitalized there, he sent white-gloved waiters up to the room with pheasant under glass and real china and silver. I always had a real good relationship with those people. Thank God.

Not everyone was so refined and considerate. My tutor Freda Garrett was startled when she was standing in the wings at the Latin Casino in Cherry Hill, New Jersey. The club's manager was slowly unzipping her dress from behind.

"I was waiting for Brenda to come off stage for her costume change, so I couldn't exactly leave," Freda explains. "And that was my first experience with a 'dirty old man.' That night, I asked Dub what I should do.

"He told me, 'Tell the boys to hang around with you and Brenda backstage after the show. Do anything you have to do, but handle it. If he'll do it to you, he'll do it to Brenda."

You can bet that Freda did "handle it," using her best steel-magnolia, Southern belle wiles, I might add. But she was also careful not to get caught alone with the man again.

Dub parlayed my nightclub success into ever more prestigious venues. I performed at the Steel Pier in Atlantic City with crooner Al Martino. I starred at the Hollywood Bowl with my old L.A. buddies the Lettermen. I even began to entertain on the Borscht Belt circuit, the famous luxury Jewish resorts in the Catskill Mountains.

The first one was the Concord, a two-week stand in their "Winter Wonderland" show in February of '62. It was like being on a cruise ship. All the dining room seating was assigned. I'll never forget it—when I got through with my first song, I heard all this pounding and clattering on the tables. I thought, "My gosh, they must hate me!" No one had told me that's how they applauded. They had little hammers that they beat on the tables. I thought they were going to start throwing stuff!

Nightclubs. Evening gowns. Jewelry and furs. I realize now that I was in the midst of an era of unparalleled glamour. President John F. Kennedy and his beautiful wife Jackie had ushered in a time of sophistication and culture. They called it "Camelot" and "The New Frontier." America was in the Space Age and a time of economic prosperity. Progress was the mood of the modernizing nation.

McDonald's restaurants were starting to open up around the country in 1961. Diet soft drinks, Polaroid color film and the electric toothbrush were introduced. *Breakfast at Tiffany's, Splendor in the Grass,* and *West Side Story* dominated movie screens, as did such stars as Paul Newman, Elizabeth Taylor, Rock Hudson, Doris Day, Tony Curtis and Sophia Loren. I've always been an avid movie buff, even back then, so I loved 'em all. On TV, westerns such as *Wagon Train, Bonanza* and *Gunsmoke* were the top-rated shows. Teased "beehive" hairdos, pillbox hats and the little black dress were women's fashion statements.

The sound of soul was entering the music mainstream at the time. Los Angeles soul singer Etta James released her torrid version of the standard "At Last" in '61; and in homage, I included that great song on my *Let Me Sing* LP. In other music capitals, the Marvelettes were singing "Please Mr. Postman" as one of the opening salvos from the Detroit hit factory known as Motown. The Crystals thundered through "He's a Rebel," illustrating producer Phil Spector's new Wall of Sound style on the West Coast. Little Eva was dancing "The Loco-Motion," representing the Brill Building pop style of New York City. In Memphis, the Mar-Keys scored "Last Night" as their first hit in 1961—the group would soon become the instrumental cornerstone of the legendary Stax soul sound. In Nashville, Clyde McPhatter ("Lover Please"), Joe Henderson ("Snap Your Fingers") and Esther Phillips ("Release Me") were recording soul monuments while my friend Roy Orbison was creating such throbbing classics as "Crying" and "Running Scared."

"By the early '60s, it was clear that rock 'n' roll was no pass-
ing fad," observes noted Nashville journalist Jay Orr. "Indeed, it
dominated the radio airwaves more than ever. Performers of
standards and jazz were practically obliterated from the charts.
In response, Billboard magazine inaugurated a new chart to list
the softer sounds that adults preferred. The first 'Easy Listening'
chart appeared in July 1961. Throughout the decade, this term
would be used alternately with 'Middle of the Road' to describe
this musical niche. The chart is now called 'Adult Contemporary.'

"So the timing of Brenda's new career direction could not
have been better. In 1962, her ballads 'Everybody Loves Me but
You,' 'Heart in Hand' and 'All Alone Am I' all hit the top of this
new hit parade and also registered high on the teen-dominated
pop charts. For the next eight years, Brenda was one of the Adult
Contemporary field's biggest hit makers. Her discs were ranked
alongside those of such showbiz legends as Tony Bennett, Nat
'King' Cole and Dean Martin."

Over the years, I became nearly as close to these established
vocalists as I was to my rock 'n' roll pals. In March 1963, for instance, I was presented on NBC's *The Bob Hope Show* alongside
Frank Sinatra and Robert Goulet. In a comedy skit, Hope portrayed teen idol "Humphrey Dacron." I idolized him in my role as
deejay "Tina Tuna." We sang the Four Seasons' chart-topper
"Big Girls Don't Cry" as our duet. But for my solo, I chose the
1928 chestnut "Lover Come Back to Me." Sinatra sang his new
easy-listening hit "Call Me Irresponsible." During this same period, I also appeared on the national variety programs of Red
Skelton and Tennessee Ernie Ford. So that gives you some idea
of the kind of audience Dub and Decca were courting.

I also met Jimmy Durante. He heard that I was doing an impression of him in my act. He wanted to meet me and invited me
to his nightclub show in Las Vegas. Needless to say, I was

stunned. He was this vaudeville legend, and I was in awe. Anyway, backstage he asked me what I did in my show, and I did a little impromptu version of "One of Those Songs," waving my hand like he did and doing his walk. He smiled and said, "To make that really authentic, you need my hat." He took his fedora off his head that he'd been wearing in his act for fifty years and autographed it to me, right on the spot. It was a piece of show business history that I just couldn't travel with. It went right under a glass dome in my house.

One of my biggest thrills was getting to know Ella Fitzgerald. It was at the Fairmont Hotel in Dallas. I was following her, so I went to see her closing-night show. To my amazement, Ella knew who I was and said she enjoyed my music. This from one of the greatest jazz vocalists who ever lived! Not only that, Ella began a tradition of sending me two dozen yellow roses as a good luck gesture of friendship every time I played that room. I don't know how she found out that they were my favorite flower, but her gift always made me smile.

Because of my new persona as a "legit" entertainer, I performed alongside a lot of artists who were considerably older and more established. My costar on a 1963 Perry Como taping, for instance, was "The Nashville Nightingale" Dinah Shore. She said she was afraid to follow me on Perry's stage, and she had the cutest quip about that. Dinah said, "Gosh, why doesn't she pick on someone her own size?"

♪

The domain of stars like Red Skelton, Dinah Shore, Robert Goulet and Frank Sinatra was the Las Vegas showroom. In the 1960s, Nevada's gambling mecca rose to become the ultimate definition of entertainment success. Even Elvis aspired to Vegas stardom.

Dub Allbritten and Dick Barstow thought my new show was a natural for the casino trade. And scheduling an engagement was no problem since the William Morris Agency was the leading supplier of talent to Las Vegas, thanks to its connections with the mob bosses who controlled the casinos. So in December 1961, I was booked to headline for three weeks at the Sahara Hotel.

I had lots of hit records. I had my newly sophisticated stage presentation and my hot band. But I was frightened and intimidated when I arrived in the Nevada desert. I was booked to follow the legendary Judy Garland's triumph in the venue, which had been held over for six weeks.

Because I was following her into the Sahara Hotel, I went to see her the night before she closed. If you want to know what she sounded like, listen to *Judy at Carnegie Hall*, the album she did that year. It had been No. 1 on the charts all that summer and later won the Grammy as Album of the Year. Judy was in spectacular voice, as good as she ever was in her life. Before she even came on stage, she had that audience in the palm of her hand—the overture was enough. You should have seen the communication that woman had with those people. She was thrilling, that's what she was.

She's such an inspiration to all female singers. She certainly was to me; and I was a little bit hesitant about asking to meet her. But I did. They said, "Well, she really doesn't meet people after her show, but tomorrow we'll set up a meeting." That was even better. So I met Judy and her daughter Liza Minnelli on the terrace by the pool, and we talked.

I was really nervous. I'd been working with Dick Barstow, and he had worked with her. Dick had told me all about her, great things. Judy was one of the people I'd been listening to since childhood. At any rate, somebody took me to her, and then they left us alone. I tried not to let my nervousness show, but I was definitely starstruck.

She was wearing a Chanel suit and high-heel shoes. Judy appeared very fragile to me, but she was every inch a star. She was very friendly, but definitely a star. We talked about Dick at first. Then she started opening up to me. Liza was only a year or so younger than me, so maybe Judy looked at me like a daughter.

I was shocked that she knew of my recordings. I would never have dreamed that. But she was wonderful to me, so kind and complimentary.

We two had a heartfelt conversation about the effects of being a child star. And I remember her saying she was disillusioned by some of her childhood experiences in the business. She advised me to beware of who I associated with and to try to have a life that was not all show business.

"You know, we have a lot in common," said Judy. "I started as a child entertainer, too. Whatever you do, *be* a child. Don't let them take that away from you."

She and I had one more connection. I took on Judy Garland's "Dorothy" character in the touring musical *The Wizard of Oz* during the summer of 1963. I loved the theater, and it was even more special because I was playing a role originated by one of my idols.

I'm so glad I got to meet Judy when she was at the top of her game. After the early '60s, she went into her downward spiral. I read everything I could about her, kept up with all her marriages, the overdoses, her life in Europe. Poor Judy. She didn't even live out the decade.

After she died in 1969, I put a special tribute to her in my show. They completely blacked out the stage, even me. There was a single spotlight shining on an empty place on the stage where Judy should have been. In the darkness, I sang "Some-where Over the Rainbow." It made people cry.

Despite my fear of following a living legend, that 1961 Sahara engagement turned out to be almost as much a triumph for me as it had been for Judy. Said *Variety,* "Brenda Lee had the adults in her opening night audience on her side from the very first song . . . She radiates personality and sells a song like a vet, adding a certain winning tonal trickery. She's at her best as a belt-er." Dick Barstow's staging was also cited as "a strong plus fac-tor." And that was the God's honest truth.

The Los Angeles Herald & Express also gave my show ex-tensive coverage. You couldn't buy a better write-up than Jimmy Starr's review, "Brenda Belts Out Ballads," which appeared on December 6, 1961:

> Las Vegas—Brenda Lee, the baby belter of ballads, who sings like a million dollars (that's how much she has in the bank), rocked the blase audience last night at the Hotel Sahara, where in the spirit of Christmas, the slot machines play "Jingle Bells."
>
> . . . The idea of such a youngster (she isn't allowed in the gaming casino) was somewhat of an experiment on the part of Producer Stan Irwin. He didn't have any worries after the first show.
>
> . . . Brenda's a little business woman, and her busi-ness is selling songs. And she does that in a big, big way.

Don Rickles and Kay Starr were among the people who came to see me. I was just the same; I'd hit all the other casino shows myself. During my off-time in Vegas, I'd go to see Moms Mab-ley. She was this incredibly raunchy black comedian, like the fe-male Redd Foxx. She dressed like an old bag lady and the most outrageous things would come out of her toothless mouth. Moms made a lot of jokes about sexual infidelity and such. I don't know why I was allowed to go. I was only sixteen, but I loved it; I'd go to see her time and time again.

I met Wayne Newton in Las Vegas, too. He was just starting out. A magazine there asked if I would pose for a photo spread with a teenager about my age who was an up-and-comer. So Sandy Ferra and I went to this ranch to be photographed horseback riding with Wayne and his brother Jerry. Wouldn't you know it? I fell off the horse.

Well, it was just like you'd see in a movie. The man who ran the stable came running up to me. But he didn't say, "Are you hurt?" or "Are you OK?" Instead, he said, "Miss Lee, I'm a songwriter and I have this song that would fit you perfectly!" I guess he figured he had me on the ground, so he had a captive audience. No matter what, he was going to tell me about his song.

We laughed about it afterward. That night, Wayne and Jerry Newton came to see my show. Then Sandy and I went to see theirs at the Fremont. What's funny is that none of us were old enough to be in the audiences of these showrooms. Somehow, I always snuck in. At Wayne's show, they put chairs for us backstage in the wings.

Needless to say, Las Vegas was a showbiz wonderland for me. I wanted to see every performer that I could. Moms Mabley and Wayne Newton were just two among a banquet of celebrities I experienced there. I can remember applauding Fats Domino, Henny Youngman, Shecky Greene, Sammy Davis Jr., the Treniers and dozens of others. Because I'd done so well, I was able to return to Las Vegas as a showroom favorite for years to come. I headlined at the Flamingo in 1962 and later played such rooms as the Frontier, the Silver Bird, Bally's, the Fremont, the Golden Nugget, the Aladdin and the Mirage.

The Sahara tossed me a seventeenth birthday party during my 1961 engagement there. And my Philadelphia buddy Bobby Rydell was on hand to help me cut the cake. We had been tour mates, and his career was red-hot with "Volare," "Wild One," "Swingin' School" and the like. In 1963, Bobby landed one of the lead roles in the movie version of the hit teen musical *Bye Bye Birdie*.

I have to confess that I desperately wanted to play opposite him on the screen. In 1962, I performed in *Bye Bye Birdie* in summer stock, playing the role of Kim, the starstruck teen who falls for an Elvis-type singer. The production played the 6,000-seat Starlight Theater in Kansas City for six weeks to standing-room-only crowds.

I loved summer stock. This was a whole new thing for me. The acting didn't come as hard for me as it had in the movies, because there was an audience I could emote to. I was pretty darn good, if I do say so myself.

My costars were Paul Lynde, who did wind up in the movie version, and Chita Rivera, the great Broadway star. Paul was hysterically funny, on stage and off. And that's rare. Most comedy people aren't funny at all when they're offstage, but he sure was. Chita was a fantastic dancer and a beautiful lady. She'd created the role of Anita in *West Side Story* on Broadway.

Both Chita and Paul came from the original Broadway cast of *Bye Bye Birdie*. Believe me, they had a lot more experience with that type of thing than I did. But they held my hand and guided me through it. I was only seventeen, but they treated me with respect.

I yearned to play Kim when they brought *Bye Bye Birdie* to the screen that year. Bobby Rydell was cast as Hugo. We were buddies; we'd toured together. I thought I should have been his Kim. It made so much sense to me. I felt comfortable in the role.

I knew those songs by heart—"One Boy," "How Lovely to Be a Woman," "Got a Lot of Living to Do" and all the rest.

I was seriously considered for the part in Hollywood, but it got back to me that the producers thought I looked too immature to play the role. And who could compete with Ann-Margret? She's the one who ended up playing opposite Bobby Rydell on the big screen. That was a bummer for me. But, of course, she was great.

One of the highlights of *Bye Bye Birdie* occurs when Kim's whole family is invited to appear on *The Ed Sullivan Show* with the teen idol "Conrad Birdie." That scene is an ode to the most powerful name in variety television of the era.

Known as "the great stone face" because of his constantly dour expression, Ed Sullivan was extremely eager to sign all the top talents of the day. Mr. Sullivan was determined to beat all competitors in the cutthroat game of TV ratings by luring the massive teen audience to his influential show. So I suppose the king of Sunday night TV was in my corner from the get-go. At any rate, by the end of 1962, I had already appeared twice on the top-rated program. But my third Ed Sullivan booking on January 13, 1963, is the one that I remember the most.

They were doing that particular broadcast from Convention Hall in Miami Beach, and I was one very nervous little girl. I had to follow Sophie Tucker. She was the legendary vaudeville star who was the original "Red Hot Mama." Sophie was the role model for just about every female song belter of the twentieth century. Her appearance on the show was to celebrate her seventy-fifth birthday, and she was going to sing her signature song, "Some of These Days."

I had recorded that song and had such enormous respect for Sophie. All that awe was just too much for me to take at the time. I was very frightened. Someone must have told her, because she came back to my dressing room before the show and talked to me for about thirty minutes. Sophie Tucker meant a great deal to me—she gave me courage when I needed it.

Later on, I wrote down the things that she said to me in poem form. It became a tribute to her in my show. It went like this:

I was rehearsing a show one day, and everything was going wrong./I was just about to give up and quit when this great lady came along.

She put her big arm around me and then she gave me a smile./And she said [and here I'd go into an impression of her voice], "Honey, I think we should chat for a while.

"This business we're in, it's not all glamour and gay./And believe me, you'll get many a bump along the way.

"But if you'll just take it as it comes and to yourself be true,/You'll find the whole world will applaud for you.

"Oh, there'll be bad times. It can't always be fun./But that's when you'll be judged for the job that you've done.

"For the top of the heap is awfully small/And when you get pushed, you get a hell of a fall.

"Some people will call you a nobody; others will call you great./They'll put you in a glass house and wait for it to break.

"But you just keep your feet on the ground and your head in the clouds/And a part of your heart out there with the crowds.

"Be nice to everyone. Don't ever let them see you frown./'Cause remember, honey, you meet the same people going up that you meet when you're coming back down.

"And remember it's better to be a has-been than a never will be/ And life is just what we make it for folks like you and me.

"So when the show's going badly and you're really in a spot/I'll give you a song that's helped me a lot.

"You just square your little shoulders and you look straight ahead./And you sing 'em this song, and it'll knock 'em dead."

That's when I'd go into my own rendition of "Some of These Days." It was always a showstopper.

Even *Time* magazine nodded approvingly at me as a newly sophisticated stylist. This is what its write-up said: "Brenda Lee peers at the world through mascaraed eyes of ageless innocence while crooning her mating songs in a voice that is part whiskey, part Negroid and all woman." Britain's *Record and Show Mirror* was more succinct. On September 3, 1960, its headline had read "Brenda Lee: The New Judy Garland."

But I wasn't the new Judy Garland. I wanted something else out of life. I wanted roots and stability and normalcy. Hollywood, supper clubs, musical theater, TV shows and Vegas were an overwhelming whirlwind of activity and emotions. I would have needed superwoman strength to continue to do it all, the way Judy had done.

Maybe I could have been as big as Judy Garland. But you know what? The business killed Judy. I made different choices. And I'm still here.

Offers continued to come in as a result of that new image everyone had created for me. NBC offered me a role in a TV pilot

called *Working Girl*. A movie called *Valencia* costarring me with
Paul Anka was announced.

I turned my back on them. Nashville wasn't Manhattan or
Hollywood, but maybe going back there is what kept me at least
halfway sane. My life had become a blur. I wanted to go home.

My mother and daddy, Grayce and Ruben Tarpley, take a stroll with my big sister Linda. It's 1942, and the city of Atlanta is booming.

Here's my older sister Linda and me enjoying a rare treat of popcorn at the Greene County Fair in Georgia. I was already singing around the house by the time this picture was taken when I was two.

BRENDA LEE ARCHIVES

My first TV appearance occurred in 1952 on WAGA-TV in Atlanta. The show was called *TV Ranch*. I was seven.

Here I am at *The Ozark Jubilee* in 1956. On the left is country singer Carl Smith. On the right is Red Foley, the show's host and the star who discovered me.

COUNTRY MUSIC HALL OF FAME & MUSEUM

We all enjoyed playing with baby Robyn, who was the center of attention here. Left to right are me, Linda, Mother, and Randall in our little home on Brunswick Drive in Nashville.

BRENDA LEE ARCHIVES

My first magazine cover billed me as "The Burning Star." It was the July 1957 issue of *Country and Western Jamboree.* I was twelve.

COUNTRY AND WESTERN
JAMBOREE

BRENDA LEE
The Burning Star

"One Special Attraction"

Do Free Country Music Shows Hurt Everybody?

BRENDA LEE ARCHIVES

THE FLAMINGO HOTEL
LAS VEGAS, NEVADA

At age twelve, I became the youngest headliner in Las Vegas history. Check out those high heels.

BRENDA LEE ARCHIVES

In 1956 on my first trip to New York, I posed in front of the Palace Theater, where my idol Judy Garland was playing. I later got to meet her.

Manager Dub Allbritten did his best to entertain me on tour. But you can tell I'm having more fun at this amusement park than he is.

I wore my Sunday best to the Davidson County Courthouse to straighten out my legal status as a minor. From left are my stepfather, Jay Rainwater, Mother, me, my manager, Dub Allbritten, and my guardian, Charlie Mosley.

I'm all ears for my buddy Patsy Cline. We're seated in the wings of the Ryman Auditorium, the longtime home of the Grand Ole Opry.

Like every girl in America, I was nuts about Elvis. This was taken on December 22, 1957, backstage at the Ryman.

The Casuals pose during our Alaska tour in May 1961. From left are Richard Williams, Tony Moon, Joe Watkins, Buzz Cason, Billy Smith, and Perry Potts. My band was the first rock 'n' roll group formed in Nashville.

DUB ALLBRITTEN, BRENDA LEE ARCHIVES

This is the "Sweet 16" birthday party at the Crescendo in Hollywood. Fabian is grinning over at Dodie Stevens while I get ready to cut the cake.

Chubby Checker was one of my steadiest touring partners in the early '60s. We've stayed in touch ever since, as this recent snapshot attests. I can still do the twist the way he taught me.

RONNIE SHACKLETT, BRENDA LEE ARCHIVES

DUB ALLBRITTEN, BRENDA LEE ARCHIVES

American Bandstand honored me with Brenda Lee Day on February 12, 1962. Host Dick Clark got a chuckle out of a delighted fifteen-year-old.

Here are just six of the more than 250 Brenda Lee albums that have been released around the world. In chronological order they are my 1961 collection *Emotions*, my first "sophisticated" album jacket on 1962's *Sincerely*, 1964's long-lived *Merry Christmas* LP, the 1967 "supperclub" look of *Reflections in Blue*, my 1969 New York album *Johnny One Time*, and the 1980 "makeover" portrait on *Even Better*.

Queen Elizabeth II meets the "younger generation" of female singers. From left going up the steps are Cilla Black, Millicent Martin, Kathy Kirby, and me.

Comedian Bob Hope dressed up like a teen to sing "Big Girls Don't Cry" with me on his national TV special. From left are funnymen Stumpy Brown and Butch Stone, me, and Bob Hope.

The legendary Jimmy Durante gave me his fedora to wear in my nightclub show. Needless to say, it's behind glass as one of my most treasured mementos.

I turned twenty-one in style with Dick Barstow, the choreographer who transformed me into a real chanteuse.

I've done twenty-nine tours of Japan and am in love with that country's culture. This ceremonial kimono is just one of the souvenirs I've brought home.

Here's the famous coat, the chocolate suede number that Ronnie gave me for Christmas in 1962.

Ronnie and I were just newlyweds when this shot was taken in our suburban backyard.

We give our fans our best during the annual Fan Fair celebration in Nashville. This backward bend is a trademark of my performing style.

Kris Kristofferson gave me "Nobody Wins," the song that launched my country hit-making career.

Willie Nelson and I "traded" songs. He introduced me to "Johnny One Time." I gave him "Always on My Mind."

I've been a dollhouse collector for more than twenty years. It's the perfect hobby for someone of my size.

From left are Lou Ferragamo, Gladys Knight, me, and Barbara Mandrell jamming it up after a charity celebrity softball game.

This plaque salutes me as a member of the Country Music Hall of Fame. I still can't believe that happened to me.

I pause to take direction while broadcasting at the massive FarmAid benefit concert in 1985. More than fifty stars participated.

I performed 1,212 shows and never missed a performance during my three seasons at Opryland. The musical revue featured me as "Dorothy" singing "Over the Rainbow."

I have no idea what was so funny at this moment, but I do recall that we had a ball recording the "Honky Tonk Angels" medley. From left are Loretta Lynn, Kitty Wells, Owen Bradley, k.d. lang, and me.

"Girls Just Wanna Have Fun." And I sure did when Cyndi Lauper asked me to perform with her at Vanderbilt University.

In Branson at the Mel Tillis Theater, I was once again billed as "Dynamite." Mel and I go back a long way.

"The Legendary Ladies of Rock 'n' Roll" pose for the camera. Back row, from left, are Lesley Gore, Freda Payne, Shirley Alston, Mary Wells, and Ronnie Spector. Center row — Grace Slick and Belinda Carlisle. Bottom — me and Martha Reeves.

STUART GOODMAN

The family got together for this portrait during the production of my A&E Biography in 2001. From left are Ronnie, Jolie, me, and Julie.

DUB ALLBRITTEN, BRENDA LEE ARCHIVES

This is one of my favorite photographs. It's the way I say "Thank You" night after night.

TEN

A Sweetheart Falls in Love

The home at 5234 Anchorage Drive in the rolling green hills of southeast Nashville was the American suburban dream.

It wasn't Hollywood luxurious, and not palatial by any means, but the modern ranch house was located in a pristine new subdivision, with quiet, curving streets winding through rolling hills. The surrounding homes were state-of-the-art ranches and split levels with manicured front lawns, faux shutters and wrought-iron trimmed porches. With its low-slung homes, paved driveways and blooming perennials, it was the quintessential "Leave It to Beaver" neighborhood.

Here, back from Hollywood, I was reunited with my younger siblings Randall and Robyn. My older sister Linda was back at home, too. She and her husband Ralph had returned from his Marine tour of duty in 1961. Along with their two young children, they were temporarily living with Mother. I delighted in playing with my toddler niece and baby nephew.

For me, life back home in Nashville went on as before—visits to Dub's office to answer fan mail and autograph photos, concert tours to promote my chart-topping singles. I was consistently booked into the finest nightclubs in North America. Even though my money was still being funneled into a trust, I earned $300,000 in 1961. Using the Consumer Price Index, this sum would be approximately $1.8 million in today's dollars. My concerts commanded $3,000 per performance. And I even topped the *Cash Box* and *Music Reporter* charts as the top female vocalist of the year.

I was considered a superstar.

But life for a teenage girl should have been so much more. And I did yearn for something else. Looking back at an *Esquire* 1962 interview, I sound almost wistful.

"I'm not going steady with anyone," I said. "I think it's silly to go steady with a boy, because I travel around so much . . . Maybe my standards are too high . . . I mean, I'm normal. I've got eyes for a cute boy just like anybody else . . . I just don't happen to be dating right now."

No wonder. I was only seventeen, and my experiences with the opposite sex had been limited to a few double dates to school functions. Many of my so-called dates had been little more than photo opportunities. When I was on the road, I was rarely allowed to socialize outside of business circles. Dub still locked me into my hotel room after performances to make sure I did my homework, got my rest and didn't get into trouble. My manager seemed all-knowing and everywhere. To say the least, I led a rather cloistered life.

But lightning struck nonetheless—and sooner than anyone expected, especially me. In October 1962, I went to the Fairgrounds Coliseum in Nashville to see the electrifying black stylist Jackie Wilson. On the other side of the arena sat eighteen-year-old Ronnie Shacklett, whom I later found out had just been voted the best-looking guy in his Central High School senior class. At six foot three with black wavy hair, he cut quite a dashing figure.

I didn't go there looking for a boyfriend or anything like that. I was just a huge, huge fan of Jackie Wilson's. That guy was one of the most dynamic, energetic performers that I'd ever seen. With his big, muscular tenor voice, Jackie had hits like "Reet Petite," "Lonely Teardrops," "Night" and "Alone at Last." And he worked us kids up into a frenzy doing splits on stage, twirling and dancing up a storm.

I talked a group of girlfriends into going to the show with me. And one of the girls in my group just happened to know some of the boys Ronnie was with. I asked my friend Kay to take a note over to him. It said something like, "Hi, I think you're really cute. My name is Brenda Lee, and I'd like to meet you. Call me sometime." I included my phone number.

I know it sounds outlandish for a girl of that time to do that, especially me. But you have to understand that he was unbelievably good-looking, just breathtaking. I certainly was not well versed in the art of dating, but I knew I wanted to meet him.

"I wasn't a big concertgoer; I wasn't even that big a music fan," says Ronnie. *"That show was on a Sunday, and we were hanging around the service station, waxing my Corvette. Tommy Jarrell, who was a good friend, wanted to go see Jackie Wilson. I had on Levi's and a white T-shirt. I said, 'I don't even have a jacket.' He said, 'Here. Wear mine.' It was a black motorcycle jacket, and my parents wouldn't allow us to wear anything like that. I guess I had the 'James Dean look' going on.*

"At the show, a girl who knew one of my buddies gave me this note. I never saw who it was from, never laid eyes on Brenda that night. I only vaguely knew who Brenda Lee was. Like I said, I wasn't that big a music fan.

"But about two weeks later, I called Brenda for a date. I picked her up in my 1961 white Corvette and took her to the Dairy King and a movie downtown at the Tennessee Theater.

"We had a great time, and Brenda was a lot of fun. I remember she was kind of hard to get in touch with. Maybe she was out

of town. I do remember that her mother was dead set against us having a date. But we had a good time that night."

It was the first solo car date that I had ever been on. And for me, it was love at first sight. I didn't say anything to anybody, but I knew from the moment that I saw him that he was the guy I wanted to marry.

Mother was so worried over my sudden infatuation. She thought that a seventeen-year-old was way too young to be thinking about a serious relationship. And Dub was livid. In his opinion, the No. 1 female vocalist in the world did not need this type of distraction.

Despite such disapproval, Ronnie and I started dating steadily. He took me to my first drive-in movie, to my first circus performance and to my first drag race. One thing I particularly remember about our dates is that Ronnie would eat like a field hand, but I wouldn't touch a morsel of food. I was petrified that I'd do something sloppy and embarrass myself.

I was just completely mesmerized by him right off the bat. Other than his drop-dead-gorgeous looks, one of the things that immediately drew me to him was his family. To me, they looked like the perfect "Happy Days" clan who had the roots that I had been searching for. The daddy worked. The mama was in the kitchen cooking. The boys were playing football and working on their hot rods.

The reality was somewhat more colorful. Earl Shacklett, Ronnie's dad, was a self-made man who'd risen from tenant farm roots to the Nashville City Council. Today, if you drive south out of Music City on Nolensville Pike, you encounter a sign just after crossing over Interstate 440 that identifies the road as the "Earl Shacklett Parkway." This blue-collar district known as Woodbine was Earl's power base as a politician for more than thirty-five years.

"My dad was the closest thing to John Wayne of anybody I've ever met," says Ronnie. *"He said what he thought and did not back down from what he believed was right."*

Earl was a successful construction contractor by trade and a classic "old school" Dixie politician. He made headlines when he punched Nashville's mayor in the nose following one heated political discussion. Earl would never back down when he frequently clashed with fellow legislators over what he believed to be unfair zoning issues and licensing fees.

The Tennessean newspaper once characterized the quick-tempered councilman as "fair but firm" and as "his own man." Earl was enormously popular with his constituents, because he campaigned, "I will fight for this district with no obligation to outside sources."

The power behind the throne was his wife, Helen. She kept the company's business books and worked alongside him every step of the way. Helen was far more than the aproned housewife I initially thought she was. Her fiery determination to succeed was the match of her husband's. She was the force behind all of his reelection campaigns and helped Earl build an empire that includes numerous commercial buildings along Nolensville Road and dozens of rental properties lining the neighborhood's side streets. In addition, Helen Shacklett was once voted Tennessee's Woman of the Year and was elected to the state's constitutional convention.

She and Earl raised four sons. Buddy, the eldest, became a successful contractor and served a four-year term in the State of Tennessee General Assembly. Ronnie also followed his father into the construction business as well as becoming a real estate investor. Steve ran a popular Woodbine restaurant and sports bar. David became a champion stock-car racer.

To this day, the Shacklett name remains widely known in the

Woodbine neighborhood. Most old-line Nashvillians can still recall the days when the Shacklett family made headlines.

After meeting Ronnie, I wrote him warmly from the stops on my concert tours during the fall of 1962. And when I was home, our romance heated up rapidly. Ronnie attended my gala eighteenth birthday party on December 11.

The party was at my guardian Charlie Mosley's house out in the suburb of Brentwood. All the record-company people were there, plus my family and teenage girlfriends. Marty Robbins, who topped the charts with "El Paso" and "Don't Worry," came to cook Mexican food for us. Best of all, Ronnie was there as my date.

At the party, Decca Records gave me a white Thunderbird convertible with red leather interior. I couldn't believe it when I saw the car sitting out on the Mosleys' driveway with a huge red bow on it. The Thunderbird in those days was considered a really hot car. That and the Corvette were the sportiest things around. What a spectacular present, really over-the-top. It was the first car I ever owned. And a convertible, to boot!

I found out later that Decca deducted that Thunderbird from my royalties. So I really bought myself the car!

On Christmas Day that year, I got another nice surprise. Ronnie had purchased me an extravagant gift. I wasn't used to getting presents from boyfriends, so I was almost beside myself when he appeared on our doorstep with a big shiny package for me. I didn't even care what was inside. The fact that he had bought something just for me really put me in a spin.

I tore the package open. Inside, there was a gorgeous chocolate suede coat with a mink collar and cuffs. I wore it everywhere. It was the nicest coat I had ever had. I still have it.

Needless to say, my heart was in a whirl. But my carefree delight would be overshadowed by tragedy within a matter of days.

It was New Year's Eve day in the wee hours of the morning. Like many times before, I'd had an argument with Mother about my seeing Ronnie so much. My bedroom was upstairs, but because I was mad, I slept downstairs in the den. It was a tri-level house. Downstairs was a laundry room, a bedroom, a bathroom and the den. A few steps up were the kitchen, breakfast room and living room. Up another flight of stairs were the three main bedrooms and two baths. At about 12:30 in the morning I woke up because I smelled smoke. The room was hazy. I made the mistake of opening the door to the laundry room. Flames and smoke gushed out in my face.

I went into the downstairs bedroom and woke up Randall, who was twelve at the time. I told him to go out the front door. The downstairs door was blocked by flames. Next, I knew I had to go upstairs, but by that time it was so smoky I had to crawl. Mother, Robyn, Linda and Ralph and their kids were all asleep on the third level. Also, my little toy poodle CeeCee was alone in my bedroom up there.

"It was really frightening," Linda remembers. "By the time Brenda woke us up and I got the baby in a blanket and came down the steps, it was so smoky that you couldn't see the front door. If you didn't know where it was, you might not have gotten out.

"There was snow on the ground and more coming down. We didn't have any coats on, and by now the flames were visible from the front yard.

"Brenda had saved our family. But she remembered that her little dog CeeCee was still inside. Brenda dashed back into our burning home to save her pet."

I couldn't find CeeCee. He must have been huddled under my bed or overcome by the smoke. But I desperately called for him. Anybody who's ever loved a pet will know what I'm talking about. I loved that little silver dog. We were inseparable. CeeCee had been a gift to me from Charlie Carpenter, the man who'd written "You Can Depend on Me." And that toy poodle always traveled on the road with me.

The smoke was getting thicker and thicker. My hair and eyebrows were singed. There was no time left. Instead of CeeCee, I grabbed the only other thing I cherished at that moment, the suede coat that Ronnie had given me for Christmas.

Our family's suburban dream house, the one I'd worked so hard to get, burned to the ground. All of our possessions, my souvenirs, photos and memorabilia, were completely destroyed. I suffered smoke inhalation trying in vain to save CeeCee. I remember that *Tennessean* reporter Frank Ritter was on the scene and went to our neighbor's home where we all had gathered. Mother said that she told him specifically not to ask me about the dog. But he did anyway. I'll never forget that I was standing there barefooted and just burst into tears. No matter. Frank had a front-page story.

My homeless family rented rooms at the Alamo Plaza Court motel on Murfreesboro Road. Later that year, I petitioned the court to let me buy a $15,000 home for them. It was in the same neighborhood as the fire-ravaged house on Anchorage Drive. For the next eighteen years Mother lived there and devoted herself to raising Robyn and Randall. My guardian arranged for their financial support.

After my frightening ordeal in the house fire, I immediately went back to work. In the early months of 1963, I was scheduled to tour Europe and the British Isles.

I was a mass of emotions as we left Nashville. I was head over heels in love with a guy who was completely unacceptable to everyone around me. It wasn't because of him personally. If Ronnie had been "Jim," "Tony," "Bobby" or "Frank," it wouldn't have made any difference. Mother and Dub made it completely miserable for me to have a date with anyone. They knew this was serious, and I think that was frightening for both of them.

I was torn between my loyalty to them and my loyalty and love for Ronnie. They were frightened that my career would be over if I married. Besides, Mother thought I was just too young. Heck, I'd been making a living since I was eight—I felt old! The more they balked at it, the more determined I became to make my own life. I was fed up with being bossed around. I was fed up with being lonely, like a character in one of my love songs of un-requited love. Why couldn't I have what everybody else had? Deep inside there was this knot of fear and intimidation. But out in front of me was this brass ring of happiness that I felt I had to grab right then and there.

Hidden in my purse as I boarded the transcontinental flight was a one-carat diamond engagement ring. During the early weeks of the year, Ronnie had started kidding with me about get-ting married. I guess like most guys, he was still a little frightened of making the commitment. We were, after all, only eighteen and had been dating just three months.

But we were engaged; I had the ring to prove it. We just didn't have a marriage date set. I kept the whole thing secret. Mother and Dub never knew. Ronnie's parents didn't know. I knew if I told anyone, I'd be overruled or talked out of it. It's very hard for me to keep a secret, but this was one that I knew I had to keep. I did not tell a single soul.

It was pretty stressful. On top of everything else, I was terri-fied I'd lose my purse with that ring in it. At night in my hotel room, I'd take it out and put it on and gaze at its little Tiffany set-ting for hours. "How are we ever gonna pull this off?" I'd won-der. Ronnie wasn't a big letter writer at all, but he would write me notes sometimes. He'd put at the end, "P.S. Just kidding about the marriage." He has a really strange sense of humor.

A supper-club return engagement at the Deauville Hotel in Miami Beach was scheduled after the European tour. My entourage and I arrived there on April 16. The next day Ronnie drove down from Nashville with two friends.

"I was going down there to see Brenda, and I invited them to go with me," Ronnie recalls. *"I borrowed my dad's car. I remember that the Deauville was really swanky—only the biggest stars worked the showroom there. We stayed in a little motel, not at the Deauville.*

"Brenda had her own cabana out by the pool. One afternoon, I went over there to talk to her. It's the only time I got to be alone with her the whole time I was there. Dub and Grayce wouldn't let me near her. Brenda and I decided that afternoon that we were going to set a date."

Because Charlie Mosley was my legal guardian as appointed by the court, I had to get his permission. Anything regarding contracts, money or in this case, marriage, had to be approved by him. I was still considered a minor. So I called him. I dreaded making the call. But I wanted this so badly I knew I had to. For once in my life, I stood up for myself. I didn't exactly ask him. I basically told him this is what I was going to do.

I was in luck. He knew the Shackletts and liked Ronnie. Looking back, I realize how gutsy Charlie was to give us his permission. After all, he was going to have to face Dub and Mother, too.

Everything was enveloped in this veil of secrecy. I was scared and excited at the same time. I think I knew this was going to hurt a lot of people, especially Mother. So instead of her, we went to Ronnie's mother. She was out sweeping the walk in front of the house.

"Mother, do you think you can get to the church by four o'clock this afternoon?" asked Ronnie. Helen Shacklett kept sweeping.

"Yes; what for?" she replied, without looking up.

"Brenda and I are going to get married," Ronnie said.

Helen kept sweeping. She looked up just for a moment and said, "Oh, OK."

"I need someone to go with me downtown to get some clothes," I said to Helen. "I don't have anything with me, and I can't go home where they'll see me packing. Do you have a suitcase I can borrow?"

Helen took me to downtown Nashville and bought me a two-piece white suit and some honeymoon outfits. She told the clerk that all of it needed to be altered in an hour. The store got it done.

Ronnie and I were married at the Radnor Church of Christ in Nashville on April 24, 1963, with only his family in attendance. As I walked down the aisle for the ten-minute ceremony, my newly purchased purse still had the shop's paper stuffing inside. There was no music. Ronnie wore a carnation in his lapel and gave me a white orchid corsage to pin on my suit. Other than that, the only other flowers were those remaining from the previous night's church service. And, despite the secrecy, there were newspaper reports. To this day, we don't know who tipped off *The Tennessean*. But somebody did. When we came out of the sanctuary, there was a photographer.

I didn't want Mother and Dub to think I'd been kidnapped or something, so I called them right after the ceremony. I couldn't just leave town and not tell them I was leaving. When I telephoned Dub from the Shackletts' house, there was a long silence on the other end of the line. I could almost feel his rage. I could just see him biting that cigar in two. Finally, all he said was, "Don't forget—you have that benefit to do for the synagogue in Paducah in three days. Be there."

Needless to say, and despite his disappointment, Dub had my marriage splashed all over the papers the next day. He even had a photographer follow us on our honeymoon.

"Brenda Lee Honeymoons in Springtime Setting," trumpeted
The Tennessean:

> Teenager Brenda Lee, whose songs of unrequited love
> shot her to the top in the record industry, is on her hon-
> eymoon.
>
> Spring beauty of clear mountain streams and
> panoramic views of the Smoky Mountains welcomed the
> singing star and her husband Ronnie Shacklett to their
> honeymoon retreat.
>
> The world famed singing idol and her 18-year-old
> bridegroom chose the privacy of the Holiday Hill Motel,
> tucked away from the main section of the business dis-
> trict [of Gatlinburg, Tennessee] for their honeymoon.
>
> They were receiving no visitors nor taking telephone
> calls unless determining the name of the caller before an-
> swering. This posed something of a problem for local
> businessmen who wanted to present them the key to the
> city. And local florists besieged with orders from all over
> the world for the couple were unable to deliver the
> arrangements.

Per Dub's telephoned instructions to me in Gatlinburg, Ronnie and I dutifully posed for *Tennessean* news photos. On April
28th, the paper pictured us signing the guest book at the motel and
getting into Ronnie's car "for an automobile trip through the pic-
turesque streets of this hamlet and into the towering mountains."

I guess Dub figured what was done was done, and he might
as well get some publicity mileage out of it. But reading about
my honeymoon in the paper must have been quite a sting to
Mother. It must have felt like I was rubbing the whole thing in
her face.

"It did hurt my feelings when Brenda ran off and got married," confirms Grayce. *"Charlie Mosley gave her permission to get married without telling me. I never suspected that they would do anything like that. I didn't dislike Ronnie. I just thought that Brenda was too young to marry him, or anyone else, for that matter.*

"I knew how much she worked. She was on the road all the time. When you're gone so much of the time, how do you know a marriage will work, especially when you're that young?"

Looking back, I know how much I hurt my mother. I will regret that the rest of my life. Mother had devoted so much of herself to me—unselfishly and to the detriment of her other children. Mother's not bitter about it, but that makes me feel even worse.

Dub Allbritten immediately started fretting about the effect of the marriage on my career. Would my fans desert me now? He began obsessively tallying the contents of Brenda Lee fan letters following the wedding. But his worries were groundless. He later boasted to *The Music Reporter* that during the month following the marriage, I had received 1,137 letters. Of these, 1,066 didn't even comment on the nuptials; 68 letter writers said they were glad for me; and only 3 were sad that I got married. Don't you know those three would have been from Dub, Mother and the Prince of Arabia!

When we came back from our honeymoon, Ronnie and I moved into an apartment in South Nashville to begin life as a couple. It wasn't anything grand—the Elysian Fields complex was a nondescript two-story series of brick buildings. Each unit had a tiny cement patio porch surrounded by pierced concrete block walls. But I was a giddy newlywed on my own; to me, it was better than any mansion. I couldn't wait to set up housekeeping. Unfortunately, I didn't know how.

No one ever taught me to cook. I had been eating in restaurants and ordering room service since the time I was a kid. My mother was a great cook, but I had never helped out. I was always working. Even so, I was not a bit intimidated by being on my own as a newlywed. I figured, "How hard can it be?" But I was a disaster in the kitchen.

The first chicken I cooked, I cut up into thirty-something pieces. I cut wings apart. I cut legs in two. I completely mutilated that bird. Another time, I cooked a casserole and went right by the recipe. It said "top with frozen biscuits," but it didn't say to cook them first. So when I put the biscuits on top of the heated casserole, they just all melted down into it. The dish was automatically ruined, of course.

It's a wonder that one of my worst cooking moments didn't kill us all. I thought that if you battered pork chops and browned them quickly in the skillet, they were ready. I didn't know you had to let them cook awhile in order to get them done. To me, when they were brown, they were ready. But they were bloody inside. That we didn't contract trichinosis is a miracle.

On another occasion, one of us had a cold, and Ronnie had heated up some Vicks VapoRub on the stove and left it there. It had congealed, and I thought it was lard. So I was cooking cabbage and just plopped a dollop of what I thought was grease down in the pot for seasoning. I thought it smelled kinda funny, but sometimes cabbage does. I actually brought it to the table and served it.

"This tastes funny; what did you put in it?" Ronnie inquired, chewing slowly.

"I didn't put anything in it except the lard on the back of the stove," I protested.

Ronnie doubled over in laughter. It took him awhile to get over the giggles before he told me about the Vicks. Then I cracked up, too.

I also cooked a turkey one time with the paper bag of gizzards still inside it. But the funniest time was when I gave away all the canned goods. I was going out on the road for a while.

"Why in the world did you give all the canned goods away?" Ronnie asked.

"Because we're going to be gone for two weeks," I replied. "They'll ruin."

I didn't know how to wash clothes. I didn't know how to use a vacuum cleaner. I didn't know how to iron. I had no clue. Poor Ronnie. His mother and father kept places set for us at their kitchen table. We would eat there almost every night of the week. Otherwise we probably would have starved.

Two weeks after the wedding, I was booked to play one of the most important shows of my life, my debut at New York's fabled Copacabana nightclub. The Copa was the pinnacle of prestige for entertainers at the time. Only the top names played there.

"Dub was afraid to play the Copacabana," recalls Charlie Lamb of The Music Reporter. *"He'd put Brenda in plenty of big places. But he was afraid of that crowd. He thought New Yorkers were too jaded. They could see top entertainment any time they wanted.*

"He asked me to handle things for him. I said, 'I'll handle the opening and guarantee you we'll have a standing ovation.' I flew up there and got ahold of the Decca Records people. I told them to pack the place with the whole staff. Brenda still talks about how I filled her dressing room with flowers.

"She tore the house down. She gave them a great show. She was sold out for the entire engagement. And she did get that standing ovation."

Raved *Billboard,* "Brenda has the fire, the drive, the movement and the vocalistics that led one ring sider to characterize her as a teenaged Sophie Tucker." *The New York Journal American* added, "Brenda Lee a Sensation at the Copa: She's a Judy Garland, Sophie Tucker all in one." *Variety* chimed in, "She has the youthful exuberance and spirit that can make a place jump. She did prove that she can work in a mature vein." *Cash Box* pictured me on its cover holding Charlie Lamb's congratulatory roses at the Copa.

During the Copa engagement in New York, I paid my fourth visit to *The Ed Sullivan Show*. Ed surprised Ronnie by introducing him from the audience as my new husband. Ronnie grinned and waved at the national TV audience. It was May 12th. He was celebrating his nineteenth birthday in style.

Something much more dramatic was happening backstage. Booked alongside me were Oscar-winning actress Vivien Leigh, comedians Myron Cohen and Rip Taylor, jazz trumpeter Al Hirt and an exciting new performer from the rising folk music movement. Bob Dylan was to make his national television debut.

All the kids my age loved him. He was writing songs about the times and about what was going on. He was a beatnik with fur Eskimo boots and a long wool coat. His hair was unruly, all frizzy and curly. Bob showed up for dress rehearsal all rumpled, but nobody seemed to care. I thought he looked adorable. I introduced myself to him and told him what a fan I was. He knew my music, too, which thrilled me.

They asked him what he was going to sing, and he performed "Talkin' John Birch Society Blues" for them. Ed Sullivan loved it. So did Bob Precht, the producer of the show. But the CBS censors said, "No." The song poked fun at the John Birch Society, a right-wing political organization. The network was afraid of a libel suit. Bob Dylan was furious. Mr. Sullivan asked Bob if he would be willing to choose another song.

Dylan snapped at America's most powerful TV host: "If I can't sing that song, I won't sing *any* song!" He stomped out of the studio.

He stood up, picked up his guitar and harmonica and just walked right out the door. Nobody could believe it. No one walked out on Ed Sullivan, especially not a new act. The bosses all stood there with their mouths open. I was amazed, too. But I thought it was great. I wished I had guts like that. He believed enough in his music that he wasn't going to have it censored by those people.

If I had walked off *Ed Sullivan,* my career probably would have been over. It made Bob a folk hero. Just a few weeks after that *Sullivan* show, Peter, Paul and Mary topped the charts with Bob's song "Blowin' in the Wind," and Bob was on his way. I was a fan then; I'm a fan now.

Three weeks after the incident, Ronnie, Dub, Mother and I flew to Los Angeles for my high school graduation ceremony. Despite leaving the West Coast, I had remained enrolled at the Hollywood Professional School. I'd completed my senior studies via correspondence courses under the tutelage of Freda Garrett.

What a weird way it was to get your high school diploma. I mean, only in L.A.—they had the graduation ceremony at the Wilshire Country Club with a TV news crew on hand! We did wear the traditional caps and gowns. I was as proud as I could be. I loved learning, loved school.

At the ceremony, I was presented with the school's Gold Key Award, which was given annually for the student with the most outstanding professional achievement. My fan club from England sent a giant floral replica of the honor. Dub, Mother and Ronnie all posed with me in my graduation robes, beaming with pride and holding my diploma.

We all looked so happy together, but Dub didn't like Ronnie

one bit. Ronnie was a nonentity, as far as my manager was concerned. He wouldn't even speak to him. Every time I wanted Ronnie to be on the road with me, Dub would try to refuse. I'd say, "Either he comes along or I'm not singing." That was the one thing Dub couldn't control. He couldn't make me sing. I especially wanted Ronnie to come along if I was going overseas. And that's how their first real confrontation came to be.

We were riding between shows in England in a hired Bentley. Dub and I were in the backseat. Ronnie was up front with the driver. I made some smart remark to Ronnie. I don't remember what it was. You know how kids are. He smart-mouthed me back. The next thing I knew, Dub had cocked his leg and with all his might kicked Ronnie in the back of the head with the hard heel of his shoe. It could've killed him.

Ronnie was dazed and looked like he was seeing stars. Then he came over that front seat in a fury. He started punching Dub in the face and didn't let up. I was terrified. I was crying and screaming for them to stop. The two most important men in my life were trying to kill each other. The driver pulled over to the side of the road. Ronnie pulled Dub out and kept beating him. They were both bloody by now.

By the time it ended, Dub was on his way to the hospital. He stayed there while Ronnie and I went on to do shows in Germany. Back home, we didn't hear from Dub for a month, which was unheard of for me. Even when I called to ask if he was all right, he wouldn't speak to me.

Finally, one day he called about business. He acted like nothing had ever happened. Couldn't have been nicer. The subject was never discussed. And from that point on, Dub treated Ronnie with the utmost respect.

"As time went on, we became friends," says Ronnie. *"In fact, we became very close. He tried to help me business-wise. He*

wanted to incorporate me into Brenda's world in some way. So he brought me in as a partner in a song publishing company that we called RonBre, a combination of 'Ronnie and Brenda.' I didn't know a thing about publishing, and here I was the 'president.' Dub ran it."

In addition, Dub got Ronnie national TV exposure as a contestant on *To Tell the Truth*. "Who is Brenda Lee's husband?" was the theme of the episode. The format of the show was that three people faced a panel. All three claimed to be the same person. Two were imposters. Ronnie was required to answer every question truthfully. Through a series of queries, the panel had to guess which man was really Brenda Lee's husband.

When host Bud Collyer famously asked, "Will the real Ronnie Shacklett please stand up?" Ronnie surprised everyone. No one had guessed him as the truth-teller, and Dub was tickled pink.

"I started traveling a little with Brenda and Dub," Ronnie relates. "I think Dub invited me at first, because he wanted me to be the driver. I was so surprised to see that Dub and the musicians were always taking 'bennies' to stay awake. For about a year and a half, I took those 'bennies' to stay up, too. My system couldn't handle it. I started seeing big pink bunnies leaping across the highway.

"Those long drives were when I really got to know Dub. He and I would talk while Brenda was asleep in the back. We talked about life, and he tried to teach me things. I'd never been around anybody like that—a show person, a wrestling promoter, a dapper dan. With Dub, everything was first class all the way. He was only in his forties, but he always seemed like an old man to me. He was very serious, a deep thinker.

"I was in over my head. I didn't know how to hail a cab, didn't know how to order in a restaurant. I remember one time they were all going out for Polynesian food and I said, 'No. I

don't like it.' The truth was, I didn't even know what it was! I wasn't worldly at all. I didn't even know how to tie my own tie— my older brother Buddy had always done it for me. Here we were, opening at the Copa, and Brenda and I struggled through this somehow. It was an ugly knot, but it was a knot.

"When I realized how big a star she was and how much went into all that, it was almost too much for me to handle psychologically. It made me grow up real fast.

"There was a lot that shocked me. Backstage at the nightclubs, the chorus girls would undress right in front of you. I'd grown up in a house full of brothers and hadn't been around girls at all. I was so surprised that the dressing room with all these beautiful women in it smelled like a football locker room.

"Here I was a nineteen-year-old kid from Nashville meeting all these big stars. Jackie Wilson came to see Brenda at the Copa, and I got to tell him what a part he'd played in our lives. I met Lucille Ball, Phyllis Diller, Nat 'King' Cole and all these celebrities. And Brenda was as big as any of them."

Oscar–award-winning actor Burl Ives knew me from the 1961–62 recording sessions in Nashville that resulted in his Grammy-winning "A Little Bitty Tear." Burl was so impressed with Ronnie's good looks that he offered him a role in one of his movies. Singer Fran Jeffries was another of my showbiz acquaintances. Fran's husband was director Richard Quine, who wanted to cast Ronnie in the 1967 epic *Hotel*.

"Brenda threw an absolute fit, both times," Ronnie reports. "She said, 'There's only room for one star in our family, and I'm it!'"

Well, I thought our marriage would have never worked if we'd both been in the spotlight. I was against all of that, and I think Ronnie was too unassuming to do any of it anyway. For his part, Dub Allbritten eventually quit pushing Ronnie into showbiz circles. As always, I was his main obsession.

Dub never let me forget that I was a Star, and he wanted his surroundings to reflect that status. He moved into a new penthouse office at 1717 West End Avenue. The suite was elegantly decorated by Freda's brother Mark Garrett.

It was lavish. There was gilded gold everywhere. I had silk faux cherry trees in my office and a tufted red-velvet princess chair behind a French, leather-topped writing desk that had been custom crafted for my height. It had my initials in gold, hand-painted on the front. Overhead was a crystal chandelier. Against the wall was a gold chaise longue.

Dub's office was hung with beautiful paintings and had a long sofa covered in raw silk. His desk was mahogany. On the wall were brass sconces and hand-carved reliefs depicting violins.

The suite had a wet bar and a full kitchen. The office tables held lamps that were taller than I was. The foyer was ultramodern with a black and chrome and white color scheme. It was all quite striking and sophisticated, especially for Nashville at that time.

I think it's significant that Dub chose not to hang his shingle out on Music Row, the business district where Nashville's country music industry was coalescing at the time. He wanted to keep me quite apart from that world.

Ever the Dub Allbritten booster, Charlie Lamb's *Music Reporter* celebrated the tony new address with a feature titled "Dub Is Manager, Star Maker." When in town, I would report to the penthouse several times a week to have career discussions with Dub, to sign autographs and to answer my fan mail. In longhand.

While I was at the top of my profession, Dub locked horns with Mother over a new Decca Records contract. Label executives flew in from New York and joined my guardian Charlie

Mosley, Dub and my producer Owen Bradley in Mother's den. The mood of the room was tense. Dub and Decca had agreed on a million-dollar renewal of my recording contract, but Mother frowned in displeasure. At issue was my legal status as a minor. Charlie kept his mouth shut, since he and Mother had had a falling out over his approval of my hasty marriage.

"Dub and the Decca men wanted me to sign away Brenda's minority status," Grayce recalls. "They wanted Brenda to be able to sign her own contract. They couldn't understand why she couldn't, since she was married. But she wasn't twenty-one. Not only that, I wanted them to make the contract retroactive, back to the first of the year before she was married. And I wanted the money to be put in escrow where nobody—including Brenda—could touch it until she turned twenty-one. Because Brenda had worked too hard. We had traveled and worked too hard for anything to happen to that money. I was trying to protect her.

"Owen was on my side, as usual. He said, 'If it was my child, I'd do the same thing.' He was always behind me. He told the others, 'You're not giving Grayce the credit for the sense she's got.' So we went before the judge."

What Mother wanted, Mother got. The new Decca contract was drafted as retroactive to the beginning of 1963, prior to my marriage. Mother wanted the funds to remain solely in my name, as opposed to being considered joint marital assets. The court approved this. The contract guaranteed me a minimum of $1,225,000, to be paid out over a twenty-year period in escalating installments starting with an annual $35,000.

"Brenda was worth more than any investment that Decca could make," states historian Diana Reid Haig. "Her albums are timeless. They were constant sellers. Her LP Brenda, That's All, *propelled by the hit singles 'Fool #1' and 'You Can Depend on Me,' had already climbed into the top-20 on the album chart. In*

1963, her All Alone Am I *collection proved to be another tremendously successful album."*

Let Me Sing, my second LP of '63, featured a cover photo taken at the Copacabana of me sitting on the showroom's piano. The collection contained "Break It to Me Gently," as well as a stunning new ballad called "Losing You."

Owen was always so ingenious with his arrangements. He would come up with a new creative twist at every session. On "Losing You," he devised this gorgeous trumpet obbligato that soars in the introduction and throughout the song. Soprano Millie Kirkham's voice is sky-high, with this angelic sighing above my reading of the lyric. The strings are beautiful in that record, too.

" 'Losing You' may have been one of Owen Bradley's greatest pop productions," says Diana Reid Haig. *"But it is Brenda's breathtaking performance that carries the record. She is totally believable as she digs into this lyric of devastating heartache with a depth of emotion almost unimaginable for someone her age."*

I was only a kid; I'd certainly never been through anything like those emotions. I would just project myself and my feelings into the situation in the lyrics. I can only say it was a gift.

"Losing You" went to No. 2 on the Adult Contemporary charts, to No. 6 on the mainstream pop hit parade, to No. 13 on the r&b charts and to No. 10 in England. My other big hits of 1963 included a blues-drenched and jazz-tinged version of "I Wonder," which had been a chart-topping r&b hit for Nashville's Cecil Gant in 1944. "My Whole World Is Falling Down" was an up-tempo, Motown-ish performance, cowritten by fellow Georgian Bill Anderson. For "He's So Heavenly" I returned to the songwriting talent of Jackie DeShannon. "Sweet Impossible You" was yet another tune from rocking Ronnie Self.

The wistful "The Grass Is Greener" came from the pen of

Brill Building pop prince Barry Mann ("Who Put the Bomp?").
For this number, Owen Bradley brought in classical harp and
flute accompaniment. "Your Used to Be" was my other single of
1963.

Looking back, I realize how much different the music business was in those days. We recorded a lot more in one year than
they do today. Counting the albums and singles, I released something like twenty-five songs in 1963. Today, an act might take
more than a year just to record ten tunes for a single album. But
the standard in the '60s was two albums and four singles a year.
And even then, I did a lot more than that. In 1964, Decca put out
eleven singles on me; in 1965, alone, I had three albums. By the
time I reached twenty-one, I'd recorded 256 sides.

My workload was awfully heavy. But I felt like I could take
on the world. My life had meaning now. I finally had someone to
call my own, someone to share my dreams with. I was in love.

Ronnie and I seized every moment of togetherness we could.
Although still working for his father's construction firm, Ronnie
often went out on weekend trips to my concert dates. But there
were still long separations, and absence did "make the heart
grow fonder." When I wasn't on the road, we were everyday
homebodies.

On November 22, 1963, Ronnie and I clung together even
more than usual. Like people everywhere, we were shocked and
devastated by the assassination of the president. The news from
Dallas came to us both over the radio airwaves.

I was out shopping and driving along Harding Road. When I
heard about it on the car radio, I pulled over to the side of the road
and cried. Jack Kennedy was the first president I'd ever really
identified with; he was a symbol of youth and vitality. As soon as
I pulled myself together, I rushed home to be with Ronnie.

"I was at work at my dad's construction business," recalls

Ronnie. *"It was a very gray afternoon, a Friday, and I was in the office. Dad had the radio on, and suddenly they broke in with the news. I went home immediately, and Brenda and I sat there for the next four days, glued to the television set like the rest of the country. Heck, like the rest of the world."*

A little bit of America died with John Fitzgerald Kennedy that weekend. The nation's lingering innocence of the '50s seemed to evaporate—the rest of the '60s would be a profoundly different decade. As a people, we turned some kind of corner in those four days, because it felt like one era ended and a new one began. People who were not alive at the time cannot imagine what a horrible and agonizing thing we experienced as a nation. Time stopped that weekend. And then history lurched on.

Ronnie and I felt the same fear and confusion that trembled in hearts everywhere. The motorcade, the bloodstained dress, Lee Harvey Oswald, Jack Ruby, the six white horses, three-year-old John-John's brave little salute, the eternal flame, the black-veiled widow—indelible images piled one on another in four days of anguish. And when it was over, what did it mean? One thing was certain: The optimistic "thousand days" of Camelot were finished.

ELEVEN

Around the World

Tracing my movements in the early 1960s creates a bewildering zigzag chart—I seem to be in a hundred places at once. I can hardly "connect the dots" myself, because it was all such a blur. It's hard to imagine that I was simultaneously courting both teen and adult audiences on unceasing concert tours, recording prodigiously in Nashville, doing summer stock, appearing on one TV variety show after another, getting married and finishing my schooling. Incredibly, during this same period, I was also touring on five continents and rising to international stardom.

"In 1963, eighteen-year-old Brenda was ranked by the readers of Britain's Melody Maker *magazine as the world's top female vocalist," observes veteran Nashville journalist John Lomax III. "Melody Maker was the mouthpiece for the U.K. music 'establishment' and often looked down its nose at teen idols in those days. Nevertheless, Brenda's victory was resounding. She received more than half of the total votes cast, easily outpacing the likes of Ella Fitzgerald and Peggy Lee. Brenda stood shoulder-to-shoulder with male winner Elvis Presley in the rankings."*

My popularity with English fans had been carefully cultivated. Ever since my childhood triumphs in Paris and Rio, Dub had kept me in front of international audiences.

With "I'm Sorry" exploding in popularity, I had returned to Brazil in the spring of 1960. The first blush of what would become a long romance with the British public came in the spring of 1960 when "Sweet Nothin's" went to No. 4 in the U.K. My first Canadian tour occurred in the fall of the year. There would be many more of those to come.

"Emotions" became a German hit in early 1961. Next came Australia, and what an experience that was. The headliners on that tour were Bobby Rydell, Chubby Checker and me. When we got off the plane in Melbourne, there were hundreds of kids screaming my name. We ran toward the terminal and an airport official whisked us into a room. We were trapped. The kids kept us in there for three hours. The police and firemen had to threaten the crowd with fire hoses before order was finally restored. I was never scared. It was just excitement to me. Back home, the *Los Angeles Herald Examiner* reported on the incident. *Cash Box* magazine later published photos of Chubby, Bobby and me teaching the Melbourne teens how to do the twist.

My international activity continued in '61 with my first tour of Mexico, and my old rockabilly sizzler "Let's Jump the Broomstick" topped the British charts that spring. "Brenda Lee is the real Queen of Rock and Roll," heralded the *London Daily Mirror* as I toured England that summer.

Too bad they didn't have frequent flyer miles in those days. In October, I went on a ten-day tour of South America. I remember that more than 3,000 fans mobbed me when I arrived at the airport in Santiago, Chile. There were similar scenes in Uruguay, Paraguay, Argentina and Brazil. Those Latin audiences were so volatile, so passionate.

When we got to Caracas, Venezuela, there were soldiers lined up on the airport tarmac toting submachine guns and semiautomatic weapons. We didn't know if there'd been a revolt or if there was about to be one. The country was always in turmoil. I didn't know if they were there to protect me or what. We had to walk right down between them. Mother was terrified.

In Paraguay, they tried to keep us from leaving the country. They told Mother that my father would have to be there before they would let us leave. She told them that Daddy was dead.

"Women don't have any say-so over here," the officials replied.

"Well, let me show you what *this* woman has," snapped Mother.

She reached down and took off her shoe. She raised that spiked heel in the air and was ready to strike him. Dub kept jerking her back. And they finally let us go.

Whether in tough contract negotiations, recording sessions or backstage with promoters, everyone knew that when Mother reached for her shoe, it was time to surrender.

Mother never wanted to go back to South America after that. But I did. I loved those cities and the people.

"The singer's Latin American popularity was stoked by tours and record releases throughout the decade," Lomax recounts. "By the end of the 1960s, Brenda Lee had been the 'cover girl' on such national publications as Mi Vida *(Mexico),* Ecran *(Chile) and* Revisto do Rock *(Brazil) and had starred on national television specials in several Latin nations.*

"Remember, this was a time when hardly any pop stars were courting the international market, never mind singers in Nashville. Brenda's discography includes more than 100 albums released in various overseas markets. She has performed in more than thirty different nations. Brenda was a groundbreaker, our first truly global pop star."

I think my emerging overseas renown led to some of Nashville's most innovative recording sessions. In the fall of

1961, Owen Bradley took me into the studio to rerecord my hits in German, French and Italian. During the next few years, I would also record in Spanish, Portuguese and Japanese.

The first song I learned to do in foreign languages was "Fool #1." In German it became "Geh am Gluck Nicht Vorbei." In French it was "La Premiere Fool." In Italian the song was translated as "Sono Sciocca." Next we did "Anybody but Me" in French and Italian. I learned the languages phonetically and was always told that my pronunciation was very good. German was the hardest for me.

Ironically, my German records were some of my biggest European hits. I even traveled to Hamburg to record "Darling Was Is Los Mit Dir" and "In Meinen Traumen" with the Bert Kaempfert Orchestra (of "Wonderland by Night" fame). My biggest German hit was 1964's "Ich Will Immer auf Dich Warten," and my other hit German releases included "Weidersehn Ist Wunderschon," "No My Boy" and "Jingle Bell Rock."

In late March 1962, I flew to England for a two-week tour with Gene Vincent. We were billed as "The King and Queen of Rock 'n' Roll," and we took those titles to heart. We really rocked out on our shows together, barnstorming theaters and creating pandemonium with those British kids.

I was thought of as a rock performer in the British Isles. A lot of my hits over there were up-tempo, not like the ballads in the States. Same thing with Australia. I did a completely different show on those overseas tours. We didn't do any of the Vegas routines. Instead, I'd open with "Dynamite" and go on from there. I'd do the hits I'd had in whatever country I was in and intersperse other well-known rock hits of the time, things like "What'd I Say" or "Great Balls of Fire," Elvis stuff and Little Richard's "Tutti-Frutti."

I was jumping around and doing all that growling and sweating, so Gene Vincent and I were a perfect pair for each other. He was one of the wildest showmen in rock history.

Even in a field noted for its intense eccentrics, Gene Vincent stands out among rock stars. Gene was the one who first wore the all-black leather uniform that has symbolized rock rebellion ever since. His menacing stage swagger, juvenile-delinquent sneer and "death-wish" angst characterize rockers to this day. Decades before punk rock, Gene Vincent was writhing on stage floors, leaping from pianos, thrashing wildly, wrapping himself around mike stands and bashing in drum kits. He'd recorded his big hit "Be-Bop-a-Lula" in Owen Bradley's Nashville studio in 1956, but by the 1960s, he was subsisting largely on his British popularity.

Gene Vincent was in a lot of physical pain on that tour. He had been in a bad motorcycle accident as a youngster. His leg had never been fixed right, and he had to wear a leg brace. If he didn't have that leg brace on, he couldn't walk. But Gene was wild, with a little substance abuse problem—pills and alcohol. The only way the show promoter could keep him in line and keep him from going out all night was to take that leg brace away. He'd take it away, and Gene would call my room.

"Brenda," rasped Gene. "They took my leg! I can't go anywhere! You've gotta get my leg for me."

"Gene . . . there's nothing I can do," I replied helplessly.

It used to make me feel so bad. But the promoter told me not to take it personally, because Gene would call and bother everybody in the hotel until he got that leg back.

I loved that British tour, but traveling in the U.K. did take some adjustments. Back in those days, the hotels you stayed in had meters for the heat. You had to put a shilling in to get thirty minutes of heat. The bathrooms were always the warmest room, so I got into the habit of grabbing the blankets and sleeping in the tub.

Sometimes you'd be given little foot warmers to put under the covers at the foot of your bed. They were like hot water bottles with small ridges on them. The first time we encountered them, Mother and I were in our room, and we heard Dub next door. There was an awful commotion with yelling and beating on something. It was late at night, so we didn't go over there. The next morning, I asked him what was wrong in his room that night. No one had told Dub about the foot warmer. So when he felt those warm ridges with his feet, he thought there was some kind of animal in the bed with him. He tried to beat it to death with a coat hanger. He kept hearing gurgling, so then he tried to smother it. We had a good laugh over that one.

By the end of the 1962 British tour, my single of "Speak to Me Pretty" was sprinting up the country's pop chart. It was to become my biggest U.K. hit. "Here Comes That Feelin'," "It Started All Over Again" and "All Alone Am I" also became British hits, in some cases surpassing their American chart positions.

After leaving the U.K., Gene and I headed to West Germany, where we were joined by Little Richard. Our trio toured U.S. military bases. Then we were booked for two weeks at the newly opened Star Club in Hamburg. On the same bill was the then unknown band the Beatles.

I thought they were just adorable. They were wearing the gray suits, pointy shoes and skinny ties by then. Plus, they were starting to sprout that mop-top haircut that was considered so unusual at the time. I loved their fire and their energy. And they all had such great senses of humor. I got a big kick out of their pranks and their antics. John Lennon used to pee out of the hotel window onto pedestrians.

It was fun being around them. They were all just a few years older than me, in their early twenties, so it felt like being around friends. George Harrison was very introspective and quiet. Paul

McCartney was a real showman, a real go-getter—and a cutie-pie. Paul was probably the most outgoing. I think my favorite was John Lennon, maybe because he seemed to be my biggest fan in the group. He was very irreverent and very intelligent. He had so much creativity just beneath the surface. He was on a different level. Pete Best was still the drummer, but I think they got to know Ringo Starr while they were in Hamburg, and he became their drummer just a few months later.

Hamburg was a seaport filled with rowdy sailors, illegal immigrants and petty criminals. It is said to have had more striptease clubs, pornography and prostitution than any other city at that time. And even back then wicked Hamburg loved to rock. The Star Club was Hamburg's biggest venue for that. The club alternated rock 'n' roll bands with lady mud wrestlers and other randy entertainments, sometimes turning over 18,000 customers a night. Gene, Little Richard, the Beatles and I always gave the teeming Star Club crowds what they'd come to hear.

The Beatles were raw musically, but I thought they really had something. After that tour was over, I couldn't get them off my mind. When Dub and I got back to the States, we begged Decca to sign them. They wouldn't listen. Same thing with the William Morris Agency.

Unbeknownst to me, the Beatles had already flunked a Decca audition in London. During the stint at the Star Club, the band learned that it was being signed by EMI's Parlophone label instead.

Years later, I found out how much John Lennon had respected me as an artist. I was so touched when he later declared in *Rolling Stone,* "She has the greatest rock 'n' roll voice of them all." I doubt that very much, but it still makes me smile to read it.

One of the most interesting international offers I ever got was to take a cultural exchange trip to Moscow in late 1962. But that

October, the United States blockaded Cuba because of Russia's military buildup there. International tensions were at an all-time high during this Cuban Missile Crisis. My proposed trip never occurred, but they did wind up releasing several of my records in Russia.

I returned to Germany in the spring of 1963. Again, I performed for GIs, and again I returned to the Star Club.

The day before I left for that trip to Germany, Patsy Cline had come over to the house. She was stopping by to visit with Mother and me before we left. I remember we talked about how far she'd come from those days when we used to tour together. She'd always been happy for my success, and I certainly was happy about hers.

Our shows in Frankfurt and Stuttgart were for both locals and U.S. servicemen. During one of my performances, my mother was standing off stage with a towel and a glass of water for me. One of the army guys went up to her and said, "Wasn't it sad about Patsy Cline?" Mother didn't know what he was talking about. He told her about the plane crash. They wouldn't tell me about it until after the show was over.

The career of Patsy Cline was cut short on March 5, 1963, when a small plane carrying her and country stars Hawkshaw Hawkins and Cowboy Copas went down in a rainstorm near Camden, Tennessee. The entire Nashville music community mourned the tragedy. But I had to mourn alone.

I couldn't even go home to pay my respects. There I was, thousands of miles away. I just couldn't believe it. Patsy had struggled for so long and was finally getting big hits like "Crazy" and "I Fall to Pieces." I was so happy for her. It was unreal that someone so vibrant could be dead. I had just seen her. I kept thinking back to all the things she'd done for us and of those times I'd play over at her house. Now that friendship was gone. I cried my eyes out; it was like losing a member of my own family.

But "the show must go on." I left Germany to tour Wales, England, Scotland and Ireland. *Disc* magazine gave me a great review after my opening date in Cardiff, Wales, in March 1963. "Fans Mob Brenda at Start of a Great Tour," read the headline.

> The tremendous Brenda Lee . . . stormed her way through two opening concerts . . . and caused fan scenes such as I have never seen before for any female singer. During a standing ovation near the end of the second house, a crowd of her male fans rushed the stage, several climbing on to it, in a scene that wouldn't have disgraced Elvis Presley!

My British fans have always been really enthusiastic. And they turned out to be some of my most loyal supporters. The fan clubs over there cropped up just as fast as they had in the United States. As soon as I started going to Canada, they developed there, too.

While in the U.K., I appeared on the popular teen show *Thank Your Lucky Stars*. My costars were Gerry and the Pacemakers, soon to top the hit parade with "Ferry Cross the Mersey," "Don't Let the Sun Catch You Crying" and other tunes. I was asked to judge talent competitions for aspiring bands. On one such occasion, I encountered a group of dandies who called themselves the Ravens. By 1964, that band was known as the Kinks and was rocking the world with "You Really Got Me."

After the Beatles broke, it seemed like there was a band forming every week over there. The whole scene was so incredible. I got to meet dozens of great bands, some of whom never did anything in the United States. But that was a tremendously explosive musical climate. And I was thrilled to be a part of it.

Another talent contest put me face to face with the ultimate "mod" band. Known as the High Numbers when I heard them in 1964, the band soon adopted a new billing as the Who. Heralded at the time for "My Generation," the group subsequently developed such ambitious concept pieces as *Tommy* and *Quadrophenia*. Incidentally, the Who was the only major "British Invasion" act that was signed by my label, Decca.

I could be wrong, but I don't think they won the contest. Even so, I know I voted for them. Their way of performing was way over the top. Even then, they were smashing instruments. Keith Moon was a maniac on the drums. He's the one I remember the most. I knew that if they ever got to America the kids would love them. And they did.

By 1964, overseas tours were annual events in my life. And travel was considerably different in those days. For one thing, transcontinental flights were agonizingly long. On the plus side, at least the planes were more comfortable than they are today. Flying back then was a luxury. They had white tablecloths, crystal and china. The first time I ever had surf and turf was on an airplane.

I've spent an awful lot of my time in the air. I've had everything happen to me in a plane that could happen. Except a crash. I've been on flights when they've had to make emergency landings on a foamed runway. I've flown through electrical storms where you'd do everything but turn upside down. There have been times when the plane would drop thousands of feet in seconds. I've been on them when they'd lose an engine.

I never gave it a second thought back then. But today it takes everything I've got to get on a plane. I will if I have to, but I sure don't like it.

I returned to Mexico City in the summer of 1964. Six days before my arrival, the nation had been hit by a big earthquake. So in addition to singing at the elegant Terrazzo Cassino, I also performed a benefit concert for the Mexican earthquake victims.

I'm not brave, so don't think that for a minute. I'm as terrified of earthquakes as the next person. The main reason I wanted
to go down there was to do that benefit. There were some after-
shocks, but the primary danger had passed. The Mexican audience had always been so great to me that I wanted to do anything
I could to lend a hand.

A "quake" was also shaking up the music world that year.
After Beatlemania erupted in 1964, the resulting British Invasion
brought me a whole new group of musical peers. It was so cool. I
toured the U.K. with some of the nation's biggest chart-toppers.
The list included Billy J. Kramer and the Dakotas ("Bad to Me"),
Manfred Mann ("Do Wa Diddy Diddy"), the Spencer Davis
Group ("Gimme Some Lovin'," featuring vocals by an eighteen-
year-old Steve Winwood), the Yardbirds (including lead guitarist
Eric Clapton), Georgie Fame and the Blue Flames ("Yeh, Yeh"),
Wayne Fontana and the Mindbenders ("The Game of Love"), the
Tremeloes ("Silence Is Golden") and a band named after my
hometown, the Nashville Teens ("Tobacco Road"). I also be-
friended dozens of lesser-known British acts.

Kids were going wild in the States over the new music idols.
I was meeting them face-to-face. In fact, I spent more time overseas in 1964 than ever before. An estimated 300,000 attended the
concerts on my European tour that year. I crisscrossed Germany,
Sweden, France, Ireland, Northern Ireland and England.

Next it was on to the City of Light. In Paris, the Councel
General de France hosted a cocktail party for me. Among the
guests was my old friend, movie star Maurice Chevalier.

Then I performed at the famed Royal Albert Hall in London
and blitzed the U.K. with media appearances on such radio and
television shows as *Easy Beat, Top Gear, Juke Box Jury, Open
House, Top Beat* and *Ready Steady Go*. On *Saturday Club* I was

reunited with my Star Club mates the Beatles. *Battle of the Giants* featured my music alongside that of Dusty Springfield.

They tried to make it a competition between us. But the truth is we loved each other. I met Dusty for the first time when she was still with her brother in the Springfields. They sang "Silver Threads and Golden Needles" on a *New Musical Express* award show in 1962 that I was on. She was so good and had that smoky, soulful voice. She also had great mod clothes. Women back then always had to share dressing rooms, so we all drew close to one another.

Over the years, I became an even bigger fan. Dusty was definitely an independent spirit. She was her own woman, and I respected that enormously. And what can you say about those records—"Wishin' and Hopin'," "Son of a Preacher Man" and the rest? Not long after she recorded her final album in Nashville, Dusty died of breast cancer at only age fifty-nine in 1999. A year later they put her into the Rock 'n' Roll Hall of Fame. I wish she could have lived to see that. I cheer every time one of my fellow female performers gets inducted.

Another highlight of that 1964 visit to England was my first London recording session. It was scheduled with Mickie Most, then one of the hottest record producers in England. Mickie was the producer of the Animals, who scored the massive international hit "House of the Rising Sun" in '64. He later produced Donovan, Jeff Beck, Lulu, the Yardbirds, Herman's Hermits and other legends of British pop.

I guess the reason that Decca wanted me to go over there and record was because of the popularity of the British Invasion. They wanted me to sound "fab" and "gear," too. Whatever the reason, I couldn't wait for the session. In fact, I went to the studio straight from the airport. I didn't know quite what to expect.

But it turned out that I really liked Mickie Most and all the musicians on that session. Jimmy Page was there as a guitarist, and you know he went on to become so big in Led Zeppelin. But he was only twenty at the time, just a few months older than me. In fact, all the players were young. I was young. Mickie was young. So the atmosphere was really hip. I wasn't nervous or intimidated. There was no pressure.

Plus, they recorded kind of like I did in the States. Every musician was there in the room, and we did it live. I recorded a rocker called "Is It True" and the Ray Charles classic "What'd I Say," both of which were targeted by Mickie for the British audience. It didn't take long, because everybody knew what they were doing, and we just did it. It was good.

My most vivid memory of any of my many trips to England is the night I appeared before the Queen. The Royal Command Performance was held at the London Palladium on November 2, 1964. Comedian Bob Newhart and singer Lena Horne were the other Americans presented to Queen Elizabeth. The Bachelors, the Shadows and Cliff Richard were among the British acts at the Palladium that night. I was to join such English female favorites as Cilla Black, Millicent Martin and Kathy Kirby in a production number that would feature each of us singing in front of a posh motorcar.

I have to admit I was, and am, fascinated by the Royals. We don't have any of that pomp and circumstance like they do over there. There was so much protocol to learn. The Queen has to walk on this carpet, never on the ground. You can't walk the same route she walks. You can't touch her. You're not supposed to look at her when you bow, just curtsy and look down.

You could only shake her hand if you wore gloves. Well, I never wore gloves, so we didn't have any with us. Dub ran around London like a madman trying to find gloves. He found some long ones. They were supposed to come to your elbows, but on me they came to my armpits. The fingers were too long and drooping down. I must have looked ridiculous.

It turned out that I was actually invited to be in the variety show by Prince Charles. He was sixteen at the time and was a fan. So there I was, at his request. At any rate, they had this revolving stage. Each of us girl singers was in a different car. The stage would revolve to the next performer in her car, a doorman would open the door and you were supposed to get out, walk to the front of the stage while your intro was playing and sing your song. When it was over, you were to curtsy to the Queen and leave.

So I get into my car. I think it was a Rolls-Royce. The turntable revolves. It stops. The guy goes to the door, and it won't open. I'm thinking, "Please don't play my overture now, because I'm still in the car." But they did. It was "All the Way," and the intro wasn't very long. Of course, I had this long fitted dress on. I had to hike it up and crawl out of the car window. I walked down and sang my song and did my curtsy. I must have been blushing beet red, but nobody laughed. After all, it was the Queen.

They said we could meet Her Majesty after the show. She was very nice, and said, "Did you have a good trip across the sea? We're very proud to have you here tonight." Never mentioned crawling out the car window at all. Prince Philip was in the receiving line. So was Princess Margaret, who later told me she used to "twirl like a dervish" dancing to "Let's Jump the Broomstick." She always was the party girl.

The British tabloid press cranked out loads of stories after that gala. *The New Musical Express* blared "Welcome to Britain, Brenda Lee!" on its cover. On December 11, my twentieth birthday, the same publication listed me as the World's Top Female Singer for the second year in a row. What a great present that was. The runners-up were Dusty Springfield, Dionne Warwick,

Cilla Black and Petula Clark. Further down the list were such notables as Mary Wells, Connie Francis and Lesley Gore. Dub put a handwritten thank-you note from me in that issue of *The New Musical Express*. Even *Billboard*'s London edition took note of the win in a story headlined, "Elvis, Brenda, Beatles Top in Newspaper Poll."

I spent my birthday doing a show at the Adelphi in London, then celebrated with a midnight party at the Lotus House. Guests included British favorites Cilla Black, Marty Wilde and Jess Conrad, plus Ronnie. The Lotus House was a swanky Chinese restaurant, and I love Chinese food. I'm a night owl, so the late hour was right up my alley. We had a ball.

The only sad thing—and I only learned this later—was that December 11th was the same day that Sam Cooke was shot to death in that L.A. motel. The last time I'd seen him was when he came to my sixteenth birthday party at the Crescendo in Hollywood. What a tragedy. What a loss for the music world.

Despite my grueling overseas travel schedule, they didn't ease up any on my recording schedule in Nashville. In fact, Decca issued more "Brenda Lee" discs than ever in America in 1964. The label apparently wanted to get as much music as possible out of its top seller.

The 1964 LP *By Request* contained my previous hits "I Wonder," "My Whole World Is Falling Down" and "The Grass Is Greener." I also recorded "Danke Schoen" for this collection. The tune was penned by my German producer Bert Kaempfert, who unfortunately did not send me his next major creation, "Strangers in the Night." Frank Sinatra got to that one first. *By Request* also included my new single, "As Usual."

"Backed by Bob Moore's steady walking bass line and a Floyd Cramer piano part that curlicues around her expressive vocal, 'As Usual' became a major pop success as well as

Brenda's eighth top-10 hit on the Adult Contemporary chart,"
reports author Mary Bufwack.

"Mindful of the perennial success of 'Rockin' around the
Christmas Tree' and of Brenda's new toe-tapping single 'Jingle
Bell Rock,' Decca finally got around to issuing a holiday collec-
tion as Brenda's second album of 1964. Merry Christmas from
Brenda Lee *remained a steady seller for the company for the next*
thirty-five years. It remains in print to this day."

Hot on the heels of *By Request* and *Merry Christmas from
Brenda Lee* came *Top Teen Hits.* Its recording sessions in
Nashville had been mainly sandwiched in between my two
British tours in the fall of 1964. Issued in early 1965, *Top Teen
Hits* was aimed more at my youth audience than most of its pre-
decessors had been.

The album contained my versions of such contemporary fa-
vorites as "Dancing in the Street," "Can't Buy Me Love" and
"Wishin' and Hopin'." I reprised my rocking British hit "Is It
True" on the package and introduced "When You Loved Me" as
my new U.S. single. Cowritten by my old *Ozark Jubilee* associate
Bob Tubert, the ballad duplicated its ten predecessors as an Adult
Contemporary airplay favorite.

"Top Teen Hits also included 'Thanks a Lot,' a rocked-up
reworking of an Ernest Tubb honky-tonk ditty," continues
Bufwack. "It was issued as a single with the complex, sophisti-
cated melody 'The Crying Game' on its flip side. The latter song
later became a chart-topper for Boy George. The unusual pairing
became one of the sixteen Brenda Lee singles where both sides
made the charts.

"Decca then issued The Versatile Brenda Lee. *It was aptly ti-*
tled, as Brenda did so many styles so well. This album contained
a little of them all. From the pop scene came Chad and Jeremy's
'Yesterday's Gone.' Country songs such as Johnny Cash's 'I Still

Miss Someone' were given the Brenda Lee treatment. From jazz
star Nancy Wilson's repertoire came 'How Glad I Am.' The Andy
Williams ballad 'Dear Heart' was recorded, as was the French-
language classic 'La Vie en Rose.' Brenda's single from the col-
lection was 'Truly Truly True,' a tune that had originated in
Russia."

A lot of my songs came from overseas. "I Want to Be
Wanted" had come from Italy. "Is It True" was given to me in
England. "Losing You" originated in France. "All Alone Am I"
was by a Greek writer and was from the stage production of
Never on Sunday. I was always open to a great melody, no matter
where it came from.

The songs were coming from everywhere, and I was going
everywhere. But I never would have predicted what happened
next. Dub Allbritten cast his eye on the large—and largely un-
tapped—music market of Japan.

Some songwriters apparently wrote this song for me over
there called "One Rainy Night in Tokyo." They sent it to me in
Nashville. There's only one line in it—the title—that is in English. The rest is in Japanese. I learned it phonetically and
recorded it in February 1965. We also recorded a Japanese version of "La Vie en Rose" and sent it to Japan as a single, too.

Naturally, Dub wanted to promote the record. After all, this
is the guy who'd paraded a pink elephant down Broadway in
New York to promote one of my discs. When we first went to
London, he had me singing on street corners to get the press's attention. So he got the idea that we should go to Japan and drum
up some business. I don't think a lot of American acts had gone
to the Far East at that point. Japan wasn't nearly as Americanized
in 1965 as it is today. The country was just starting to have a pop
scene.

If you think the flights to Europe were long, you haven't endured anything until you've flown across the Pacific. I was exhausted when we got in. I looked out of the plane when we landed at the airport, and all these people were there. They had on these little blue caps that said "BLFC." I said to Dub, "Look at that. There must be thousands of them. I wonder who they are? It must be some kind of tour group." When I got off the plane it was the Japanese version of the Brenda Lee Fan Club. They were all there for me! It was just the most amazing thing. I didn't know the song was so huge. It was a Gold Record there, a No. 1 hit. Today, "One Rainy Night in Tokyo" is considered a standard in Japan.

Anyway, there were all these reporters there. Photographers were snapping pictures. It was like a mob scene—people were trying to touch me and were yelling things, none of which I could understand. It was just unbelievable.

In concert, the audience response was something strange to me. When I first started doing shows over there in 1965, I would be up on stage and all I would hear was little pitter-patter clapping in unison at the end of each song. No matter how hard I worked, it sounded the same each time. I thought they hated me. After I got through, I told the promoter, "They hate me. They hardly applauded." He said, "Oh, no. They *loved* you."

They sat like little soldiers, all dressed alike and everybody with black hair. It was like a little beehive of all the same-looking little people. I said, "Can I sign autographs after the show?" The promoter said, "You can't do that because you'll be mobbed. I'm telling you, you don't want to do that." I said, "Please let me."

Do you know what? Every single person in the audience stayed. I was there for more than five hours after the show ended. Each person brought up a piece of stiff white poster board, outlined in gold. That's what you sign. They sell the cards at the shows expressly for that purpose, so they can all frame your autograph afterward. The fans were very respectful and reserved. Then, at the end, they all go, "Bravo!" They're so cute.

"Brenda's version of 'If You Love Me' has become one of the most widely loved and performed songs in Japanese history," reports overseas music expert John Lomax III. *"She is unique as an American artist who is revered as a legendary icon, a singer of what are considered Japanese standards, the Nippon version of a Frank Sinatra, if you will. To this day, when Japanese business executives call on her home state, Brenda is summoned to be at the governor's side as an ambassador."*

In years to come, I recorded two top-selling live albums in Japan. Eventually, I also starred in Japanese TV specials and scored further hits with "Gomennasaine" ("I'm Sorry"), "Omoide No Bara," "Akasaka after Dark" and other tunes. In all, I've released more than fifty singles in Japan. I have been honored with formal tea ceremonies and have resided in Emperor Hirohito's private hotel suite.

In 1978, I brought a Japanese student, Toshiko Wada, to live with my family and me in Nashville. We still correspond. I have also remained lifelong friends with Tom Nomura, the man who organized almost all my Japanese tours.

I later expanded my Far East touring schedule beyond Japan to include Singapore, Hong Kong, South Korea, Indonesia, Thailand and the Philippines. It really doesn't matter whether I have a current hit record in America or not. I'm always welcome in the Orient.

As odd as it sounds, Japan never really felt "foreign" to me. The language came easily, the customs felt natural. I loved the hotels. I loved the food. I felt right at home.

The etiquette was just extraordinary. I immediately started to learn to converse in Japanese so I could get to know the people better. You bow. You never let them lose face. If someone gives you a gift, you must never say, "Oh you shouldn't have done that." That makes them feel bad, insulted.

You could go into a shop and ask where a drugstore was. The clerk would not only tell you but take your hand and walk you there. Whether it was six blocks or three blocks, they'd take you to the place. Then they would go back to whatever they were doing before you interrupted them.

Everybody works, whether it's sweeping the streets or minding children. They revere their old people. They take care of them and don't put them in nursing homes. You don't get thrown out when you get old in Japan.

I loved the artwork. I started collecting wood-block prints, which are quite valuable today. I fell in love with Imari china and have also bought ivory, silk kimonos, pearls, jade sculptures and the cleverest toys you've ever seen. I love shopping for clothes and shoes there. For once, I was someplace where they definitely had my size.

They have a wonderful culture and a wonderful country. I was so innocent—I'd think, "How tragic it is that there was a war between our countries. Even though the Japanese don't show a lot of emotion, they're such a loving, respectful people."

I absolutely love it there. After 1965, I went back to Japan every year for the next twenty-five years.

I wouldn't take anything for my international travels. They not only opened my eyes, they opened my mind—they taught me tolerance and understanding. I feel like I learned more about the world and its people by being on the road as a singer than I could have learned from a hundred books.

That was my college education.

TWELVE

Coming On Strong

"You can't be pregnant, you're booked!" decreed Dub Allbritten. My manager was seated behind his desk, and I was totally crestfallen at his response to my news.

Everybody else had been so happy for me when I told them. Owen, my record producer, was thrilled. Right away he offered to buy the baby bed. Charlie Mosley, my guardian, was really happy—he and his wife had never had any children of their own. Ronnie was a little scared and proud at the same time.

Mother had mixed emotions. She thought I was too young to get married, so I'm sure she thought I was too young to have a child. And both she and Dub were concerned, because I was at the top of my game professionally.

But as for me, I was beyond being thrilled. This is what I had always wanted, a family of my own. I was just over the top with excitement and anticipation.

I never had one thought of the career, of the consequences or what it might mean to my future. I was in love, and I was pregnant. It was perfect. It was normal.

It was the fall of 1963. I was eighteen going on nineteen and a young bride of seven months. Ronnie and I were still teenagers, but we were growing up fast. After learning that I was pregnant, I asked Charlie Mosley for funds to buy our first home.

It was a rambling white brick home, what they called a "French ranch." It had columns out on the front porch, a huge den, four bedrooms, a sunroom, a breakfast room, big living and dining spaces, an ultramodern kitchen and stone fireplaces, all situated on eight acres of sweeping lawn. We had to buy a tractor just to mow it. I really felt like a proper little housewife. I even tried my hand at decorating.

It was on Kelly Road in Brentwood. I remember we went downtown to Sterchi's furniture store on Broadway to buy what we needed to fill up all those rooms. Ronnie signed a note and made monthly installments until we paid the furniture off. It was nice, but it wasn't top of the line by any means. It was all we could afford.

"Brenda was a terrible housekeeper and was on the road all the time anyway," Ronnie recalls. "So I hired a woman to come in and help out. One day I came home, and Brenda was ironing while the maid was watching soap operas! She never could boss people around."

We were just kids. One day Ronnie was out mowing the lawn on the tractor, and a salesman came by. He walked up the drive, and Ronnie stopped. The man asked, "Is your dad at home?"

Ronnie said, "This is my house!" He and I laughed a lot about that later.

Even though I was pregnant, I finished my concert commitments through the end of '63. Ordinarily, few tours are booked in the winter months such as January and February. And this proved to be very providential for me.

It was a difficult pregnancy. The doctors told me that being small was an issue. Plus, I went into premature labor several times. By the early spring, it was pretty clear that I couldn't travel at all. I'd only gained twelve pounds, which isn't considered enough to have a healthy birth.

The baby wasn't due until mid-May. But in late March, I was home alone watching TV—the doctors had put me on bed rest by then. I was having pains, but I didn't think too much about it. False contractions had happened before. But it kept getting worse, so I called the doctor. He said I needed to come on in. Ronnie hurried home from work and drove me to Vanderbilt University Hospital that morning.

I spent forty hours in labor. Finally, the doctors realized that I was unable to deliver naturally and elected to perform a cesarean section. The baby's heartbeat was growing fainter, so I was rushed into surgery. The Casuals, Dub Allbritten and my road manager Lamar Fike all joined the Shacketts and Mother in the waiting room.

"She's dilated two centimeters," reported the nurse.

"She's dilated five centimeters," came the next update.

"How big do her eyes have to get before she has the baby?" inquired Lamar in all seriousness.

None of the men laughed at the remark, since none of them were any more informed. But the nurse sure had fun telling me about it later.

Actually, the situation was quite serious. I finally gave birth to a daughter in the afternoon of April 1, 1964. We named her Julie Leann Shacklett. She was premature by almost two months and weighed less than five pounds. Unbeknownst to me, our child was in critical condition. The staff immediately whisked her out of the delivery room.

I found out much later that Julie had been born with hyaline membrane disease. In premature births, a film on the lungs sometimes does not disappear as it is supposed to, and breathing difficulties ensue. The same condition had killed the premature son of President John F. Kennedy and his wife Jackie in August of the previous year. Julie was placed under oxygen, fed through tubes, given transfusions and kept alive in an incubator.

I was told nothing. I kept asking when I could see my baby, but the doctors had instructed everyone to keep mum. I wasn't allowed to watch TV or see any newspapers. I thought that was a little bit strange, but as the days went by, I became more and more worried. Finally, a hospital employee I'd never seen before came into the room and said, "I'm so sorry to hear about your daughter."

"What are you talking about?" I pleaded.

"I heard she's not going to make it."

"Get my doctor right now," I cried. "I want to see my baby right now!"

They finally took me to see her. They had Julie all covered with blankets, because they didn't want me to see all the tubes and needles and all. Once I saw that she looked fine, I calmed down. It wasn't until days later that I found out how bad it really was.

I wasn't aware of it, but the *Tennessean* had been headlining the crisis for days. "Brenda's Baby Seriously Ill," lamented a typical story. The British tabloids screamed, "How I Nearly Lost My Baby," after Julie got out of danger.

Our baby had to remain at Vanderbilt for several weeks. I couldn't even hold her until she was a month old. Finally, we sent out a birth announcement, a pink theater ticket saying, "It's show time!"

Dub had the announcement printed up. He was always promoting something, even my baby. But it was awfully cute.

Even while Julie was still in the hospital, Dub sent me back out on the road. I still had my cesarean stitches, but my manager announced, "The show must go on." In late April, I attended the National Association of Record Merchandisers convention at the

Eden Roc Hotel in Miami Beach. I went there to pick up NARM's awards as Best Selling Female Vocalist and Top Female Singles Artist of the previous year.

They were great honors, but why on earth was I out there working so soon after being in labor? Not to mention being apart from the baby I'd wanted so badly and who needed my love and care. I mean, the child was sick! Once again, I found myself slipping into that old pattern of being controlled. Like I'd always been. Dub was telling me that if I didn't go out on the road, my career would be ruined. It was a guilt trip. He said how much he had done for me, and that I was being "selfish" if I didn't press on. I was miserable and mad at myself for doing it, but I was torn. I was young. I went along with it. I rationalized it by thinking that I had to provide for my child.

On top of everything else, Dub lied to me. He told me I was going back to work for only a few weeks. I had no idea what I was in for.

From July of 1964 until nearly the end of the year, I was away from home. I toured Europe and Mexico that summer. Then they put on a barnstorming schedule through the Midwest in August. I returned to Europe in September. After a brief stay back in Nashville (to record, of course), I flew back to Europe in October and remained overseas until December 12. Julie was an eight-month-old toddler when I returned.

My God, I sound like a monster. How horrible of all of us. I never stood up to anybody about any of this, I'm ashamed to say. Poor Ronnie—he was thrown into a situation that was completely foreign to him. So he never questioned things, either. Plus, I begged him to go overseas with me on that fall trip to Europe.

Fortunately, Dub's mother came to Nashville from Kentucky, and she's the one who nurtured Julie in those early months. We all loved "Grandmary," that's what we called her.

And thank God for her. She was a loving, trustworthy, strong, faithful and kind woman. She devoted the next fifteen years of her life to my children.

After that first awful separation, I said to Dub, "That's it. Never again. I am *not* going to be apart from Julie for that long anymore." I threatened him by saying that I would refuse to sing. I'd used that tactic before. So Julie was traveling with me by the time she was a year old. Grandmary came along, too. And it stayed that way until Julie reached school age.

With my baby in tow, I continued my hectic career pace. But at least I was finally getting to enjoy my hard-earned riches. Ronnie and I asked Mother to petition the court for the removal of my minority status. The judge agreed. From this point on, the money I made was no longer controlled by the tightfisted Charlie Mosley. We asked Dub to oversee our finances, and he proved to be a more indulgent custodian.

Whenever we needed something, we went to Dub for a check. And Dub was always nice about it. He wanted Ronnie and me to have nice things, too. He was living first class and always had. So what could he say? After all, it was my money, and I'd hardly seen a dime of it.

Almost overnight, things were better. We were in a nice home. We were able to have a new car and to entertain. After all those years of money being an issue, suddenly it wasn't. We started paying cash for everything. We never bought anything, not even a house or a car, unless we could pay for it outright.

"I'm not a teenager anymore," I scolded a reporter in 1964. "I've been pegged 'Little Miss Dynamite' for too long." After Julie was born, I left my girlhood behind without a backward glance. And when I turned twenty-one on December 11, 1965, everyone celebrated the milestone.

Decca Records threw a party at the Hermitage Hotel downtown. All the people from Music Row came—Red Foley, Boudleaux and Felice Bryant, the Casuals, Dick Barstow, my family, songwriters who'd written hits for me, the A-Team musicians who'd played on my records and, of course, my beloved Owen Bradley. Ronnie gave me a red Mustang convertible. Owen gave me an 18-carat gold charm for my bracelet that said "21." Dick gave me a set of six limited-edition hand-painted china cups that were commissioned for the 1952 coronation of Queen Elizabeth. The people who published "I'm Sorry," "Sweet Nothin's" and several other hits gave me a mink stole. Dub gave me sterling silverware and forty pieces of Baccarat crystal—after all, I'd never had a wedding shower. They'd hired a society orchestra, so we danced late into the night.

Riding high, Ronnie sold the Kelly Road house for a small profit in 1966. After a brief stay in another contemporary home, we moved into a 1930s Georgian estate. Surrounded by the spacious homes of comedian Minnie Pearl and country star Webb Pierce, as well as the Tennessee Governor's Mansion, the stately residence was located on two acres off the tree-lined boulevard of Franklin Road. Ronnie and I worked side by side, happily renovating the house from top to bottom.

That was my dream home. When I was a little girl, I used to walk to school in Lithonia, Georgia, and pass a huge antebellum home that was up on top of a hill. I used to look up at it and think, "Maybe one day I can live like that." I think all Southern girls have that dream. It's that *Gone With the Wind* syndrome.

The lawn was shaded with fragrant magnolias and was filled with ancient boxwoods. There was a riding ring out back and a little barn, so I bought Julie a pony. Ronnie and I had horses, too.

Freda's brother Mark Garrett decorated the interior with beautiful country French furniture interspersed with European antiques. As you entered, there was a marble foyer topped by an enormous crystal chandelier. A grand, curved, floating staircase took you upstairs. The house had a music room and a formal living room, which I decorated with raw silk draperies. French doors opened onto a side porch with gothic columns. All the wood trim in that house was hand-carved.

But the Franklin Road house was definitely haunted. Don't laugh. I'm serious. You could hear the ghost walking around in the attic. And at night, the attic door would open and footsteps would come down the grand staircase and walk around downstairs.

I thought it was groovy. To me, it was just an added attraction to the house. It was a nice ghost. It had a kind of shuffling walk, like somebody moving along in their bedroom slippers. It never did anything to make us afraid, but it was still a ghost. Even my levelheaded husband agrees that there was a spirit in the historic mansion.

"We used to hear things," Ronnie insists. "One night in particular we heard something in the stairwell. I got my gun. I was scared to death and looking all around, about to go up to the third floor. Brenda came out of the bedroom and said, 'Ronnie! Right where you are is right where I heard it!' I about jumped out of my skin."

We had some great times in that house. We had big dinner parties and catered receptions for hundreds of folks. But even that house couldn't hold my really big deal. Every year for several years we threw a big masquerade party in December. For those, we'd go to a big warehouse that Ronnie's father owned.

Everybody from politicians to building contractors to family to music industry people were invited. The top radio deejays in town would come. A photographer would greet guests at the door, take a picture of them in their costumes and take a dollar from each one. That was the "kitty" money. The deejays would judge and would award that kitty to the best costume.

People really dressed up. Ronnie went as Rhett Butler one year. People came as gorillas, pirates, princesses, cowboys, just everything. The costume rental places really loved us, because we brought them so much business every year. Everybody from the mayor to federal judges to Chet Atkins would come—anybody who was anybody came.

We always had great entertainment, too. One year it was Gale Garnett singing her hit "We'll Sing in the Sunshine." Another time it was Jewel Akens, who sang "The Birds and the Bees." My favorite was the time we booked the Monkees. They were the most popular group in America at the time, with hits like "I'm a Believer," "Last Train to Clarksville" and "Daydream Believer."

Needless to say, the Monkees were "fave raves" in *16 Magazine*. And since editor Gloria Stavers had long been my buddy, the gala got a photo spread in the teen magazine. After I sang with the group, I posed happily with Monkees Peter Tork and Davy Jones. Since I was a clown that year, my cheeks were dotted with red circles, and I was wearing a puffy ruffle around my neck.

This was our real party period. We don't rock like that anymore. "Been there, done that," I always say. We were living it up. I remember that Ronnie bought nineteen cars in one year.

Our old-money address meant that I—the little girl from red-clay roots—had "arrived" in society. We eventually started socializing with the blue-blood families of Nashville. We put Julie in the best private schools and maintained a full-time staff—a housekeeper, a nanny and a yard man who doubled as a chauffeur.

Grandmary or the maid would cook our meals every night. We had the dinner parties catered. In fact, it was at one of our dinner parties that I went into labor with my second child.

That time, I was pregnant for five months before I even realized it. One reason I didn't expect it was that I was on birth-control pills. For that matter, I was on them when I got pregnant with Julie, too.

Anyway, with that second pregnancy, I gained forty-eight pounds. I waddled everywhere I went, including to my own dinner party. The baby wasn't due for three more weeks, so I thought it would be OK to entertain. But the contractions started right in the middle of the second course.

"You all are going to have to excuse me," I said. "I think I'm getting ready to have my baby. Make yourselves at home. I'll probably be right back. I've had false contractions before. Eat, drink and be merry."

Jolie Lenee Shacklett was born in the wee hours of the next morning at Vanderbilt University Hospital, January 21, 1969. Although premature, she did not have the severe complications that her older sister Julie had experienced at birth.

I named Jolie after Al Jolson. That was his nickname. A lot of young people don't remember him today, but Jolson was a showbiz giant back in the days of vaudeville. Before Frank Sinatra, he was called the world's greatest entertainer. He's the one who gave us "California Here I Come," "Swanee," "My Mammy," "Toot-Toot-Tootsie Goodbye" and dozens of other standards.

It wasn't intentional that the name Jolie was so similar to Julie. I'd wanted to name my first baby after Patsy Cline, but I was talking to Loretta Lynn when she was pregnant at the same time I was. She told me she was going to name her twins Peggy and Patsy if they were girls. Well, there went my idea. So I picked Julie, which was what Patsy had named her only daughter.

Because I lived in Nashville, I was surrounded by country music legends. In addition to Loretta, I was friends with George Jones, Eddy Arnold, Marty Robbins, Kitty Wells, Bobby Bare and many other country stars of the '60s. Ronnie and I attended Radnor Church of Christ, and in 1964, his close friend and former schoolmate Carl Dean began bringing his new girlfriend to services. Fresh from her East Tennessee high school graduation, Dolly Parton was working as a waitress on Murfreesboro Road and hoping to make it in the music business.

I thought she was the prettiest thing. Dolly told me that I'd been an inspiration to her. When I heard her sing, I thought she had the most hauntingly beautiful mountain soprano. I think what's so endearing about Dolly is the same thing that's endearing about Loretta. They're not ashamed of their roots. They are just who they are. You accept them for who they are, or not, because they're not going to be any different.

She and Carl got married not long after that. He was in the contracting business, like Ronnie, and they had been teenage running buddies. I think it's interesting that both of us couples wound up with two of the longest-lasting marriages in the Nashville music community. Do you think it has something to do with the construction business?

Being a woman, I'm always interested in what other female performers are doing and what the women have to say in their music. Whenever new female performers would come to town, I wanted to support them. I'd go see them, because I also wanted to see what I could learn from their stage shows.

In 1968, somebody told me this good little singer was performing at the Black Poodle club in Printer's Alley, the Nashville nightclub district. During her show, she'd occasionally say how much she liked and admired Brenda Lee. So we went to the club to see her, and I thought her performance was electrifying.

It was Barbara Mandrell. She was so energetic and played all those instruments. You certainly didn't see a woman doing that every day. She sang great and was as cute as she could be. That next week, I told everybody I saw on Music Row, "There's this girl playing in the Alley, and you *need* to go see her." I became a big booster.

"*One night while I was working the Black Poodle, Daddy came backstage and said, 'Brenda Lee is out there,'*" recalled Barbara Mandrell in her popular autobiography, Get to the Heart. "*I had been a fan of hers since I was 10 or 11 . . . Once I sang at an album store, and they gave me my choice of two albums. I remember taking* Grandma What Great Songs You Sang *and* Emotions, *two great Brenda Lee albums.*

"*Now she was sitting in the Black Poodle and I was excited . . . Brenda was the first one to applaud and the last to stop . . . Along with servicemen, she was the best audience I ever had.*

"*A few months later, I received an invitation to her baby shower. I remember how awestruck I was at her mansion, with antiques everywhere. She was so natural, with no shoes on, and she set her plate right on her pregnant tummy.*"

Ever since I met her backstage at the Black Poodle that night, Barbara and I have always kept in touch. It wasn't long after that when she got her record contract and started having hit after hit.

About a year later, Loretta Lynn brought her little sister to Nashville to record for Decca Records. The kid's name was Brenda Webb. They told her, "We already have a 'Brenda' on the label. You'll have to change your name." Well, Gail was her middle name and Loretta liked the Krystal Hamburger fast-food chain. So because of me, Brenda Webb became Crystal Gayle. A few years later she had that huge hit "Don't It Make My Brown Eyes Blue."

During the late '60s a flood of new talents inundated Nashville. That's when Tammy Wynette arrived on the scene. That's also when Donna Fargo started recording on Music Row.

Waylon Jennings moved to Music City. So did Lynn Anderson and Ronnie Milsap. By 1965 Music City had built twenty recording studios, established 110 song publishing houses and was home to more than 1,500 professional musicians. It was amazing to watch it grow.

Stars such as James Brown (1970's "Sex Machine"), Peggy Scott & Jo Jo Benson (1969's "Soulshake") and Joe Simon (1969's Grammy-nominated "The Chokin' Kind") were recording hits on Music Row. In 1965, my friend Buddy Killen began producing a string of successes for Joe Tex that included "Hold What You've Got" and "Skinny Legs and All." In 1967, Robert Knight recorded the enduring classic "Everlasting Love," which was cowritten by my former Casuals band member Buzz Cason. Even bigger was the 1966 international smash "Sunny," sung by Nashville native Bobby Hebb.

Ray Stevens was clicking on the charts with "Gitarzan" (1969), "Everything Is Beautiful" (1970) and a string of others. Gary Puckett & the Union Gap recorded "Woman, Woman" (1967), "Lady Willpower" (1968) and more on Music Row. Tony Joe White scored with the "swamp-pop" sound of "Polk Salad Annie" in 1969. Bob Dylan recorded *Blonde on Blonde* in Nashville in 1966, which led to an avalanche of song poets descending on the city.

It seemed like every day you'd see scruffy guys with guitars on their backs getting off at the bus station downtown. Nashville was really becoming a mecca for songwriters. And it's still that way today.

You know the old joke? How do you find a songwriter in Nashville? Call, "Oh, waiter!" in a restaurant. There's a songwriter on every corner. I was even handed a cassette of a song by a guy who was in a car accident with me. I was driving down

Music Row, and this man ran into the side of my car. I'm fine, so I get out of the car and rush over—I'm worried about his car and whether he's hurt.

"Are you OK?" I asked frantically.

"Oh hi, Brenda," the driver replied. "Remember me? I was just thinking about you the other day. I've got this song that would be absolutely perfect for you!"

The guy went back to his wrecked car and rummaged through the debris. He brought a tape directly back to me. I was dumbfounded. His car was completely totaled, and he was acting like nothing was wrong. And then when the police came, he had the nerve to say it was my fault!

Needless to say, I threw his tape away.

One of the funniest stories about a struggling songwriter happened at one of my recording sessions in the late '60s. I arrived at the CBS studio on Music Row to record with Owen Bradley one night, and the janitor wouldn't let me in. He thought I was some kid who had come to bother the star. That janitor was Kris Kristofferson.

"This is a closed session," Kris said officiously. "Brenda Lee never allows any visitors to her recording sessions; you can't come in."

"I have to come in; it's my session; I'm singing; I am Brenda Lee," I sputtered.

I teased Kris about that for years. During that time he did all kinds of odd jobs. He even worked for Ronnie's dad as a roofer.

I didn't know it at the time, but Kris Kristofferson would later have a profound impact on my place in the music world. We'll get to that later.

By the late 1960s, my position in the pop top-10 was no longer assured. My 1965 singles, "Too Many Rivers" and "Rusty

Bells," fared far less well than most of their predecessors. But I had an insurance policy—both tunes became top-5 hits on the Adult Contemporary charts.

Some artists think there's a stigma attached to being Adult Contemporary, Easy Listening or Middle of the Road, or whatever you want to call it. I never did. I was glad that I had my foot in the door on that chart from the first. I don't care who you are, today's teen idol is tomorrow's A/C act. Whether you're Sting, Billy Joel, Elton John, Madonna or whoever the hippest thing in pop is at the moment, sooner or later you're going to be considered Adult Contemporary by the younger generation.

But even A/C support wasn't everlasting. In late 1965, "Too Little Time" became the first Brenda Lee single in six years that did not appear on any music charts. My follow-up, "Ain't Gonna Cry No More," struggled only as far as No. 77.

To my surprise, I bounced back in 1966 with the hit toe-tapper "Coming On Strong." The song was later quoted in the 1974 hit "Radar Love" by the Dutch rock band Golden Earring. "Coming On Strong" shared the radio airwaves with a new generation of rockers—"Walk Away Renee" by the Left Banke, "Reach Out (I'll Be There)" by the Four Tops, "96 Tears" by ? (Question Mark) and the Mysterians, "Good Vibrations" by the Beach Boys and "Mellow Yellow" by Donovan.

But that chart comeback with "Coming On Strong" was short-lived. After mild success with 1967's sprightly "Ride Ride Ride," my four 1968 releases all failed to chart. One of them was the title tune to Broadway's hottest musical, *Cabaret*.

On the album front, 1965's *Top Teen Hits* became my first noncharting LP. In retrospect, the project was probably doomed from the start. I had made so many strides beyond the teen marketplace that my presence back there seemed forced. With its Motown and Beatles tunes, that album was my only outright stab at commercialism. After the British Invasion, teen record sales exploded to unheard-of heights. Decca had wanted me out of that world, and now they suddenly wanted me back in it.

The eclectic follow-up album, *The Versatile Brenda Lee,* also failed to chart. Owen Bradley reverted to formula on 1965's *Too Many Rivers* and 1966's *Bye Bye Blues*. Both contained a new Brenda Lee single, surrounded by supper-club fare. It had served me well for years, but now the formula for my LPs was worn out.

Old-school show business was dying, and rock was being revolutionized. The Rolling Stones, the Byrds, the Mamas and Papas, the Doors, Simon & Garfunkel, the Jefferson Airplane and the Grateful Dead led a charge of long-haired, politically irreverent and musically experimental rockers. It was no longer enough to package hit singles with perennial favorites. Albums were now considered "art." The hippest acts were expected to compose and produce their own sounds. I didn't fit in.

Pop music began to reflect the turbulent times. I don't think there's a single era since the Civil War that has witnessed so much upheaval in America. The assassination of President Kennedy was followed by the killings of Malcolm X (1965), Martin Luther King Jr. (1968) and Senator Robert Kennedy (1968). Race riots inflamed the cities. The civil rights movement, the environmental movement, the women's movement and the peace movement were all born in the '60s. American culture would never be the same.

There was no longer a sense of hope and optimism among the nation's youth, and I empathized. The military buildup in Vietnam was escalating. Young people's protests against the war became ever more vocal as the decade wore on.

I was insulated from the political turbulence. Dub kept me in my own little bubble. But I certainly knew about the events of the day. I was then and am now an avid newspaper reader. Several of my high school friends died in Vietnam, and I sang at their funerals when their bodies were shipped home.

On one trip to the Philippines, I went through the military hospital at the Clark base with General Westmoreland when he was giving out purple hearts. I saw the guys that were there from Vietnam and what they had gone through. It was very emotional—many of those guys had their arms and legs off. A lot of people wouldn't want to see that, but I felt it was the least I could do for these men who were giving their lives and limbs for America. Several of them gave me the telephone numbers of their families back in the States. They wanted me to call when I got home to tell their folks that they were alive. There were dozens of families, and I called every single one.

I wanted to go to Vietnam and perform for the troops. I was the pinup girl for one of the divisions, so I used to write those boys all the time, and they'd write back. I even sent records. Bob Hope asked me to go on one of his tours to the front lines, and I was ready. But Dub said no. He thought it was too dangerous.

My generation was the one that had to fight. Thank God Ronnie was exempt, because he was a young father. Buddy, his older brother, went into the Air Force.

When the kids started protesting, I agreed with what they had to say. I was never in favor of that war. It made no sense to me.

The protesters were the most visible and vocal representatives of a generation in commotion. Young people's alienation from the political process and their disillusionment with mainstream culture led to the creation of a culture of their own. No image of the time is more vivid than that of the dope-smoking, flower-wearing, long-haired hippie. And the music that defined the times was the psychedelic hippie sound. The event that became its shining hour was the 1969 Woodstock music festival.

People who were coming of age in the late '60s were the children of the baby boom. Those were the kids who were born right after me. Their culture had such an impact because there were so many of them—one-sixth of the U.S. population by the end of the decade. A hit teen record in the 1950s might sell 100,000 copies. By the end of the '60s, hit rock 'n' roll discs sold in the multiple millions.

I tagged along. The new rockers strutted their stuff on TV shows such as ABC's *Shindig* and NBC's *Hullabaloo,* the first real network attempts to come to terms with rock 'n' roll. So I belted my new singles on these programs alongside such "youthquake" stars as the Hollies ("He Ain't Heavy, He's My Brother"), The Young Rascals ("Groovin'"), the Impressions ("Amen"), Peter and Gordon ("I Go to Pieces"), the Beau Brummels ("Laugh Laugh") and the Animals ("Don't Let Me Be Misunderstood").

I kept meeting everybody I could, just like when I was a kid. When I was in England in 1965, this Welsh coal miner came to see my show. One of my band members came backstage and said, "Tom Jones is in the audience, and he wants to meet you." I knew immediately who he was, because "It's Not Unusual" had just come on the charts as his first hit. I later recorded the song on my *Too Many Rivers* LP.

After the show, we all sat around in the club and talked. Tom hadn't been to the States yet, and he was all excited about that. I told him all about Nashville and New York and all the great places to see. I would've talked to him all night. He had that black curly hair, those broad shoulders and that little bitty waist. Looking like that, I knew he wouldn't have a problem with the female audience in America at all.

At the NARM convention that same year the hottest new group was the Supremes. We were in a huge ballroom, and the stage was set up in such a way that there wasn't much space for dressing rooms. It was kind of cramped, so we were pretty much thrown together. The Supremes were beautiful girls, and I was immediately drawn to Mary Wilson, in particular. She was so warm and friendly. But Diana Ross seemed kind of snooty. She hardly even acknowledged that I was there. I guess she was paying attention, though: She later recorded "Sweet Nothin's" as the flip side of her hit single "Mirror, Mirror."

I was a big Motown fan. I met the Temptations at the Jukebox Convention in '65. I met Martha Reeves, and she's a hoot. She's very feisty, speaks her mind at all times and is one of the funniest people I've ever been around. I met Smokey Robinson in his early days, too.

I got to know most of the "girl groups." One of my favorites was the Ronettes, who had "Be My Baby." I met them when we did *Hullabaloo* together. To me, Ronnie Spector had one of the great female rock voices. And those girls had the moves. Like so many of the acts, the Ronettes were never given the money they earned and deserved. That's one of the sad facts about the rock 'n' roll business in those days.

I loved Felix Cavaliere of the Young Rascals. He's one of the sweetest guys you'll ever know. I met John Denver in 1969 when he was a fairly unknown songwriter. Peter, Paul and Mary had made a hit of his song "Leaving on a Jet Plane," and I congratulated him on that. He was an odd guy, not terribly good at conversation. But he seemed like a gentle person, very kind.

Dub Allbritten tried his best to keep me relevant in the new cultural climate. He began scheduling "no alcohol" shows at my nightclub engagements in an attempt to reconnect me with a teen audience. More significant, he booked me for the first time on college campuses. A 1966 tour took my show to five universities. I played to more than 20,000 students, and I'm delighted to say that I earned fifteen standing ovations.

I also became a frequent guest on TV's *Hollywood Squares* in 1967–68. I performed on such new programs as *The Mike Douglas Show* and *The Tonight Show*. In the summer of 1967, I starred on a television special celebrating the tenth anniversary of *American Bandstand,* and a year later, I had my own special on Canadian TV.

I remember my opening at the Coconut Grove in Hollywood in 1967 as another highlight. Rick Nelson attended and visited me backstage. Telegrams arrived from Elvis Presley and from Sonny and Cher. "Brenda Lee Grows Up" headlined the *Los Angeles Times* review. *Variety* ran a congratulatory ad from "Elvis and The Colonel."

Decca Records toasted me with a new LP titled *10 Golden Years.* The collection saluted my tenth anniversary with the company and featured one of my hit tunes for each year from 1956 to 1966. The label declared "Brenda Lee Week," and *Billboard* magazine published a special Brenda Lee supplement on the date of the disc's release. The album became my first to earn a Gold Record award.

Here I am, only twenty-one years old, and the public is buying my oldies! I wasn't ready to be old! I felt like I still had lots of music in me.

On the fashion front, I began to frost my brunette bouffant in 1965–66. I lost weight and began wearing glamorous false eyelashes. My gowns became more form-fitting and streamlined.

When the figures were finally tallied, 1966 turned out to be my highest-grossing year to that date. I might have been doing well on the road, but there was still the nagging problem of how to get me back on the popularity charts.

In pursuit of a new direction, I embarked on a series of musical experiments. For my 1967 *Reflections in Blue* album, Owen Bradley hired the Hollywood Strings. The Los Angeles sessions also included hotshot guitarist Glen Campbell. Later that year, Glen would enjoy his first hits of his own, "Gentle on My Mind" and "By the Time I Get to Phoenix."

Reflections in Blue failed to chart. So next, I tried a New Orleans approach. I teamed up with Dixieland clarinetist Pete Fountain in 1968 for a jazz/blues LP titled *For the First Time*. The album's single, "Cabaret," stiffed, and *For the First Time* barely eked out a No. 187 position on Billboard's Top 200 Albums listing.

I was now officially "cold" as a chart artist. Fatherly Owen Bradley took me aside for a chat.

"Listen, honey," said Owen, "I've had a long talk with the label, and we feel you need to try something different. I know this might be hard for you, but it would be good for you to try and freshen things up. You and I have had a long run together, and I'll always be here for you. This isn't the end, but I do want you to meet this guy in New York we've found for you. I think you and Mike Berniker could work well together."

Because Owen thought it best, I gave up the comfort and familiarity of my longtime Nashville session players to explore new sounds in Manhattan. But when I did, I made sure I took a hit with me.

I was driving in the car one day listening to the radio, and I heard Willie Nelson singing this song called "Johnny One Time." I was immediately struck by it. I thought, "I could do that." It had everything I've always looked for in a song, a great lyric and a great melodic chorus. I tracked it down and found out it had been written by two of my favorite writers, Dallas Frazier and Doodle Owens. I don't always know a hit when I hear one, but I was as sure as I could be that this one had what it took.

" '*Johnny One Time*' is a striking lyric about a woman se-

duced and abandoned," observes Finding Her Voice *author* Mary Bufwack. *"In the studio, Brenda poured herself into her performance. The guitar and orchestral accompaniment heightened the emotion. In the space of three minutes and fourteen seconds she conveys shame, anger, heartache and bitterness in a brilliant, emotional tour de force. It remains one of the most extraordinary vocals in her career.*

" 'Johnny One Time' became a giant hit on the Adult Contemporary chart. The disc netted Brenda her second Grammy Award nomination. It also pointed the way to her future by becoming her first disc since 1957 to crack the country hit parade."

Dub was furious about that country chart attention. I think he made a special trip to New York to cuss out the Decca brass, because he thought they were promoting "Johnny One Time" as a country single. He tried to get one of the promotion men fired. He didn't want me to be associated in any shape or form with country. He wanted no part or parcel of "hillbilly," "Nashville," "hay bales" or "Southern." He had done everything in his power to take me out of that. Back then, country was really not cool. It turned out that the Decca promotion staff had nothing to do with it—country stations had picked up the single on their own.

The Grammy nomination for "Johnny One Time" delighted me. I immediately made plans to attend the prestigious event. The Recording Academy even invited me to cohost one of its celebrations.

There were two Grammy ceremonies that year. The one in New York was held in Alice Tully Hall. That's where I went, rather than to Los Angeles. It turned out to be the wrong choice. The show was slowly paced, and to top it off, the sound system went out while I was singing "Johnny One Time." I was mortified. I kept singing, even though I was holding a dead mike and nobody could hear me. After I was done, the electricity stayed off for half an hour and the music-biz crowd got more and more irritated.

"When she'd been nominated for 'I'm Sorry' at the beginning of the decade, the Grammy voters were dominated by 'establishment' music-business executives who were fighting a losing battle against the rising tide of teen culture," recalls music historian John Lomax III. "Back then she'd competed against such chart has-beens as Rosemary Clooney, Doris Day, Peggy Lee, Ella Fitzgerald and opera star Eileen Farrell. Although Brenda had the only legitimate hit record, the Grammy went to jazz legend Ella.

"Now, at the end of the decade, the Grammys were in transition between the music industry's 'old guard' and the proponents of the new music of the late '60s. Although some of that year's awards went to Blood, Sweat and Tears; Crosby, Stills and Nash; Aretha Franklin and Joni Mitchell, the ceremony also honored adult-appeal stylists Henry Mancini, Percy Faith, Art Linkletter and Danny Davis.

"Brenda was caught between the two worlds. In her category she competed against Dionne Warwick's 'This Girl's in Love with You,' Jackie DeShannon's 'Put a Little Love in Your Heart' and Dusty Springfield's 'Son of a Preacher Man' on the hip side, plus balladeers Peggy Lee for 'Is That All There Is?' and Vicki Carr for 'With Pen in Hand.' Peggy, the establishment artist, took home the Grammy."

I figured if I'm gonna lose, I might as well lose to one of my idols. I'd lost in 1960 to Ella Fitzgerald, and I loved her. Now I was outvoted by Peggy Lee, who was one of the greats, too.

The loss didn't slow me down. On the heels of "Johnny One Time," I issued "You Don't Need Me Anymore." I loved the dark emotion and the desolate lyric of disintegrating love in that song.

It became my fiftieth charted title on the pop hit parade. I was completely oblivious at the time, but now I realize what an amazing feat that was.

It hadn't been an easy ride, but it turned out that I finished the '60s as the fourth most successful chart act of the decade, right behind the Beatles, Elvis Presley and the Supremes. Little did I know that the dawn of the new decade would not be as kind.

THIRTEEN

If This Is Our Last Time

The early 1970s was an awful time in my life. I just didn't know if there was a place for me in the recording business anymore. And everything seemed to be changing around me. It wasn't just the music, it was everything.

After the New York experiment and my subsequent success with "Johnny One Time," Decca sent me to Memphis to see if I could capture some of the magic that was happening there. The city had come a long way in the music world since giving birth to the careers of Elvis Presley, Johnny Cash, Jerry Lee Lewis and Carl Perkins in the '50s. By the late '60s and early '70s, Memphis was famed for a whole new sound. It was sizzling as the recording center for Stax Records, whose house band was heating up the charts with the hits of Otis Redding ("Dock of the Bay"), Sam and Dave ("Soul Man"), the Staple Singers ("Respect Yourself") and others.

Across town at American Sound, another group of session musicians was cooking up a different flavor of Memphis soul stew. That team crafted hits like "The Letter" for the Box Tops, "Hooked on a Feeling" for B. J. Thomas, "Sweet Caroline" for Neil Diamond and "Suspicious Minds" for Elvis. In addition, my old friend Dusty Springfield had scored a huge comeback hit there in 1969 with her Memphis-recorded "Son of a Preacher

Man." So in the early weeks of 1970, I went to the American Sound studio, too.

Memphis was hot and producer Chips Moman was "happening." Those musicians were making records that were hotter than firecrackers. I was a little bit more excited about the Memphis sessions than I had been about New York. I'd loved r&b since I was a kid. Plus, those musicians were good ol' boys, like the Nashville players, with a laid back attitude but incredible musicianship.

The album that resulted was called *Memphis Portrait*. I still like that record, but it was a bit of a departure. It was composed about half-and-half of hit Memphis soul tunes and newly written songs. I remember that we lived in that studio, recording around the clock for about a week. We practically slept there. We had food catered in, and we had plenty of good times. It was exhausting, but it was fun.

Too bad it was all for naught. It turned out that 1969's "Johnny One Time" was my swan song as a pop hit maker—the Memphis single "I Think I Love You Again" failed to duplicate its success. In fact, the track stalled way down at No. 97 on *Billboard*'s "Hot 100" chart. But I kept plugging away. I promoted *Memphis Portrait* by performing "Proud Mary" on Johnny Cash's national TV series. I poured my heart into it. Looking at that clip today, man, I was really rocking. But as good as it was, my "soul" LP was a commercial failure.

That was it. I told the record company, "I'm tired of all this experimentation. I want to go back where I belong. I want to go back with Owen."

So that's what I did. I returned to Nashville, reunited with Owen Bradley and issued the folk-pop "Everybody's Reaching Out for Someone," the wistfully aching "Misty Memories" and the profoundly sad "If This Is Our Last Time." That last one was ironically titled, since instead of becoming a new hit, the record was just about my "last time." All three singles withered on the charts in 1971–72. Even when I introduced a future classic, I "couldn't get arrested."

Johnny Christopher had been on my sessions in Memphis. He and Wayne Carson Thompson and Mark James had written this touching love song called "Always on My Mind." Owen and I both liked it a whole lot and decided it should be my next single. I knew it was a good song, but by this time, I was feeling pretty pessimistic about things. Right after I put it out, Elvis did his version.

Looking back, I realize we both missed the real tenderness in it. When Willie Nelson slowed it down and put it out later, I thought, "That's the treatment I should have done with it." I'm kind of ashamed to say that, because usually I try to give the lyric the best reading I can. I think it had a lot to do with my state of mind at the time. My failure with that single completely demoralized me—by the fall of 1972, I felt thoroughly frustrated.

I didn't know what else I could do. The charts were becoming more and more specialized. You were either rock or soul or country. I didn't know where I belonged. I got real discouraged with the business, and I thought I might quit recording completely. I was at a crossroads. I thought maybe it was time to rest, time to rethink my music.

I was musically adrift. Glam rock, heavy metal and psychedelia were raging on the charts by the early 1970s. Pop/rock became ever more fragmented as the scene splintered into various genres. In addition, Los Angeles and London solidified their positions as pop music capitals. The influence of regional pop centers like New Orleans, Memphis, Chicago and Nashville diminished.

The hit parade now belonged to Grand Funk Railroad, David Bowie, Sly & the Family Stone, Rod Stewart, Pink Floyd,

Chicago, Santana, Led Zeppelin and the Woodstock acts. Pioneers like Fats Domino, Chubby Checker, Connie Francis, Pat Boone, the Everly Brothers and the Shirelles had vanished from radio. The Beatles and the Supremes broke up. Ray Charles, Chuck Berry, Roy Orbison, the Monkees and the Beach Boys went into eclipse. Uncertain of where to turn, I simply "dropped out" as a recording artist.

The world I'd known as an entertainer was fading away. Rock 'n' roll package shows ceased to exist. Variety television was gradually losing its clout. The once mighty *Ed Sullivan Show* was canceled in 1971, and its host died three years later. Perry Como and Steve Allen had long since disappeared as staples of variety programming. The supper clubs that had been my mainstays for years were closing down.

Even my record company was no longer the same. The powerful Music Corporation of America had purchased the majority of Decca's stock, and the once independent label officially became a division of MCA in 1966. On March 1, 1973, Decca ceased to exist entirely. "Brenda Lee" was now the property of MCA Records.

Many of the stars of my girlhood were twinkling out. Sophie Tucker had died in 1966. My old mentor Red Foley died in 1968. My idol Judy Garland passed away in 1969. Paul Cohen, who'd signed me to Decca Records, was diagnosed with terminal cancer in 1970 and died a year later. Jimmy Durante suffered a debilitating stroke in 1972 and faded from public view. Columnist Louella Parsons expired in '72 and so did my French friend Maurice Chevalier and my childhood idol Mahalia Jackson. In 1973, Bob Wills was felled by the stroke that crippled him, and he died from it two years later. While performing on stage in 1975, Jackie Wilson suffered a stroke from which he never recovered. Even some of my peers were passing away—singers like Frankie Lymon (1968), Gene Vincent (1971) and Bobby Darin (1973).

That wasn't the end of it. My manager Dub Allbritten underwent "exploratory surgery" at the respected Scott-White Hospital in Temple, Texas, in September 1970. Four months later he was hospitalized again there, for partial paralysis on his left side. He told me nothing about this.

I knew something was wrong. When we were on the road, at the Fremont Hotel in Las Vegas, he told me he was having some problem with his arm. I had to button his shirts for him. But every time I asked him if he was OK he'd say, "Oh, I'm fine." I didn't know for months how sick he really was. I guess I was in denial—it was inconceivable to me that he might be dying. It turned out that he had inoperable lung cancer.

During his first visit to the hospital in Texas for the surgery, they gave him six months to live. And he did die almost six months to the day from the time he came back from there. Dub was very private. He never confided in me that he was dying. He told Ronnie; then Ronnie told me. But I never talked to Dub about it. He didn't want to discuss it. The only time I saw him mad about the disease was when he couldn't drink his beloved espresso. It made him sick to his stomach.

Eventually Dub was confined to his bed in his elegant apartment at Windsor Towers on West End Avenue. One by one, his old comrades paid their respects. Bob Beckham, who had spent so many hours driving overnight with his old manager, sat with Dub for days at a time. Charlie Lamb came. Billy Smith called on the boss of the One Niters talent agency, too.

So did I. I wanted Dub to talk to me about his dying, about everything. Our life together was coming to a close, and he wouldn't even say it. To the very end, Dub just couldn't be emotional. Not with me, anyway.

He worked right up until the end. And I was just expected to keep doing my job, too. But I'd have much rather been with him than on the road. It might have been a dysfunctional relationship, but I still loved him. And I kept holding out the hope that he would finally tell me he loved me.

I still can't help crying whenever I think about the death of Dub Allbritten. He was more than a manager. He had been the central male figure in my life since I was only twelve. He had quite literally raised me, in addition to making me the star I was.

On the eve of his death, Dub summoned Ronnie and me to his spacious West End apartment. Dressed in his silk pajamas, Dub rose from his couch and took Ronnie's arm.

"Ronnie, I've been saving some money for Brenda all these years," said Dub. "And I want you to have it."

"He walked over to this walk-in closet and inside was a large safe," Ronnie reports. *"I just glimpsed it and suddenly the doorbell rang. Two of his lady friends were there and they came in chattering away."*

Dub said, "Don't worry Ronnie. They'll be gone in a minute."

"Oh, that's OK," said Ronnie. "I'll see you tomorrow. We'll get it straight when you feel better."

He was just so weak and fragile. We didn't want to seem like vultures about whatever was in the safe. I think it was thousands of dollars he'd been paid at overseas dates.

That same night, Dub was rushed to the emergency room, and we were called immediately. Ronnie was with him to the end, by his bedside at Baptist Hospital. I couldn't face the reality of Dub breathing his last, so I held vigil in the waiting room.

"He would take a gasping breath," Ronnie recalls. *"Then a long time would go by. I would think that was his last breath. But then another one would come. He never spoke. It was like he was in a coma. This went on for hours. Finally, he gave a great sigh and never breathed again."*

William Dumas Allbritten died in the wee hours of the morning on Friday, March 19, 1971, at age fifty-four.

The money in the apartment safe was mysteriously gone the next morning. I have no idea who had access to his penthouse, so to this day, nobody knows how it disappeared. Was Dub trying to give me money he'd kept that was rightfully mine? Was the gesture a dying man's attempt to clear his conscience? Was he giving us the cash to help us avoid estate taxes? No one will ever know.

The mainstream Nashville press ignored Dub's passing. But the music community gathered en masse at the Roesch-Patton Funeral Home near Music Row for the funeral.

The reading of Dub's will occurred a few weeks later. My grief turned to surprise and hurt when I learned of its contents. Although Dub left something in his will for everyone else around him, there was little mention of me in the will at all.

He bequeathed small amounts of money to Casuals alumni Richard Williams, John Orr, Joe Watkins and Billy Smith. He gave his car to Bobby Fuller. Julie and Jolie were given partial royalties from "I'm Sorry" and the other songs Dub had shared with Ronnie Self. Dub's brother and his mother were provided for as well.

But for Ronnie and me, there was only this sentence: "I give and bequeath all of the stock that I own in RonBre Music, Inc. (even though it is my opinion that the said stock has no present value), equally to Ronald Shacklett and his wife, Brenda Mae Tarpley Shacklett, also known as Brenda Lee." In short, he left me nothing.

It wasn't that I wanted his money. It was just such a slap in the face.

As the years went by, Ronnie began to believe that Dub had lived high on the hog at my expense. Dub's custom-decorated penthouse office, his suburban Brentwood home and pool, his yearly automobile purchases, his handmade Italian suits and silk shirts, the stylish apartment and all his other fancy trappings had come as a result of my success. To be sure, Ronnie and I had spent money on parties, houses, antiques, hired help, private schools and cars. But we were still stunned to learn after Dub's death that the biggest female pop star of the '60s had only $40,000 to her name.

To add insult to injury, Dub's estate claimed that I owed him money! To say that I felt betrayed is an understatement. It was one of the lowest points of my life.

It was so painful. I thought about fighting it in court. But Grandmary, Dub's mother Mary Allbritten, had devoted years of her life to caring for my children when I was out of town. She was almost as important to our family as my own mother, and the children truly did think of her as their grandmother. I hoped the money would go to her. It didn't.

It turned out that Dub didn't even have enough money in the bank to cover the bequests in his will. So the cold-blooded estate lawyers came after us, claiming that I owed the estate $250,000 from my Decca contract that Dub had negotiated. Since my children were included in the bequests, and to avoid a court battle, we settled on paying $100,000. That was money we simply didn't have. So I made a deal to pay $20,000 a year for five years. Ronnie was scared, and we were in over our heads, but we did what we had to do.

I already felt adrift in the music world in the early 1970s, and Dub Allbritten's death left me lost at sea. Now his wind in my sails had stopped buoying me onward. I was in a downward-spiraling emotional and psychological whirlpool, as well as a professional one.

Three years earlier, Ronnie had sold my dream mansion for a

big profit, which broke my heart. But someone made him a huge offer that he couldn't refuse. We were young and dumb. Then we had moved to a spacious new residence down Franklin Road. And now, uncertain of our financial future, Ronnie and I downsized even further. He sold his Jaguar, and we decided to move to a small Victorian clapboard home next door to his parents. So our family moved back to the Woodbine neighborhood where Ronnie had been raised. Julie, eight, cried bitterly. Jolie, three, didn't know the difference. But I did. I felt distraught and disheartened.

The financial pressures put a strain on our marriage. Ronnie was trying to spread his wings as an independent businessman. He'd formed his own contracting company and was building custom luxury homes on speculation. He was also deep in several investment ventures involving apartment complexes. In addition, he was "Mr. Mom" at home with Julie and Jolie while I traveled.

I was gone an awful lot, and he was there with the girls. He was trying to keep his career going and was increasingly helping me with mine. He was having to juggle too many balls in the air, I think. So there was a lot of stress there.

We were young, in our twenties, and didn't know what to do. We just had to start all over again, and that was hard. Thank God we were still young enough to bounce back. You just do what you have to do.

I think it was hardest for Ronnie. In his world, the wife stays home, cooks the meals and raises the kids. I think he always imagined marrying somebody like that. The husband was supposed to be the head of the family, just like his father had been. That was the atmosphere he grew up in. I don't think he ever resented taking care of the girls. But I do think there was a part of him that resented my being gone all the time and being a professional career woman.

He never asked me to quit. But every time he was thrown

into my world, he'd act really frustrated. My show business world had been centered on Dub while he was living; not Ronnie. In those early days of our marriage, Ronnie was jealous of the showbiz people around me. And he couldn't understand how fickle show business can be—people patting you on the back one minute and stabbing you in it the next. You have to be a good actor to put on that smile and survive in show business. Ronnie wouldn't play that game. He couldn't pull it off. I wanted him with me, but he just hated the music business.

It got to the point where I felt like it just wasn't going to work. I was torn between two worlds. For a time, I thought I would have to either give up my marriage or my singing. But I was so busy. I mean, you have no idea. I barely had time to eat, never mind thinking about divorce. It's like I've always said about having a nervous breakdown: "I don't have time. I'm booked."

Every marriage has its rough spots. And if anyone tells you different, they're living in a dream world. A relationship and a family are hard work.

Despite our reduced circumstances, I insisted that the children remain in private school. Education has always been so important to me. Our housekeeper and groundskeeper/driver were retained. Dub's mother continued as a nanny when I was on tour.

And now, more than ever, I needed to work. The relentless concert schedule continued. Although absent from the popularity charts, I was still a "draw" as a live attraction. I added Puerto Rico, Spain and Holland to my international schedule. The yearly trips to Japan, England, Canada and Germany continued as well. Australia and South America remained on my route, too. For instance, in the first half of 1970, Dub had me on the road for seven straight months of one-night appearances. When I returned, my baby Jolie had begun to walk in my absence. That cut me to the quick.

And Dub had arranged for a full schedule to continue even after his death. Dub was even negotiating contracts the week he died.

But fifteen years of constant touring were taking their toll on me. Even as a teenager, Dub's grueling pace had sometimes gotten to me—in the early '60s I'd contracted pneumonia and been hospitalized with stomach problems. In 1970, I was hospitalized for exhaustion.

Now it got worse. During a three-week stint at the Fairmont Hotel in New Orleans in 1972, I was desperately ill. I sang in the evenings and underwent extensive medical testing by day at Touro Hospital there.

I'd been experiencing abdominal pain for months and had been going to the doctors in Nashville for quite a long time. They could not find anything wrong with me. When I got sick in New Orleans, I was referred to two specialists there. They'd do tests on me all day long, then I'd go do my two shows that night and check back into the hospital the next morning. For three weeks they did every test known to man and finally decided to schedule exploratory surgery to try to find the cause of my nausea, pain and stomach distress.

A month later, I had to cancel my European tour and returned to the Crescent City for surgery at Touro Hospital. I was operated on for abdominal adhesions and internal repair. I had adhesions, scar tissue, that were probably the result of my cesarean operations. There were knots wrapped around my digestive tract, and the doctors had to remove a part of my intestines. I was very, very sick.

Then in 1973, I developed kidney stones. I had no symptoms until one day I was doubled over in pain. That same day they put me in the hospital for emergency surgery in Nashville.

In 1974 came my most serious physical problem of all. I was

driving on Music Row on my way to a meeting with Owen Bradley. I got what I thought was a charley horse in my calf. I couldn't rub it out and the pain was excruciating. When I got to his office, Owen insisted that I go immediately to the hospital.

A blood clot had developed in the major artery leading to my heart. I was only twenty-nine, but my life was in danger. At Park View Hospital, an emergency regimen of blood thinners was administered around the clock to save me. But I was severely weakened.

While hospitalized with the blood clot, I came face-to-face with another nightmare. A demented fan had been stalking me for a year or so. He sent me a string of threatening letters, each one postmarked closer to my home or tour location. The letters had all been written on the same stationery, with roses on it. The stalker vowed to kill both me and himself.

Stalking laws were nonexistent at that time. My family and I were closely guarded, with the help of the police and FBI. Now, sick and helpless as I was, I looked up to find the man at the foot of my hospital bed. Despite a posted guard, he burst into the room, threw a small briefcase at my feet on the bed and ran. The box held silverware and other items for my "last supper."

His previous letters indicated that he believed I was the Virgin Mary and that I had to die for all the sins in the world, hence the "last supper" reference. When I'd turned the letters in to the FBI, agents had informed me that there was nothing they could do until he acted.

After I was released from the hospital, I was scheduled to sing at the Top of the World club in the Contemporary Hotel at Disney World. I was taking the whole family, and the girls were so excited. About a week before our departure I got another letter with those dreaded roses. He said, "I know you're going to be in Orlando, and that's where you'll meet your end, and we'll finally be together." Then I didn't want to go, but I had a signed contract. The FBI men accompanied us everywhere we went, even into the park and onto the rides. They walked me to my shows and back. They stood outside the penthouse suite where we stayed.

I was terrified. I had never gotten a good look at him in that hospital room. So he might have been there, and I never would have known it. If he wanted to shoot me while I was on stage, I assume he could have. I sweated bullets on stage, no pun intended.

Police eventually tracked the stalker to his home in Florida where they discovered a religious shrine to "Brenda Lee." The tiny residence was plastered with my pictures, as well as a collection of newspaper clippings detailing gruesome murders. Amazingly, the authorities deemed him "harmless." He eventually quit bothering me, thank goodness.

Those letters that I turned over to the FBI were spooky. I felt threatened by the weirdo, but a lot of fans want to feel close to you. Other than the stalker, most of the things you get are just off the wall. I once received a picture of a naked man holding one of my albums. Also in the package were a couple of marijuana cigarettes. Since he'd sent an autographed picture of himself, he wanted one of me. Ronnie told me to throw it away. But I thought it was so hilarious I stuck it in the bottom of the picture drawer. It's probably still there. And I did send him an autographed photo, clothed.

Other fans have asked me to autograph body parts. There are fans who have tattoos of my whole head on their body. Fans name cars and children after me. Fans tell me they've gotten married because of my songs. Some say they got through the Vietnam War because my music helped them.

The most amazing story probably belongs to Marian Rose White. This was a woman who was locked up in a mental institution in San Francisco from the time she was a little girl. Her mother had died, and her stepmother had put her away there, because she didn't want her. She spent almost her whole life there until a nurse took a special interest in her when Marian Rose was in middle age. She had her tested, and they found that there was nothing wrong with her. She'd been medicated and sterilized and abused.

I was at home watching television one night in 1982, and this movie came on about her life. It starred Nancy Cartwright, who later became famous as Bart's voice on *The Simpsons*. I was glued to that movie. Marian's sad story just gripped me.

The next day, Bob Beckham called from his office on Music Row and said, "There's a lady named Marian Rose White who is trying to get in touch with you." I knew immediately who he was talking about. I don't know how she knew to call Beckham's publishing company, but he gave me her number, and I called her back.

Marian told me the amazing story about her life. She said that when she was in the institution, what kept her going was playing my records all through the 1960s and 1970s. The mental patients would have talent shows for therapy, and Marian would always sing my songs. She had my records and played them constantly. I guess that's what kept her sane.

We began corresponding regularly. Finally, a friend brought her to see one of my shows in Reno. She stayed at the hotel for a few days and came to every show, two shows a night. Marian sat at ringside and sang every song right along with me. Loud. Like there was no one else in that casino but her and me. She'd come backstage and talk, and then she'd go to her room. The next night, there she'd be again.

That movie had really touched me, and to meet the person who it was about was so special. She even made me a three-foot-tall Brenda Lee rag doll that has curly hair and a glittery stage costume.

The tragic story of Marian Rose White and of how my music was her sustenance still moves me every time I think of it. She was such a sweet lady, not at all bitter about what was done to her. And she taught me to never feel sorry for myself or for whatever bad situation I was in.

FOURTEEN

Country Comeback

I had the blues, and I had 'em bad. I'd sacrificed my youth, my health and many of the joys of young motherhood. I'd worked my tail off for nearly twenty years in a nonstop marathon of traveling, performing and recording. And for what? A house on a nondescript little street in an ordinary neighborhood, a scrapbook full of fading clippings and forty thousand bucks in the bank?

Ronnie was able to dust himself off and move on. But I couldn't shake the feelings of bitterness. Everything I'd worked for was gone. For a year after Dub died, I'd catch myself dialing his number. I wanted to ask him why he'd left me this way. After all the years of doing exactly what I was told, why hadn't he taken better care of me? Then I'd realize he was gone, and I couldn't ask him. Ronnie kept telling me, "Just get over it." But all the hurt and confusion wouldn't leave me alone.

I was depressed. I found myself crying at odd times of the day. I had a lot of guilt feelings. I was crushed by Dub's death, but I also felt a weird sense of relief. It was almost like, "Well, now I can make some decisions, and maybe I can have a life without someone ruling me with an iron hand." It sounds awful. I didn't want him dead, certainly. But there was something oddly liberating about it.

To this day, I am haunted by the memory of Dub Allbritten.

And back then I was consumed by it. I didn't know if Ronnie and I had the ability to continue my career. I thought about trying other managers, but Dub's brand of all-encompassing career guidance virtually died with him. They just don't make 'em that way anymore. Today an artist has a manager, a publicist, a financial advisor, an agent, a road manager and an image consultant. Dub was all of those things and more. He was the last of his breed.

I was twenty-eight years old at the dawn of 1973. That is an age when many artists are beginning their careers. And here I was, trying to reinvent mine. The future loomed like a vast black unknown, and I felt utterly lost in the present. I'd wandered in musical experiments from one city to another—L.A., New York, New Orleans, Memphis. Nothing seemed to work.

It turned out that my musical salvation was right in my own backyard, in the form of one of my old touring partners. By the 1970s, Bob Beckham had become one of Nashville's most successful song publishers. And among his protégés was the former janitor at Columbia Studios, Kris Kristofferson.

"I wasn't buying any of Brenda's talk about 'dropping out' or quitting recording," says Beckham. "I knew that the best therapy for her was what had always been her best tonic. Music.

"I knew Brenda was at a real low point in her life. She'd lost Dub, and he was like the only father she'd ever known. I could tell she was really depressed. On top of everything else, Owen Bradley got sick with colon cancer. And she loved him more than anyone.

"I really wanted to find Brenda a hit. So I called her up and asked her to drive down to Chip Young's studio in Murfreesboro, Tennessee, with me. I produced four songs at the session. As usual, Brenda sang great. When Owen got better soon after, he

*praised me to the skies for the work I'd done. Then he rerecorded
every damn one of them."*

Among the tunes Beckham brought to me was "Nobody
Wins." Written by Kris Kristofferson, the lyric told the tale of a
disintegrating marriage. The desperately sad song was right up
my alley. Especially since I was so down at the time.

I actually cried when Beckham played it for me. It's such a
great song, and I just love Kris Kristofferson. He's one of the
most talented people I've ever met. But when I first met him,
back when he tried to keep me out of my own recording session,
he was just this ruggedly handsome guy who was trying to get in
the business.

Kris had drifted into Nashville in 1965. By the beginning of
the 1970s, he was revolutionizing country songwriting with
frank, poetic compositions like 1970's "For the Good Times" and
1971's "Help Me Make It through the Night." My old friend
Roger Miller had helped Kris get a foothold in Music City by
making "Me and Bobby McGee" a country hit in 1969; two years
later Janis Joplin would make the tune a pop smash. Another
longtime friend, pop veteran Ray Stevens, recorded Kris's "Sunday Morning Coming Down" in 1969, but it was Johnny Cash
who took it to No. 1 in 1970.

Kris was hot as a writer, so the record company put out "Nobody Wins" immediately after I recorded it with Owen. Everyone was excited. It turned out that 1973 was a good year for
everybody involved. Owen got his health back. I got a hit record.
And Kris married my old high school friend Rita Coolidge that
summer.

That recording of Kris's desolate divorce song brought me
back into the top-10 in early 1973. But this time, it was the country music charts that embraced me. Quite by accident, I was re-

turning to the music of my childhood. I don't think that my
singing style changed so much. It's just that country music had
become broader.

Country music had come a long way from the days when
honky-tonks and truckers dominated its lyrics. Artists like Charlie Rich, Ronnie Milsap, Dolly Parton, John Denver and Anne
Murray were appealing to a wider audience and giving the style a
more sophisticated image. Both Johnny Cash and Glen Campbell
were stars of their own series on national television. Roy Clark
was invited to guest host on *The Tonight Show*. Country acts
began to appear routinely on *The Midnight Special,* which debuted on NBC in 1973 as music's influential new television
showcase.

The style was invading the music mainstream on three fronts.
Artists like Ray Price, Lynn Anderson, Olivia Newton-John and
Eddy Arnold were developing classy stage shows that opened
doors in Las Vegas. On the other hand, singers Waylon Jennings
and Willie Nelson were adopting a renegade blue-jeaned look,
growing their hair, experimenting with drugs and fashioning a
new country sound that appealed to the vast youth market. And
meanwhile on the West Coast, rock acts like the Byrds, Linda
Ronstadt and the Nitty Gritty Dirt Band decided that country was
hip and began recording in the idiom.

*"Country record sales soared during this era," reports long-
time Nashville journalist Jay Orr. "By 1970, the style's annual
dollar volume had risen to $100 million a year. During the next
fifteen years, that figure would more than triple. Nashville down-
played its hay-bales image and redefined country as the music of
Middle America. As the nation became more suburban, so did
country music. Symbolizing its uptown aspirations, Music City
opened a Disney-like theme park called Opryland in 1972. Its attractions were all given musical themes, and troupes of freshly*

scrubbed young performers entertained daily there. More than a
million people went through the park's turnstiles during its first
season, and over the next twenty-five years Opryland helped turn
Nashville into a major tourism destination."

I was right in the middle of a major musical shift in my
hometown. For the first time in its history, country music was becoming Big Business.

No one ever told me, "You're going country." They just released "Nobody Wins," and it flew up the country charts. I felt
like I fit in there, and so did the fans.

I'd been in country music when I was a child, of course. My
roots were there. But in the 1960s, Dub had taken me far away
from that world. I certainly wasn't averse to being on the country
charts. It might have been a departure, but I was just glad to get
my career going again.

The other artists were incredibly warm to me. I felt welcomed by the country performers from the start. And if I thought
the rock world was full of characters, the country field could sure
give it a run for its money. When the movie *Nashville* came out in
1975, a lot of the country music people didn't like the outrageous
ways they were portrayed. But it really wasn't that far off the
mark. The city really was that colorful.

It was a very diverse community in those days. Charley Pride
was black. Freddy Fender and Johnny Rodriguez were Mexican
American. Olivia Newton-John and Diana Trask were Aus-
tralians. And their records were as huge as anyone's. Ronnie Milsap was this unassuming blind man having hit after hit. Kris
Kristofferson was a Rhodes Scholar. Mel Tillis stuttered.

The women were larger-than-life characters, too. Loretta
Lynn, Dolly Parton, Jeannie Seely, Connie Smith, Skeeter Davis,
Dottie West and Jean Shepard were all unique individuals. They
were strong and beautiful with lives full of drama.

Tammy Wynette was "the heroine of heartache" with her emotional performances, her personal tragedies and her having had five husbands. Tammy and her husband George Jones were neighbors when we lived on Franklin Road. We'd vacation together in Florida. Georgette, Tammy and George's daughter, was the same age as my daughter Jolie, so Jolie used to go over there to swim all the time.

We also took Jolie and Julie to weekend cookouts at the home of Jerry Reed, who was hotter than a pistol with the 1970–71 hits "Amos Moses" and "When You're Hot, You're Hot." Prior to his stardom, Jerry had provided me with such tunes as "That's All You Gotta Do" and "Born to Be by Your Side."

The children usually didn't accompany us to "outlaw" Waylon Jennings's house. Waylon's wife was Jessi Colter, who had divorced my old heartthrob Duane Eddy in 1968 and married Waylon a year later. Throughout the '80s and '90s, Waylon and I would get together regularly to have what he called "meet and eat." These dinners, singing sessions and ultracandid storytelling times were closed to anyone who wasn't an entertainer. And that included family members.

Charley Pride became a fast friend as well. I had been visiting his Dallas home for years, and this relationship blossomed as my country career accelerated. Charley and his wife Rozene would often babysit Julie when I played the Fairmont Hotel in Dallas.

I kept up with Elvis, too, of course. As Jolie got older, she became one of his biggest fans. She was that way, literally, from the age of three or four. I can't explain it. Anyway, on April 6, 1975, I took her and Julie to see him in concert at the Murphy Center in Murfreesboro, Tennessee.

Jolie, who was six, was fascinated with the scarves that he'd throw into the audience. We went backstage, and the girls got to meet him. Elvis couldn't have been sweeter—he treated us like members of his own family. And for years afterward, Jolie kept pestering me about those scarves. I finally wrote Elvis to ask for an autographed scarf for Jolie. It was so eerie—it arrived in the mail the day after his death in 1977.

If I'm in town and there's a concert, you can bet I'm going to try and get a ticket. And I'm always trying to get backstage and collect autographs. I was a big Elton John fan, so when he came to Nashville in November 1972, I got front-row center seats. The marijuana smoke in the auditorium was so thick, I almost choked. But I was determined to meet him.

To my shock, he spotted me and introduced me from the stage. He dedicated "Crocodile Rock" to me. He told the crowd that I was the inspiration for the song. He asked me later that night if I'd like to sing a duet with him. We were both on MCA, so I called the label and told them. But for some reason it never panned out.

I kidded with Elton, saying that I felt like I had "discovered" him. I had bought his debut album when I was on tour in England in 1969. It was never a hit in the United States, but I kept my copy. Every time he came to town or was anywhere near where I was, I loved getting together with him. We threw a big birthday party for Elton at the Minnie Pearl Museum at Opryland when he played the Opry House in 1979.

Johnny Cash and June Carter became close friends as well. Even so, the couple once surprised me with the intensity of their kindness and commitment. In 1979, I was admitted for abdominal tests at St. Thomas Hospital. The next day, my daughter Julie was admitted to the same facility. Doctors thought that my fifteen-year-old had a malignant tumor and told me that Julie was possibly terminally ill. Evangelist Billy Graham was in town, appearing at Vanderbilt Stadium. After the service, Johnny and

June organized an all-night prayer circle on Julie's behalf at their home.

Early the next morning, Julie was prepped for surgery and en route to the operating room. The radiologist rushed to meet her there. He'd reread her X rays and declared that the cancer diagnosis was a complete mistake. Julie got off the stretcher and walked to my room in her hospital gown. "Guess what?" she said as she opened the door. "They said I'm fine." I must have looked like I'd seen a ghost. Then I got a clean bill of health, too. We went home together the next day.

To this day, I think Johnny and June's prayers worked. It was a miracle.

I guess I'm just incurably sociable. I love hanging out with my fellow entertainers. And since I'm a fan of all kinds of music, that means I've met just about everybody. But because of my background, I've always been particularly supportive of youngsters who want to be in this business.

In 1972, Tanya Tucker came on the scene with "Delta Dawn." She was thirteen years old. I was at the Peddler steak house near Music Row, and someone brought her over to meet me. She was very sassy and cute and perky. Tanya said, "Oh, I know who *you* are!" I was shocked, because she was just a kid. That started a wonderful friendship. It was like Patsy Cline and me in reverse. Now I was the older gal giving advice. Not that Tanya needed much of it. She was much stronger willed than I ever was.

She sends me flowers. We talk on the phone. I've sent baby gifts for her children, and she's always written me the sweetest notes back. She has invited me to travel with her, too. The one thing about Tanya is that she is a woman of her word. If she tells you she's going to do something, she'll move heaven and earth to get it done.

A lot of people in Nashville think Tanya's too much of a wild child. But I love her and all her rowdy ways. She has a heart of pure gold.

Little Tanya Tucker was the first of many child stars who sought my advice. To this day, stage mothers knock on my front door. When I open it, there will be the latest Shirley Temple of Iowa or Little Rock, standing there in full stage regalia. Without a word of introduction, the tot in her starched crinolines will burst into song. It's usually a "Brenda Lee" number, often accompanied by vigorous tap dancing. Believe it or not, I always invite these people in, much to the amazement of my family. They think I'm nuts. But I have a long-standing policy of always trying to give starry-eyed children positive and helpful guidance. Who am I to rain on their parade? I figure if they've got enough guts to come to the house and do that, then go for it. Who knows? They might be the next LeAnn Rimes.

A lot of these kids didn't know that I'd been "Little Miss Dynamite," the pop star. The ones who came along in the 1980s knew me only as a country hit maker. I was surprised at how fast I became known in country music.

"Nobody Wins" became the centerpiece of my comeback LP, *Brenda.* I was stunned when the album climbed all the way to No. 7 on the country charts. Now I realize that it was only the beginning of a whole new career for me.

In 1973, MCA Records also repackaged twenty-two of my pop hits on the LP *The Brenda Lee Story.* The collection earned me a Gold Record and remains in print to this day.

"Nobody Wins" was followed by a second country smash for me, the upbeat "Sunday Sunrise." It kicked off my third album of 1973, *New Sunrise,* which made it to No. 3 on the country hit parade.

In Germany, MCA's European division issued a double-LP

set called *Brenda Lee: Legends of Rock*. The collection was dominated by my early rockabilly sides and up-tempo hits. It, too, appeared in 1973.

To top things off, I was invited to cohost the Grammy Awards that year. Andy Williams, Roger Miller and I presided at the historic Tennessee Theater in downtown Nashville over a talent lineup that included Roberta Flack, Helen Reddy, Isaac Hayes, the Temptations, Johnny Cash, Aretha Franklin, Charley Pride, Curtis Mayfield and the Fifth Dimension. CBS network officials were worried that big pop stars wouldn't make the trip to Tennessee for the event, but that night the attendees included Ringo Starr, Don McLean, Roy Orbison, Smoky Robinson, Loggins & Messina, Rod McKuen and David Clayton-Thomas.

Moms Mabley came. So did Dusty Springfield. To get to be in the same room with all those people made me just giddy. That's the night I got to know Art Garfunkel. He later married my doctor's daughter. And it was great to see Ringo again, and the Temptations. I'll never forget it, Loretta Lynn's husband wore a bright yellow suit to the black-tie ceremony.

Roger Miller and I hosted the post-telecast awards, which is when most of the forty-seven awards were given. Only eleven were given on the air that year. That was the first internationally televised Grammy celebration. And it holds the record for the highest-rated Grammy show in history.

I'd started the '70s feeling completely down and out. And now here I was with three hit albums, two huge country hits in a row and a spotlight at the Grammy Awards. You know what they say about the music business—it's chicken one day and feathers the next. One minute nobody will give you the time of day; then you get a hit, and you're everybody's little darlin'. It's still that way. That's why there are numbers on the charts after No. 1. No one stays on top forever.

My 1973 *New Sunrise* album also contained my third straight top-10 country hit. In early 1974, I issued "Wrong Ideas," a hardcore barroom song underscored by steel guitar that was my most "country" performance to date. It was written by the colorful *Playboy* magazine cartoonist Shel Silverstein. With his shaved head and bare feet, Shel cut quite an unusual figure in Nashville. We must have seemed unlikely friends. But like the bohemian Kris, Shel became one of my most steadfast buddies.

Shel was an old hippie, a real free spirit. He had several homes, and he drifted around between them—you never knew where he was, in New York, on his houseboat in Sausalito or at some other place he owned. I don't think Shel drove. When he'd come to Nashville, he stayed with Bobby Bare, who is quite a character himself. Shel was always barefoot, even in the dead of winter. He'd arrive at my door with his guitar to play me his songs and have a meal. You never knew when to expect him. He'd just show up.

Believe it or not, I was an avid *Playboy* reader—the magazine had great articles—so I knew who he was before I met him. And as we got to know each other better, I became as big a fan of his children's books as I was of his songs.

That song, "Wrong Ideas," got me in a little hot water with my fans. It was pretty racy. The woman's alone in a bar, drinking with a stranger whom she takes home. That was a real big departure for me and my "sweetheart" image. But that's what country music is, real-life situations faced by adults. And it was so cleverly written.

The thing about Shel's songs is that he insists that they be performed exactly as they are written. When he brought me "Big Four Poster Bed," it was over four minutes long. A song of that length was unheard of to be programmed on radio, so we wanted to cut a couple of verses. Shel said, "If you cut it, you can't do it." I respected that, so I took a chance and recorded it in its entirety.

Shel's four-minute story song, "Big Four Poster Bed," became my fourth consecutive top-10 country hit and the centerpiece of my 1974 album, *Brenda Lee Now*. That collection also included "Enough for You" and "Please Don't Tell Me How the Story Ends," both of which came from Kris Kristofferson, who was becoming one of my favorite sources of material. The opening track of the collection was "Rock On Baby," a salute to my bopping past.

I turned thirty celebrating the top-10 success of "Rock On Baby" and entered the spring of 1975 with my sixth consecutive top-10 country hit, "He's My Rock." Rewritten as "She's My Rock," the tune also entered the hit repertoire of black country stylist Stony Edwards, and later became a No. 1 smash for George Jones.

"Bringing It Back" was a swaying two-stepper that rolled up the charts in the fall of 1975. The background chorus featured the then-unknown Janie Fricke, who began having country hits of her own two years later.

I next tried the up-tempo "Find Yourself Another Puppet." The song was the first real success for its young Nashville writer Jimbeau Hinson. Ironically, he had grown up as a child performer in Mississippi whose act consisted of "Brenda Lee" song tributes.

I first met Jimbeau because he wrote me the greatest fan letter. He told me about the act he'd had when he was a kid, and that he was an aspiring songwriter. He said he would be honored if I'd just listen to his songs. So I called him.

"When I was a little boy, I saw Brenda on TV, and I zeroed right in on her," says Jimbeau. "We had the same timbre in our voices, so I thought, 'I can do that.' I was singing at honky-tonks in Mississippi by the time I was ten, and she was my first major influence. What did I learn from Brenda? She's one of the best

vocal phrasers in the business; I learned that from her. Her timing on stage was the best. And she always picked great songs.

"I moved to Nashville as soon as I graduated from high school in 1969, and one of the first things I did was pitch songs to her. Brenda called me, and I couldn't believe it. She's one of the few artists that personally ever called me about a song. She invited me over to her house, and I couldn't believe that, either. That's when I played 'Find Yourself Another Puppet' for her. She was so kind, so sweet and so real. She did not disappoint me; she was everything I'd dreamed she would be and then some. Sometimes you meet your idols, and you wished you hadn't."

I eventually recorded four of Jimbeau Hinson's songs for singles and several others as album tracks. Jimbeau has since written for Patty Loveless, Kathy Mattea, Steve Earle and many others. But he still says that I'm his favorite.

Jimbeau made a name for himself at a time when income for country tunesmiths was dramatically on the rise. As the '70s progressed, country music's popularity continued to expand. In 1976, *Wanted! the Outlaws,* costarring Willie Nelson and Waylon Jennings, became country's first million-selling Platinum Record. Southern rocker Charlie Daniels stormed the country hit parade with "The Devil Went Down to Georgia" in 1979 and crossed over to top the pop charts as well. Johnny Paycheck snarled "Take This Job and Shove It" in 1978, and the tune was later made into a movie. Emmylou Harris brought her hip California sensibility to Nashville with a string of 1975–79 chart-toppers. Hank Williams Jr., whom I had known since childhood, altered his traditional style and reinvented himself as a rowdy hell-raiser who sold millions.

It is a truism in the music business that country does well in times of economic recession. Its boom as a genre in the 1970s echoed similar prior periods. Country first flowered as a style during the Great Depression in the 1930s, and it enjoyed another blip upward in popularity during the postwar recession of the late 1940s, when my idol Hank Williams ruled the hit parade. Now country music was in an upswing again at a time when the American economy was struggling. During the 1970s, the nation dragged through a prolonged period of "stagflation"—rising prices and falling wages. The oil producers in the Middle East conducted an embargo against the United States and incredibly long lines at gas stations resulted. U.S. Steel closed thirteen factories, and the government bailed out the failing Chrysler Corporation and Lockheed Aircraft.

That decade was a kaleidoscope of social trends. Abortion was legalized. Joblessness plagued the country. Crime rose to new heights in American cities. Church attendance fell. I especially remember music fans dancing to the rhythmic sound of disco or to the blues-based, amped-up style called Southern rock. Spurred by high grocery prices, home gardening boomed. Even I planted in those days. Jogging and fitness activities became popular. I didn't join that craze. Unrest on college campuses was more pervasive than ever. Drug experimentation permeated all levels of society.

Believe it or not, I really wasn't exposed to marijuana in the 1960s. When I was on tour in Australia in 1970, I went to a private party for the touring cast of the musical *Hair*. It was in a huge apartment in downtown Sydney. I walked in and I thought, "They must be burning the heck out of toast or something. Are they making sandwiches and burning the bread up?" I had no idea whatsoever that the smell was pot.

When I found out, I couldn't have cared less. Back home in the States, some guy at one of the nightclubs gave Ronnie a joint, and we decided to try it. We brought it home and pulled all the drapes closed and locked the door and turned out the lights. It hurt my throat horribly. I think the main reason I never smoked again was that I was afraid it would hurt my vocal cords. It's not that I didn't want to. But I was always really disciplined about my throat. Plus, somebody told me that smoking pot makes you hungry. I thought, "Oh great, that's all I need. I've been yo-yo dieting and struggling with my weight as long as I can remember. Get hooked on something that makes me even fatter? No, thank you." It definitely had its drawbacks.

When cocaine came along, I never tried it. There was a dinner party in L.A. when I was recording out there. And for dessert, they laid out lines of cocaine by everyone's plate. I was flabbergasted.

At recording sessions in Nashville, musicians thought that coke made them play better. So it was sometimes around. But I was the original "Just say no." I figured I'd better not do it because I was scared that I'd love it too much. Everybody else seemed to, and I knew a lot of music people who got hooked.

As the decade wore on, worry piled on worry for many Americans. Is it any wonder that people turned to comfort in the lyrics of country songs like "Big Four Poster Bed"? Or that country stars became national icons of stability and normalcy?

I decided to use my newfound country stardom to campaign for change. I stumped for Georgia governor Jimmy Carter when he ran for president in 1976.

When Jimmy came to Nashville during his campaign, I was one of the music people who lent their support. He told me he loved country music and seemed pleased that so many of us were behind him. The Georgia governor didn't forget my efforts. To my surprise, Jimmy's staff called to invite me to his election-night party in Atlanta.

I almost didn't go because it was a bad, stormy night. At the last minute, I called a friend who owned a private plane, and I flew down with Ronnie's dad, the politician. The plane ride was so bumpy, I thought we were going to fall out of the sky. But the party was great. I was surprised at how few people had been invited. It was in a three-room suite with ultramodern decor at a downtown hotel.

I felt so honored to be there. I was in the suite with the Carters when it was announced that he had won the presidency.

Actually, I'm not very political. As an entertainer, you don't want to alienate any fans by taking sides. Dub had taught me early on to avoid controversy.

So I've made friends with both Republicans and Democrats over the years. Former Georgia governor Zell Miller and I are good friends. He's now a U.S. senator.

I also really like Max Cleland, who is another Georgia legislator. Max is respected for his heroism in Vietnam and serves in the U.S. Senate despite the handicaps of losing both legs and one arm during the war.

Max went to school with my sister Linda back in Lithonia, so I've known him all my life. We both have streets named after us there. He's one of the most inspirational men I've ever known.

I also got to know President Ford while he was in office. Later, we even did a show together—he was the speaker, and I was the singer. Ronald Reagan invited a big group of country stars, including me, to a White House dinner. Then later, I attended one of his presidential dinners there. I also know both Al Gore and George W. Bush.

You wouldn't call me an activist, but I'll usually step up to the plate to lobby for issues that directly affect the creative community. In 1976, the U.S. Congress attempted the first major reform of copyright legislation since 1909. I went to Washington to garner support and wrote letters urging lawmakers to update the nation's statutes. The resulting legislation extended copyright protection significantly and set new royalty rates for record makers.

I've always been willing to help when I'm asked. I stay abreast of what's going on and think I'm pretty well informed. Ronnie and I worked hard on his father's city council races for years. It was a lot of fun to get out and get the votes for "Pop."

But Jimmy Carter was the first national politician I really campaigned for. A big reason for that was that he was a fellow Georgian.

Jimmy Carter campaigned on a platform of moral honesty. He called for energy conservation and tried several measures to turn the ailing economy around. But the 1970s ended in the same recession-caused doldrums in which it had begun. And country music, conversely, was bigger than ever.

In 1976, the MCA brass suggested I record with West Coast producer Snuff Garrett, who was then hot with Cher's hits "Gypsies, Tramps and Thieves," "Dark Lady" and "Half Breed." Snuff had been in the business ever since the Gary Lewis & the Playboys days with "This Diamond Ring," and was one of the most successful pop producers of all time.

In Nashville, Owen Bradley was retiring, so I knew I had to go somewhere. But I admit I went to L.A. reluctantly. I'd already been through these experiments before and hadn't had much luck with them.

The resulting album was titled *L.A. Sessions*. It was not a notable success. It wasn't me; it wasn't "Brenda." I didn't like the L.A. scene of recording. They wanted me to overdub my vocals, sometimes one word at a time. That drove me crazy. I said, "I can't record this way. I have to sing as if I'm living the lyric I'm singing." Records like that get so slick that they lose all the basic musical energy and raw emotion. It was a prostitution of everything I believe in, musically.

I was used to having the say-so in the song selection. And when I got out there the songs had already been chosen for me. It was the first time my independence as a song selector had been taken from me, and that a recording project was out of my control.

Two of the better tunes, "Ruby's Lounge" and "Takin' What I Can Get," were chosen as singles. Neither one set the charts on fire.

So next, I tried the recording scene in Muscle Shoals, Alabama. But the soul tune "Left Over Love" barely scratched the top-60 on the charts, and the Muscle Shoals album was never issued.

The producers tried everything on those Alabama sessions. They tried to make me disco. They tried to make me rhythm and blues. I was frustrated. I kept thinking, "Why are they trying to change who I am as an artist? What's wrong with the style I've got?" It was almost like I was a nonentity. It was like, "Let's bury Brenda Lee and come up with somebody else." That was a sad feeling for me. Once again, I wanted to go back to the place I knew the best and where I'd had the most success. After all, Nashville—then and now—is where the great songs are.

It wasn't that I was opposed to change. On the contrary, I think I embraced it enthusiastically during this era. In line with my new career, I'd adopted a new look. I'd become a redhead in 1968 when I was experimenting with new sounds in New Orleans and New York. So when the spree of country hits began in the 1970s, I had a fresh visual style to go with them. Instead of gowns, I now wore casual clothes on the cover photos of my LPs and on stage. When pantsuits came along, I was in heaven. My act was very energetic, and it's hard to kick up your legs when you've got a dress on.

We changed the nightclub act, too. The ever faithful Dick Barstow made my presentation even more elaborate and sophisticated than it had been before. He incorporated some of the country hits but emphasized my extensive repertoire of pop classics more. He also wrote specialty material that united the band and me in skits and invited audience participation.

There was one set that was a giant clock—it must have been ten feet tall and fifteen feet across. It was our "Tick Tock" set. The clock had a big pendulum that went back and forth. Then the orchestra leader went into a big speech about the hands of time. It had something to do with me withstanding the test of time and with my songs enduring through the years. That segued into me singing "All the Way" from backstage. Then I'd appear and go into an upbeat tune like "Higher and Higher" or "You Are the Sunshine of My Life." It was one of the best shows I ever had.

I was still a top draw in Vegas. But now I also joined my fellow country stars on the state fair circuit. I also added venues like Harold's Club in Reno, the Playboy Club in Dallas and Burt Reynolds's Bachelors III nightclub in Fort Lauderdale. One show really stands out in my mind: When I played Madison Square Garden at the thirteenth annual Rock 'n' Roll Revival concert in 1977, 18,000 attended. Six years earlier Rick Nelson had been booed at the same event when he tried to perform new material. In response, he penned "Garden Party" and "went country." He showed them.

One of the high points of my '70s touring career was a tour packaged as the Festival of Music. This paired me with guitar legend Chet Atkins, the "Yakety Sax" man Boots Randolph and "Last Date" pianist Floyd Cramer.

We had a blast working together. I closed my part of the show with the moving medley "American Trilogy," which is "Dixie," then "All My Trials," followed by "The Battle Hymn of the Republic" as the finale. It usually brought down the house. Boots was supposed to follow me. The first time I rehearsed it, Boots came by and listened.

"I have to follow *that*?" bellowed Boots. "Well, thank you a lot: They'll be throwing babies up on the stage when you do that one." And you know what? It did always get standing ovations.

In addition to touring, there was lots of TV work to do. My television appearances in the '70s included *The Merv Griffin Show, The Tonight Show, The Joey Bishop Show* and Eddy Arnold's network special, as well as all the major syndicated country variety series. In 1975, I was invited to do *The Midnight Special*. Two years later I returned to the program. They asked me to participate in a special salute to my career, which I thought was awfully nice. Costarring on that episode were David Bowie, Stevie Wonder and Paul McCartney & Wings.

As a result of the television work, the hit country records and my concert tours, the money began to pour in. And this time it was in far greater amounts than I'd earned as a pop music performer.

The business had changed so much. Music was so much more important in people's lives. All the major cities had built auditoriums and civic centers. Music festivals were sprouting everywhere. And the international scene, which I'd courted since I was a child, was suddenly important to everyone.

On my tenth annual tour of Japan in 1975, I recorded a live album that became an overseas favorite. Today it is one of the most sought after "Brenda Lee" collectibles. Two years later I recorded a second Japanese LP, *Just for You, Something Nice*. It mixed Japanese songs with American pop ditties like "Tie a Yellow Ribbon," "Song Sung Blue" and "Take Me Home, Country Roads."

In 1978, I returned to France. "I'm Sorry" had been rereleased there and became a No.1 pop hit all over again. In 1979, *Amusement Business* reported that I had appeared in fifty-six countries to date and was "a black-market star" in Czechoslovakia. That was certainly a surprise. I'd never bothered to count.

The '70s were awfully good to me. It was a tough time in America, but in my little corner of the world, things couldn't have been better. The girls were becoming young ladies, and watching them grow was the greatest pleasure of my life. Julie was a cheerleader and ran track at Brentwood Academy. Jolie was a loving little sprite at Oak Hill Elementary School who brought every stray critter home to stay. Thanks to her, we had a duck, a raccoon, rabbits, gerbils, a parakeet and a pair of St. Bernard dogs.

Even though I was on the road so much—and felt guilty about it—the girls actually had a very stable home life. They were surrounded by family and were typical, energetic young girls. I kept them out of the limelight and made sure their upbringing was as normal as possible. I'd seen too many times how bratty and screwed up the children of showbiz people could be.

I never wore my "Brenda Lee" hat at home. I was "Mrs. Shacklett"; I was Julie and Jolie's mother; I was the obnoxious cheerleader with the cowbell at their basketball games. I became a master at helping with school projects—I can tell you everything about King Tut that you'd ever want to know.

I never missed a major school function, whether it was a play or a sporting event or an art show. I even skipped dinner with Frank Sinatra one night to see Julie win the big award at her sixth grade science fair.

Everything seemed to be going our way. Ronnie had invested in a profitable liquor store and established a big lumber company that specialized in custom millwork. And my career had a new beginning.

In 1977, *Newsweek* compiled a list of the "Top 20 Artists of the Past 20 Years." I was astonished when the magazine put me at No. 7 in its ranking. The magazine also credited me as one of the top-five American artists who had best survived the British Invasion.

Against all odds, I was back.

FIFTEEN

Urban Cowgirl

In late 1979, filming began in Texas on a John Travolta movie called *Urban Cowboy*. It was to mark the beginning of a new era for Nashville music. Travolta was then the hottest young star in Hollywood, having starred in two previous musical blockbusters, 1977's *Saturday Night Fever* and 1978's *Grease*. By turning his attention to country music, he was drawing millions of new fans to our genre.

He wasn't alone. *Urban Cowboy* was one of three major Hollywood hits that showcased country music on the nation's movie screens in 1980. Loretta Lynn's cinematic life story, *Coal Miner's Daughter,* earned an Oscar for Sissy Spacek in the title role. Dolly Parton costarred with Jane Fonda and Lily Tomlin in *9 to 5,* her silver-screen debut. Dolly's theme song was nominated for an Academy Award.

That kicked off a whole trend in moviemaking. And since I'm such a movie buff, I was tickled to see so many of my peers on the silver screen. Willie Nelson starred in *The Electric Horseman* in 1979 and *Honeysuckle Rose* in 1980. Close behind in the early '80s were *Honkytonk Man, The Best Little Whorehouse in Texas, Rhinestone, Songwriter,* the Patsy Cline biographical film *Sweet Dreams* and the Oscar-winning *Tender Mercies.* These weren't cheesy B-movies; they were A-list Hollywood productions. Overnight, it seemed, country music was hip.

The wave of popularity that country rode in the 1970s crested in the early '80s. Suddenly our music seemed all-pervasive. On television, *Barbara Mandrell and the Mandrell Sisters* ruled the Saturday night airwaves in 1980–82. The countrified 1979–85 comedy *The Dukes of Hazzard,* featuring Waylon Jennings as "The Balladeer," was the highest-rated TV show in America. The country series *Hee Haw* became the longest-running variety program in television history.

I became active in the Country Music Association. That's where I learned that the number of country radio stations was dramatically increasing. In 1980, there were 1,534 full-time country broadcasters in the United States. By the end of the decade, there were 2,108 country stations, more than any other musical style. A fourth of all the radio stations in the nation "went country," and the style's weekly listenership swelled to 43 million. In 1970, country record sales were $100 million per year; by 1989, they were $500 million per year. In 1983, country launched two cable television channels, the Nashville Network (TNN) and Country Music Television (CMT). During the next fifteen years they would grow tenfold in size, faster than any other cable franchises. I loved the new opportunities and did as many cable shows as I could.

In Nashville, they called it the "Urban Cowboy" era—Wall Street brokers were donning cowboy boots and heading for country music ballrooms. Country nightclubs sprouted in cities everywhere. Jeans became fashionable. People who'd never seen a horse looked like westerners.

And in the thick of it all was me, newly restyled as an "Urban Cowgirl." After a brief flirtation with Elektra Records, I rejoined the MCA roster in early 1979. Jim Foglesong had become the head of the label by then. He was, and is, a true gentleman—as honest as the day is long. Jim was a singer who had toured with Fred Waring's Pennsylvanians, so he was a big fan of other vocalists. Lucky me, he respected my music and my accomplishments. He was always so kind to me and sincerely made me feel like an important artist. He valued my contributions to the label.

Jim was performing in a chorus on *The Ed Sullivan Show* back in the days when I performed on it. He said that's where he first saw me, and that he'd been a fan ever since.

"Jim Foglesong just loved Brenda," confirms former MCA Records executive Ron Chancey. "I remember that shortly after he took over the company, we were in a meeting talking about the label's artist roster. We both kind of looked at each other when we got to Brenda's name, and Jim said something like, 'Why isn't anyone making records with Brenda?' He started to talk about how great she was."

I don't know how, but Jim had an intuitive sense of what would work for me musically. He knew I wanted more from a producer than simply a contracted working arrangement. Having spent all those years with Owen Bradley, I needed a personal relationship in the studio. Ron Chancey took the job.

"I grew up listening to Brenda," Ron recalls, "so before meeting her for the first time, I thought she was a lot older than she actually was. And boy was I shocked. I had her in the Rosemary Clooney or Teresa Brewer era, but when we got together, Brenda was only thirty-four. And I was even more shocked at what a great singer she still was. What a talent.

"Owen Bradley had retired. So I was a little bit nervous about producing her, trying to fill Owen's shoes, because I think he's the greatest country record producer of all. But Brenda made it easy for me. After I got to know her and Ronnie, we became great friends. We'd hang out on my boat at the lake, or I'd

go over to their house. We were kind of like family. It was just a
wonderful way to work. I don't think it's much like that with too
many people these days."

I hit it right off with Ron Chancey. He wasn't bossy. He let
me be a part of the entire process, just like the relationship I'd
had with Owen. Ron is very sweet-natured and also extremely
talented in the studio. We were a great match.

And Ron Chancey's fears of stepping into Owen Bradley's
shoes proved to be groundless. The two producers created completely different sounds. Like me, Ron had grown up as a huge
fan of rhythm and blues. And although he had country credentials
as a record maker, he took the savvy step of injecting his musical
tracks for me with a healthy shot of soul.

He also had a keen ear for songs. When he ran into Ben Peters one day, the songwriter asked him who he was recording.
Ron told Ben that he'd just taken over my record production.

"Boy, have I got a song for her!" exclaimed Ben.

He came to Ron's office the next day with a sultry lament
called "Tell Me What It's Like," and Ron seized it for me at once.
Ron called and told me he'd found a song that could be really
great, so I went right over to hear it. I immediately agreed with
him after hearing it just once.

We recorded it in July 1979 at Woodland Sound in East
Nashville. That was the "happening" new studio at the time.
Ron's sessions were the first time I recorded in the modern way
in Nashville. Before, every vocal on every record was me singing
live with the old A-Team band on Music Row. Now I had the
luxury of coming back in and polishing my performance if I
needed to. They'd just tape over the old one. It was a little hard
for me to get used to. I was used to getting my vocal energy from
working live with the musicians. So most of the time, Ron would

wind up using my very first attempts, when the musicians were there with me. We call those "scratch vocals."

"She always sang her best when we had the whole band in there," Ron agrees. "It turned her on. For the most part, we never could beat her scratch vocals. Everybody back then was doing it for the music. The song publishers were eager to give Brenda their top-drawer songs. And Brenda couldn't have been nicer to all the new session players I introduced her to. Everyone was so excited to be recording with her, especially since she hadn't been in the studio in a long time. Even Glen Snoddy who owned the studio was all excited. He even had a photographer come in, so that he could use Brenda's being there as advertising for the studio."

The recording sessions were like big family get-togethers. I would sometimes bring Julie and Jolie. Ron's son Blake was interested in audio engineering, so he was always around. By the time he was in junior high school, he had a studio in the basement of his parents' home and was recording local bands.

Blake Chancey was just precious. And he must have been paying very close attention indeed. In years to come, Blake produced hit records for the multiple-million-selling Dixie Chicks.

"Brenda made her sessions fun," continues Ron. "She was just so sweet and lovable and down-to-earth. You'd never know she was any kind of star. That's the best thing you can say about a person. I was pleasantly surprised, because I know too many that are the other way. Believe me, I've seen the opposite."

I loved "Tell Me What It's Like," because it took me back to the old days of dramatic recitation. The lyric was extremely different for me—it was a girlfriend-to-girlfriend story about one woman going to another for advice and consolation as she feels heartache coming on. And it was so melodic, with a strong bluesy feel.

With what they believed to be a surefire hit song "in the can," MCA decided to give me a makeover. The label had big plans for my record's fall release. And I was eager for the change. I did think I needed an update. It never hurts to try and reinvent yourself every once in a while. The company flew in the top stylists from New York, a makeup artist, a hairdresser and famed fashion photographer Frank Laffitte. I felt like a queen with them fussing over me.

Tennessean music reporter Laura Eipper flipped when she saw the results: "Gone is the bouffant, lacquered hairdo, the cute dresses and the dimpled grin, replaced with a seductively tousled mane, slinky outfits and a come-hither pout . . . The new image was such a success that a whole new look to her show will be built around it."

I told Laura that I couldn't believe how great I looked. She did a big story in the paper and quoted me as saying, "It's every woman's dream to be able to look beautiful . . . But there's just one problem with the whole thing. I've got to learn how to do it all myself. It's the first time in years I haven't sprayed my hair. I used to be a slave to my head, and I love not being one, but it's going to be hard to live up to that [publicity photograph]. I may just cut it out and wear it around my head." Actually, I've felt that way about most of my publicity pictures. The wonders of airbrushing!

MCA introduced the "new" Brenda with my new sound at the annual Country Music Week festivities in Nashville in 1979. The label presented me in full production at the Opry House to a packed audience of radio executives and Music Row power brokers. "Tell Me What It's Like" was released a week later.

Jim Foglesong and his staff beefed up MCA's promotion with full-page ads in the music trade publications, blaring: "AbsoluteLee! PositiveLee! MCA's little dynamo is blasting her way up the charts . . . and back into your hearts . . . With a new look, new producer, and new single, 'Tell Me What It's Like.' "

"It's a gorgeous performance," says Diana Reid Haig. "Over a pulsing bass and electric piano intro, Brenda begins the record with another heartfelt recitation. As Bergen White's shimmering string arrangement begins to soar, she sings with a new depth and maturity. Her voice, that magnificent instrument, is even more powerful than ever. And, as always, she pulls you into the song. This record blasted up the country charts and hit the top-10 just before Christmas in 1979. As icing on the cake, 'Tell Me What It's Like' earned Brenda a well-deserved third Grammy nomination."

I felt great. I was so excited. Coming right out of the chute with my first record with Ron Chancey, we had a top-10 and a Grammy nomination. I was right in there, competing with real country queens like Barbara Mandrell and Crystal Gayle. Billie Jo Spears was nominated that year for her country-disco hit "I Will Survive," which is a song I've always loved. The winner was Emmylou Harris for her remake of Loretta Lynn's "Blue Kentucky Girl." I've always liked and admired Emmy, because she walks to the beat of her own drummer. She has such integrity about her music. It's not about stardom with her; it's about music, period.

Like many of my cohorts, I was caught up in Hollywood's new fascination with country music. During Barbara Mandrell's inaugural season as a TV variety diva in 1980, I'm happy to say that I was one of the first guests she invited to appear. My old friend Dick Clark also asked me to guest on his national television special. Mike Douglas called again and so did *Hollywood Squares*.

I took my turn in front of the movie cameras when Burt Reynolds offered me a cameo role. For years I'd performed at his Florida nightclub Bachelors III, and we were fast friends. Burt had filmed a string of hit country movies, including 1975's *W. W. and the Dixie Dancekings,* 1976's *Gator* and 1977's box-office smash *Smokey and the Bandit.* When he cast its sequel in 1980, he told me that his *Gator* costar Jerry Reed and I were among the first people he thought of.

I'll never forget how it happened. Burt was coming in to Nashville, and I was heading out to a concert date. We ran into each other at the airport. We stopped, hugged each other and talked for a minute.

"We're going to do a 'Smokey II,' and I want you to be in it," Burt said to my surprise.

"Oh, Burt, you know I'm not an actress," I protested.

"You don't have to do much; I just want you to have a little part in it," he replied.

I actually thought he was joking, but I still said OK and told him to call me when he was going to film it. Burt called all right, and asked me if I could be in Las Vegas the next week. So Ronnie and I got on the next plane out of Nashville. We filmed in Vegas for a week in the summer of 1980.

Smokey and the Bandit II featured Sally Field, Dom DeLuise, Jackie Gleason and Paul Williams in a strange plot involving transporting a pregnant elephant to Texas. I portrayed a frumpy little church lady and provided "Again and Again" for the movie's soundtrack.

The most wonderful thing about that movie experience was working with Jackie Gleason. Burt introduced us on the set.

"Mr. Gleason, do you know Brenda Lee?" asked Burt.

"Do I *know* her?" barked Gleason. "She was a star when you were in knickers, Sonny."

All my scenes were with him. Jackie's rule was that he would not film after noon—that's when he started drinking. So we would have to get up before dawn to start shooting. You know, he had a photographic memory.

He had this man, what you might call a valet, who followed him around everywhere. He'd flick Jackie's cigarette ashes for him; and you had to communicate to Jackie through this guy all the time. It was bizarre, but I thought it was wonderful. Jackie called the shots. Everybody stood up and saluted when he was around.

Jackie was my defender on that set. There was one place where I was supposed to say "shit" in the movie. I didn't know how to get out of it, so I went to Jackie.

"Mr. Gleason, I have children who are going to be watching this movie, and I just can't say curse words," I said meekly.

"Don't worry about it, honey, I'll get that all changed," replied the gruff showbiz legend. Gleason marched right up to Burt, the movie's star, and gave his ultimatum in thunderous tones.

"She doesn't want to say 'shit,' and she's not going to! Find something else for her to say!"

Ronnie wasn't along for the movie junket simply as my husband. At my request, he was now managing my career. I went to him in tears one day in 1979 and told him I couldn't handle things by myself anymore. I knew he was head over heels in building projects and taking care of the children. But I was miserable. I was overwhelmed.

After Dub Allbritten died, I tried letting the booking agency handle my whole career. When that didn't work, I tried a couple of managers, who only lasted a few months. Then I tried to do it myself with my office help. But I couldn't deal with things all alone. I needed somebody to run interference for me. And I needed somebody I didn't have to second-guess all the time, someone I could trust. So I asked Ronnie outright if he would just take on the management job.

Ronnie was a good businessman. He might not have understood show business that well, but he promised me he'd do everything in his power to help me.

Because show business management is a full-time job, he had to give up his own career. If I had realized that at the time, I probably wouldn't have asked him to take on so much responsibility and to give up something he truly loved doing. I understand now what a sacrifice I asked him to make for me.

To this day, he's never once thrown it up to me that he might have been a hugely successful builder and contractor. If he'd shown as much dedication to that as he has to my career, there's no doubt in my mind that Ronnie would have been incredibly successful on his own. As it was, he gave up the lumber mill, his home restoration work and his building projects; everything.

Some people on Music Row kept Ronnie at an arm's length. I guess they'd seen too many examples of family members who interfered with a singer's career.

But I never thought Ronnie got in the way, and some of his moves were very smart. His lumber mill was located on a hill a few blocks from the Tennessee State Fairgrounds, which is just a five-minute drive from our home. Although he turned the business over to others in 1980, he held on to the buildings and property. He converted two of the structures to house a business office for Brenda Lee Productions and a rehearsal studio for the band and me. From there, Ronnie slowly and methodically restructured my finances.

He helped renegotiate my MCA contract in 1979 and coordinated the label's big push behind me in the '80s. My new look and new sound marked a new career direction. And Ronnie was by my side for this challenging new phase of my professional life.

By this time, the top country stars were making far more as concert attractions than even the biggest pop stars of the '50s and '60s had. My earnings in the 1980s astonished me. Even when I was the world's No. 1 female pop vocalist, I never saw that kind of money. Another big change was the introduction of what we call "concessions." We sold ball caps, T-shirts, glossy tour books and cassette tapes. Sometimes you'd make more money with those than you would for doing the concert itself. Plus, we changed the way we traveled. Ronnie thought airplanes were too extravagant.

We started leasing two tour buses in 1979. Then Ronnie went looking for one to buy. We bought one from one of the gospel acts and completely customized it for me, complete with my own stateroom in the back. We kept that thing for ten years and put 585,000 miles on it.

Ronnie proved to be as frugal as Charlie Mosley had been with my burgeoning income. In fact, he often went to my former guardian for financial advice. We also relied on the counsel of former Decca chief Owen Bradley.

"If you were to look at our income on a graph from 1980 to 1990, it would go up at a forty-five-degree angle," Ronnie relates. *"I tried to run Brenda Lee Productions more as a business. And Charlie Mosley was my mentor. One of his main things was his frugal Scottish attitude. He was a saver who watched every dime. So that's what I did."*

Unlike most country stars of the day, I didn't tour as part of a "package," with opening acts or warm-up attractions. I continued to headline almost all my own concerts, giving country audiences the same type of performances that I had given to pop fans for so many years.

The dates poured in as my country hits continued to multiply. I followed "Tell Me What It's Like" with "The Cowgirl and the Dandy." The song was originally written and performed by Bobby Goldsboro as "The Cowboy and the Lady," but his version stalled at No. 85 in 1977. When I turned the tale around by reversing the genders, the tune went into the top-10.

I certainly wasn't a cowgirl by any means. But the idea of the two lovers from different sides of the tracks appealed to me. Once again, it was a bit of a departure. And once again, the song has had enduring appeal. It was later recorded by artists like Dolly Parton and John Denver.

The two top-10 hits were packaged together on my 1980 LP *Even Better*. This was the album that introduced that alluring and stylish new image. And instead of "cover versions" of others' hit tunes, this was the first of my albums to feature all original material. *Even Better* included songwriting contributions by such celebrity Nashvillians as Eddy Raven, Deborah Allen, Jim Stafford, Troy Seals and Linda Hargrove.

"Rather than terming this . . . a 'comeback,' Brenda Lee is in fact simply marking yet another milestone in a musical odyssey that's almost unparalleled in the music industry," wrote Jackie Monaghan in my album's liner notes. "Now entering the decade of the '80s, Brenda Lee . . . is personally embarking on touching a fourth decade as a household name . . . from Seattle to Singapore."

Even Better really did mark a new beginning. During the next three years, Ron Chancey and I would craft some of the finest albums of my career. Immediately after the success of "Tell Me What It's Like" and "The Cowgirl and the Dandy," the label urged us back into the studio. We emerged in the fall of 1980 with the hit album *Take Me Back* and its smash single "Broken Trust."

"The situation with that song was a little bit delicate," says Ron Chancey. "It was owned by the Oak Ridge Boys' song-publishing company. Jimbeau Hinson, the writer, had pitched it to the Oaks. So I had to be real careful how we did this. I asked them if we could record it with Brenda, and when they said, 'Sure,' I said, 'Well, why don't ya'll sing harmony on it?'"

The Oak Ridge Boys were a highly successful gospel quartet who had "gone country" in the 1970s around the same time I had. Their highly energetic stage performances prefigured the romping concert presentations of Garth Brooks and his peers in the '90s. The Oaks were also one of Nashville's acts that successfully crossed over to the pop hit parade. When I recorded with the group, the quartet had already topped the country charts with a string of hits, including "Leaving Louisiana in the Broad Daylight." Six months after the Oaks backed me on "Broken Trust," they roared up the pop charts with "Elvira."

"Broken Trust" was by Jimbeau Hinson, the songwriter who'd sung Brenda Lee hits as a child in Mississippi. I was always lucky with Jimbeau's tunes. He also wrote "Just for the Moment," "Find Yourself Another Puppet" and "Don't Promise Me Anything (Do It)," which was one of my most rocking singles in the early '80s.

"One of my biggest thrills ever was going to see her in Birmingham, Alabama," recalls Jimbeau fondly. "As she sang her hits, I remembered every talent contest I'd ever won singing her songs. And then she ended with 'Broken Trust,' my song! It might sound corny, but it was exactly like a dream come true."

"With 'Broken Trust' becoming yet another solid top-10 country success, Ron Chancey and Brenda Lee 'pushed the envelope' for country when they selected the songs for that album," observes Mary Bufwack. "The LP's title tune, 'Take Me Back,' came from the pen of Brenda's buddy Elton John. Her old Mem-

phis producer Chips Moman cowrote 'Staring Each Other Down,' a song of pent-up lust. I think Brenda's soul-saturated performance is the equal of anything ever cut in either Muscle Shoals or Memphis. The rasping rocker 'What Am I Gonna Do' came from the pen of Kim Carnes, who was then just one year away from stardom with 'Bette Davis Eyes.' Having r&b backup harmonies was unusual on Nashville country records at the time, but just as she had done on the Even Better *sessions, Brenda enlisted the support of soulful Donna McElroy, Vicki Hampton and Yvonne Hodges."*

I think that "Broken Trust" introduced me to a new decade of music lovers. That hit meant I was being played alongside such new country icons as Kenny Rogers, Lacy J. Dalton, John Conlee, Tanya Tucker and Sylvia.

That song shared the top-10 with two of the singles that best epitomize the decade. During Thanksgiving week in 1980, Anne Murray was singing "Could I Have This Dance" as the love theme from *Urban Cowboy,* and Waylon Jennings was singing "Just Good Ol' Boys," the anthem for TV's top-rated show, *The Dukes of Hazzard.*

I would soon have my shot at a Hollywood theme tune, too. In 1981, the producers of Neil Simon's bittersweet comedy *Only When I Laugh* came to Music City to ask me to be on the film's soundtrack. The movie is now highly regarded for its fine performances by Marsha Mason, Kristy McNichol, James Coco, Joan Hackett and Kevin Bacon. And "Only When I Laugh" became the title tune for my next album.

If you blink, you'll miss the song in the movie. Still, it was a good song. And I thought the movie was terrific.

That was the start of a new aspect of my career. I made many more soundtrack appearances in the '80s. The 1980 science fiction comedy *UFOria,* featuring *Laverne and Shirley* TV star

Cindy Williams, included me singing "Break It to Me Gently" on its soundtrack. I recorded the Ben Peters tune "Again and Again" for *Smokey and the Bandit II* in that same year. The soundtrack for the 1982 film *Missing* prominently featured my oldie "My Whole World Is Falling Down." The Oscar-winning film starred Jack Lemmon and Sissy Spacek in a tale about the fascist government of Chile.

If only I had known what those South American governments were really like during all those years I toured there, I'd have been scared to death to go. I think the movie *Missing* opened up a lot of people's eyes. It certainly did mine.

The soundtrack appearances continued with me singing "Jingle Bell Rock" in the hit Eddie Murphy/Dan Aykroyd comedy *Trading Places* in 1983. Also that year, "I Want to Be Wanted" was heard on the soundtrack of the biker movie *The Loveless*. Later in the decade "Bigelow 6-200" was used in the 1987 baseball comedy *Long Gone*. In addition that year, TV's *Our World* used "You Can Depend on Me" as a soundtrack tune.

I guess when you've been around long enough, your past comes around full circle. There was practically a full-scale revival of Brenda Lee songs on the charts of the 1980s as well. Diana Ross's version of "Sweet Nothin's" appeared in 1982, and in the same year Juice Newton topped the country charts with her revival of "Break It to Me Gently." Willie Nelson scored a pop and country hit with "Always on My Mind" that same year, and in 1984, George Jones revived "She's My Rock" on the country hit parade. The Forester Sisters brought back "Too Many Rivers" as a top-10 hit in 1987. A year later, the Pet Shop Boys took "Always on My Mind" to fame once again.

It just goes to show you what I've always said. If the song is there, it can be rock; it can be pop; it can be country; it can be r&b. It can be anything.

Hearing my "golden goodies" being revived was nice. But I was busy making lots of new music, too. The *Only When I Laugh* LP included the rags-to-riches waltz "From Levi's to Calvin Klein Jeans," which became my debut single of 1982. The collection also featured "Shine On." I never issued my version as a single, but George Jones reprised it as a top-10 hit the following year. It was one of the few times I'd "missed" as a song expert.

By this time, the press was calling me things like "Nashville's Song Magnet." I have been pretty good at spotting hits over the years. But I'm not always right.

Bob Montgomery wrote "Misty Blue" especially for me, but I turned it down. Eddy Arnold, Wilma Burgess, Joe Simon and Dorothy Moore all had big hits with it, so there you go. Shel Silverstein offered me "One's on the Way," and I passed on that one, too. So Loretta Lynn had a No. 1 hit with it. I turned down "Here You Come Again," and look what Dolly Parton did with that. I've missed with tunes throughout my career, from "Bye Bye Love" back in the '50s to "She's in Love with the Boy" in the '90s. I blew it on "Rose Garden," which Lynn Anderson had such a big hit with. "Jose Cuervo" became a smash for Shelly West after I passed on it. I even goofed with "He Believes in Me," which Kenny Rogers later took to the top of the charts as "She Believes in Me."

In many cases, I knew they were great. It was just that at the time I couldn't get around to recording them. I held on to "Here You Come Again" for six months and finally let it go, because I was embarrassed to hold it any longer. I felt sorry for the songwriters. A lot of times songs just got lost in the shuffle, particularly during those days in the late '70s when I was between Owen Bradley and Ron Chancey as producers.

So in my show in the 1980s, I did a "hits and misses" medley. I'd set it up by talking about how lucky I had been in getting great songs from great songwriters. Then I'd say I've made a few mistakes in my career concerning songs that had been offered to me first. I always ended that by telling the audience, "You know, we're not always as smart as we think we are."

I credit producer Ron Chancey for providing me with choice songs throughout this period. Ron also ran a side business creating national ad jingles. He thought I would be a natural as the singer behind top brand names. So you could hear my vocals touting the praises of Coca-Cola ("It's the Real Thing!"), McDonald's ("You deserve a break today!"), Starkist Tuna (for which I modified "I'm Sorry" to fit the "Sorry Charlie" ad campaign), Nestlé's Crunch candy, Chevy Trucks, Huggies diapers and other products.

I was seen as well as heard as the spokesperson for Beanee Weenees. This Van Camp's lunch snack was designed for moms on the go, which certainly fit my lifestyle. Magazine ads pictured me posing with the product and extolling its virtues.

I figured if Loretta Lynn could plug Shake 'N Bake and Crisco, well, why not? It turned out that the job came with a lifetime supply of Beanee Weenees. I've still got cases and cases of them in my pantry. Chili Weenees, too.

That company sponsored my national radio show, *Brenda Lee's Country Profile,* which debuted in 1982. The syndicated program ran weekly on hundreds of stations nationwide throughout the early '80s. The format was that I would "interview" other artists and see what was happening on the musical scene with them. Alanna Nash, who wrote and produced the show, would get the sound bites from the other artists. Then I'd come in and record my introductions and such. I think the show was so successful because the little interview snippets were short and easy for the radio stations to drop into their programming throughout the day.

"Having Brenda Lee's name attached to the program didn't hurt," states her Nashville contemporary John Lomax III. "At this point, Brenda was one of a tiny handful of artists who remained on the charts twenty-five years after they'd first appeared in the mid-1950s. Johnny Cash, Jerry Lee Lewis, George Jones and Marty Robbins were her only musical peers 'left standing,' and by 1983, Marty was dead and Jerry Lee was in a commercial tailspin.

"The fact that she'd attained the status of a living legend was reflected in her induction into the Georgia Music Hall of Fame in 1982. She shared the honor that night at the Colony Square Hotel in Atlanta with fellow inductees Duane Allman and songwriter Boudleaux Bryant."

Duane Allman had died by then, but his brother Gregg took the stage, played the piano and sang so soulfully. I thought back to all those times when the Allman Brothers had played in Nashville in the '60s. They were called the Allman Joys back then and were one of the "show bands" that Dub Allbritten's One Niters agency booked. I don't think Dub handled them personally—Billy Smith probably booked them. Billy had become Dub's partner in the agency after leaving my band, the Casuals.

Ronnie, my husband, was crazy about the Allman Joys. He used to go see them in this little joint where they played in downtown Nashville.

"It was a little club called the Briar Patch," Ronnie remembers. "I called it 'a chainsaw joint.' There was hardly a night that went by that there wasn't a fight or some kind of trouble there. But that place was always packed. That's where the group was discovered. I thought they were really cool. I was a big fan.

"I thought they were as good as the Beatles. There are only a few people I've seen where I felt I was seeing a star before they became one. And this was one of those times. Duane and Gregg

*were originally from Nashville, you know. They even boarded at
Castle Heights Military Academy in Lebanon, Tennessee, for a
while."*

Soon after Ronnie and some of the Music Row people saw
them at the Briar Patch, the Allmans were offered some
recording-studio time. It was at Bradley's Barn, the studio that
my producer Owen Bradley had built in Mt. Juliet, east of
Nashville. I think the Allmans were one of the first rock groups to
record there. I always liked those guys. The Allman Brothers
were Southern rock, and I appreciated what they did with their
sound.

Besides Duane Allman, another inductee at the 1982 Georgia
Music Hall of Fame awards was the legendary songwriter
Boudleaux Bryant. I'd known him ever since I was a little girl.
Boudleaux and his wife Felice were responsible for such great
songs as "Bye Bye Love," "All I Have to Do Is Dream," "Rocky
Top" and "Wake Up, Little Susie." Ronnie and I used to go out to
the Bryants' house when they lived on the lake outside Nashville.
They were such fun people, and boy could Felice cook. Then
after they moved to Gatlinburg, we visited them there in the
mountains.

As for my own induction into the Georgia Music Hall of
Fame, it was one of the few times in my life that I've been truly,
truly surprised. I can usually figure out what's up. But I thought I
was going down there to Atlanta to present an award to someone
else. When they said my name, I lost it. It was like I was glued to
my chair. I couldn't get up. I thought they'd made a mistake.
Until I looked back at the videotape, I had no idea what I said. I
was crying profusely, but somehow or another I made a coherent
speech.

The awards they gave us in Georgia were beautiful. They
were tall crystal obelisks made by Tiffany. One of my saddest

days was when I was having my house painted, and the painter knocked over my "Georgy" and broke it. I called Zell Miller, the Georgia governor, in tears. He said, "Oh, don't worry about it, honey, we'll get you another one." They're worth, like, fifteen hundred bucks apiece, I think. Anyway, darned if another painter didn't knock the second one over and chip it. I'm too embarrassed to call and ask for another one again.

I was so honored to be recognized alongside the legends who were in there. Ray Charles, Otis Redding, Johnny Mercer, Joe South and the Reverend Thomas A. Dorsey had already been inducted. And believe it or not, I got in there before James Brown, Little Richard, Gladys Knight, Ma Rainey, Fletcher Henderson and Gram Parsons.

♪

In 1982, I was teamed with three of my favorite people in the world on a double-LP package titled *The Winning Hand.* Lucky me. I got to collaborate with Kris Kristofferson, Dolly Parton and Willie Nelson on the records.

Artist Barry Buxkamper painted striking likenesses of all four of us for the album's jacket design. We were each depicted as a face card from a gambling deck. I was the Queen of Diamonds.

Johnny Cash provided poetic liner notes for *The Winning Hand,* praising all four of us. The collection became the basis for a two-hour TV special. In addition to the original "Winning Hand" of Dolly, Kris, Willie and me, the special featured the charismatic Cash as both host and performer.

On the special, I participated in a number of set pieces. Dolly and I portrayed secretaries at typewriters for our number together. Willie and I were cast as an estranged married couple at the breakfast table.

One of my personal highlights of the production was singing

"Help Me Make It through the Night" with Kris. We stood in dim lights holding hands and gazing into each other's eyes throughout the number. Kris was grinning. He's just precious. He doesn't even know how hard that was for me. It's difficult to sing directly at someone, and it's even harder when that someone is such a spectacular hunk. Kris doesn't even realize the sex appeal he has, and that's what makes him so darling.

The album turned out to be quite successful. Propelled by its TV special and my duet single with Willie, "You're Gonna Love Yourself in the Morning," *The Winning Hand* climbed to No. 4 on the country hit parade. Critics praised it as "a piece of history," saying it was "one of the most durable albums ever recorded." The collection made the *Boston Globe*'s list as one of the ten best albums of 1982.

But *The Winning Hand* never achieved its full potential. Monument Records filed for bankruptcy in early 1983. Dolly and Kris were listed among the 659 creditors. The company fought valiantly during the next four years but wound up selling its master tapes to CBS in 1987. I was never paid for *The Winning Hand*. Neither were any of the other stars, as far as I know. Ronnie and I never pursued it. We figured it was water under the bridge.

While I was busy on *The Winning Hand*, MCA Records marked time by issuing my *Greatest Country Hits* collection. It included the ten tunes that had brought me a new audience between 1973 and 1981. But my next three singles sputtered out in the lower reaches of the charts.

I took that as a sign that it was time for another change. So I went to producer Jerry Crutchfield. Ronnie and I had known him for years, and I really admired his work with Tanya Tucker. Jim Foglesong was all for the idea, so I went in and did a whole album with Jerry.

Our collaboration began with 1983's swaying, wistful "Didn't We Do It Good." That single became the basis of my first music video. MTV had gone on the air in the summer of 1981 and created a new type of pop idol, the video star. Eighteen months later, both the Nashville Network and Country Music Television bowed on the cable dial. Practically overnight, music marketing was transformed.

Suddenly, we all had to become video stars. So they took me to the estate of a friend of ours, Margaret Henley. Ronnie played my lover, and in flashbacks we were shown holding hands, picnicking and feeding Margaret's horses. The production was pretty grade school by today's video standards. I lip-synched the song in a restaurant called Darryl's, and the cameraman kept shooting its logo.

But you know what? It made a star out of Ronnie. We'd walk into a truck stop and people would yell, "I saw you in a video!" People would recognize Ronnie before they would me. I knew this video business wasn't my gig.

I've never been one of those "pretty" singers. The reason I got the nickname Little Miss Dynamite in the first place was because of the energy I had. Other female stars could glide around in designer gowns and never muss their makeup. They'd look just as beautiful at the end of the show as they did at the beginning. Not me. I'd come off stage wringing wet with my makeup running down my face.

When I'm done with a show, I look like I've played a football game. Ronnie says I glow. I say it's sweat. I would have done better in a performance video than trying to act in one. That never was my thing.

Despite airplay for the "Didn't We Do It Good" video in '83, producer Jerry Crutchfield and I didn't hit our stride until "A Sweeter Love (I'll Never Know)" a year later. It was written by

Jerry, and I promoted it via an eleven-city Learjet blitz. The soaring, torchy tune became a comeback hit for me.

The music world was now a profoundly different place than it had been even five years earlier. The video revolution was creating an entirely new generation of celebrities. And many of the pioneers who'd shared stages with me either left the scene or were passing away.

John Lennon was shot and killed in December 1980. Rockabilly pioneers Bill Haley and Ronnie Self died in 1981.

Then in 1982, I got a call from Dick Barstow's nephew. Dick had suddenly died of a heart attack. There went the colorful man I'd leaned on for so many years as the creative genius behind my shows. I have so many fond memories of Dick. We had a lot of laughs, and he taught me so much. If the truth be known, he really taught me how to be an entertainer. I'll carry him in my heart always.

Late that same year, I joined the crowd of mourners at Woodlawn Cemetery for the funeral of my old friend Marty Robbins. A cold rain fell as thousands gathered to pay their last respects to the Grand Ole Opry's greatest showman. I sang "One Day at a Time" at the request of Marty's son and widow.

Figures from "old school" showbiz like honky-tonk legend Ernest Tubb, *Nashville Banner* columnist Red O'Donnell and *The Ozark Jubilee*'s Ralph Foster all died in 1984. Much more personal to me was the passing of "Grandmary."

That was a dark time in our whole family's life. Grandmary, Dub's mother, had not only helped raise my children. In another way, she helped raise Ronnie and me, too. She was buried in Paducah in the pink lace pajamas that Julie and Jolie had given her the Christmas before. At her request, she held a picture of the girls in her hands in the coffin. The pall on top of the casket had a pink banner with "Grandmary" written in silver glitter.

We drove up to Paducah in shock and sadness in the early fall of 1980. She'd died of congestive heart failure at age seventy-nine. She'd had heart problems for years, but we were still shocked. We'd taken a cruise to Bermuda with her just months before.

The girls were devastated. Jolie was eleven years old then. When they lowered Grandmary's casket into the ground and began to cover it, Jolie tried to climb down into the grave with her. It was just awful.

An era was ending for me in other ways, too. After years of living alone in Nashville, my mother moved back to Georgia in 1980. My sister Linda had relocated back to Lithonia ten years earlier. My brother Randall and little sister Robyn and their families would soon join the rest of the Tarpley kin there.

Although I was still having country hits, I remember this whole time period as being fraught with uncertainty. I was wistful and nostalgic when I took to the highways in my tour bus during the peak of the "Urban Cowboy" era. Out on the road, I'd sometimes run into old friends, and it would make me sad to see them playing in little joints. I vowed right then and there that I would never let that happen to me.

In 1980, I was on tour in Japan, and I ran into Tina Turner. That was before she got to open shows for the Rolling Stones and started to have her comeback. Like a lot of American artists who worked that market, she was always big in Japan. She didn't have any hits as a solo artist yet, but Tina had a positive attitude. She'd left her husband Ike and was trying to get into the public eye again. Tina had tried recording a country album in Nashville but really hadn't found her niche.

All of us have hit that period in our lives, when we're not doing anything and nobody wants us. That's when we try and reinvent ourselves. And that's exactly what Tina did four years later with "What's Love Got to Do with It."

Back on tour in the States, I was going into some completely different venues thanks to the "Urban Cowboy" explosion of country popularity. When I played Gilley's, the Houston dance hall that became so famous because of the *Urban Cowboy* movie, it turned out to be a really weird gig for me. Even though I had country hits, my act wasn't really "country." So I was kind of like a fish out of water in a place like that.

Plus, I've always hated it when people dance while I'm singing. That's why I've never liked to work on New Year's Eve, because people are up dancing. Now, I don't care if they're eating. That's a different deal. I watched them do that for years in the supper clubs. But when they're up and dancing, you feel like you might as well be a jukebox.

Your whole career flashes before your eyes and you're wondering, "What am I doing here?" You could be any faceless local band. Mind you, the Texas honky-tonk acts feel that if the dance floor isn't full, they're not doing their job. Me, I'm like, "Please, don't get up and dance! And forget about getting down on your back and doing the Gator on the floor while I'm up here singing!"

I spent the early 1980s coheadlining at big country shows with the Statler Brothers. The quartet had graduated from Johnny Cash's road show and could entertain crowds with hit after harmony hit like "Class of '57," "Flowers on the Wall" and their soundtrack smash from *Smokey and the Bandit II,* "Charlotte's Web."

The Statlers also joined me as a guest on Jerry Reed's television special of 1982. Glen Campbell, Burt Reynolds, Faron Young, Jimmy Dean, Vicki Lawrence and Louise Mandrell also took turns at the mike.

Later that year, I played the World's Fair in Knoxville, Tennessee, with superstar Ronnie Milsap ("It Was Almost Like a Song"). At the Westbury Music Fair in New York, I coheadlined with mellow crooner Don Williams ("Tulsa Time"). At the annual Fan Fair festival in Nashville, I would take the stage with my fellow MCA recording artists George Strait ("Does Fort Worth Ever Cross Your Mind"), Lee Greenwood ("God Bless the U.S.A.") and John Conlee ("Rose Colored Glasses").

Another concert highlight of this era was appearing at the 1981 Sugar Bowl in New Orleans. In addition to singing the National Anthem, I cheered the Georgia Bulldogs to victory over Notre Dame. The winning school would soon welcome my daughter Julie as an undergrad.

In the fall of 1982, Ronnie and I rode down to Athens, Georgia, with Julie, and it was the saddest day because our little girl was "leaving the nest." But looking back, it was pretty funny, too. I had never been to college, so I had no idea what to pack, what to take or anything. Julie didn't know, either. So we took everything she owned. We figured she was going to be there for four years, after all. What's even funnier is that we took Julie and all her stuff down there in my tour bus. We must have looked ridiculous.

When we got to the school, we found out her dorm room was the size of a postage stamp. We had this huge TV for her that wouldn't even fit in there. We didn't let her take a car, and Julie had to bum rides from her classmates just to get to a drugstore or a shopping mall.

But we learned our lesson. Five years later when our younger daughter Jolie entered Southern Methodist University in Dallas, we towed her BMW down there and put her up in her own condo!

That's because Ronnie went purple when he found out that Julie was assigned to a coed dormitory. He certainly wouldn't have allowed it if he'd known in advance, and he didn't want Jolie repeating her older sister's experience.

"We might as well leave her downtown on Broadway!" wailed Ronnie when he and I deposited Julie at the University of Georgia.

My last vision is of leaving Julie standing under a little tree and waving at us with tears streaming down her cheeks. The next thing I know, Ronnie is bawling his eyes out and trying to drive this huge bus.

Back home in Nashville, I decided to attend a sold-out concert at Vanderbilt University by "new wave" pop stylists Cyndi Lauper and the Bangles in the fall of 1984. Cyndi was blessed with a penetrating voice and a delightfully kooky stage presence.

Ever the fan, I went backstage to greet the singer before her show. Cyndi squealed loudly with delight when she saw me walking toward her.

"'Girls Just Want to Have Fun' was written just for you!" chirped Cyndi earnestly. She added that "Let's Jump the Broomstick" was one of her all-time favorite records, and I was her idol.

"Will you sing 'Girls Just Want to Have Fun' with me at the encore? I'd be so honored."

"Gee, I don't know, I came here to listen, not to sing," I replied in surprise. "Besides, your hair is redder than mine," I added with a laugh.

"Ooooh, listen! I've got some pink hair spray. You want some?" Cyndi piped up happily before coaching me with an a cappella rendition of the song's chorus.

"Don't worry, I know the song," I replied. And we two redheads traded verses enthusiastically, prancing all over the stage together before my hometown crowd later that night.

It was usually either at such backstage encounters or at multiartist awards programs and benefit shows that I got to indulge in my incurable fan-worship of other performers. I presented Willie Nelson and Merle Haggard with their Duo of the Year prize at the 1983 Country Music Association Awards Show. At the American Music Awards in 1984, I got to chat backstage with Michael Jackson. I'd always liked the music of the Jackson 5, and I could relate to Michael, because I'd been a child performer, too. Of course, I was still doing the bop, and he'd gone on to the Moonwalk.

"I'm so proud of you!" I exclaimed. "I love where you've taken your music. My daughter Jolie plays *Thriller* at our house from sunup to sundown." She did, too.

"Oh, thank you," Michael said in that soft little voice. "It's so great to see you again. I'm a fan of yours, too, you know." He's so shy—conversations with Michael are few and far between for most of us.

A lot of times, the place to meet other acts was at benefit shows. Country music artists are famed for their tireless charity work. Long before the pop world was singing "We Are the World," country musicians were donating their talents on behalf of prisoners, orphans, disaster victims, social causes and medical problems. When I became a country act, I plunged into the style's unending round of benefits with gusto.

There was no shortage of opportunities. During the Reagan presidential era of the 1980s, the plight of the homeless became a major social concern for the first time since the Great Depression. In 1984, a virulent new disease was identified called AIDS. The American people were made aware of the ravages of world hunger. These and other causes were embraced by the country stars of the day.

My feeling about benefits is that I've been so blessed that it's the least I can do to give something back. I do just about anything that anybody asks me to do, no matter what the cause.

Charlie Daniels and I cohosted the first Country Music Radiothon to benefit the National Kidney Foundation in 1981. When I staged the Brenda Lee Celebrity Auction at the 1984 Fan Fair festival, generous donations by my buddy Barbara Mandrell helped raise thousands of dollars for the YWCA's displaced homemakers program.

I tried to return the favor by participating in the Barbara Mandrell Softball Tournament. This star-studded event raised money for Vanderbilt Children's Hospital.

The party afterward featured a who's who of the sports and entertainment worlds. Dallas Cowboys quarterback Danny White, Rams quarterback Vince Ferragamo, Los Angeles Raider Ray Guy, Chicago Bears star Walter Payton and Philadelphia Eagle Dennis Harrison mingled with music makers. The gala was held on the terrace behind the gracious Southern mansion belonging to BMI music chief Frances Preston.

Dottie West was there; so was her daughter Shelly. Gosh, there were more than a hundred people around that pool. Brooke Shields was taking pictures for her scrapbook. Patrick Duffy, from the TV show *Dallas,* said he couldn't wait to tell his family about all the stars he met. Steve Wariner said he was having a blast. So was I. There were Japanese lanterns and umbrellas and fresh flowers everywhere. Tons of fried chicken, beef tenderloin, fried corn, food to just die for. I remember it was Barbara's wedding anniversary and Gladys Knight's birthday.

I've known Gladys forever; she's such a sweetheart. She had a bad gambling addiction for a while, but she's managed to survive. I love to see her show in Vegas when we're both there. I'm such a fan. So it was a real highlight for me that she and I and

Barbara sang that old Ray Charles song "What'd I Say" as the finale at that softball party.

The charity I'm proudest of is the one that bears my name in Nashville. The Brenda Lee Scholarship Fund, which still exists today, gives money to needy college students who are studying for careers in the music industry. The fund was established by the Nashville chapter of the National Academy of Recording Arts and Sciences (NARAS). The organization, best known for its Grammy Awards, voted to give its prestigious Governors Award to me in the fall of 1984. Monies raised at the black-tie ceremony were earmarked for my scholarship fund.

The Governors Award is reserved for lifetime achievement and is given very seldom. Prior to me, only four Nashville music personalities had been given the honor—Roy Acuff, the King of Country Music; Kitty Wells, the Queen of Country Music; *Billboard* music-trade editor Bill Williams; and NARAS cofounder Wesley Rose.

The Recording Academy dubbed my big night "Tribute to a Legend." At the Vanderbilt Plaza Hotel ballroom, I was so touched and felt so loved by my fellow entertainers and by my music industry friends. Ray Stevens hosted the show, which featured the Oak Ridge Boys, Lee Greenwood and Reba McEntire, as well as me.

The Oaks were hilarious that night. They surprised me by coming out in red, curly Brenda Lee wigs and singing "One in a Million." Mother was there to sit with me. I told the audience about all that she had been through with me and about all the sacrifices she had made. It kinda felt like "This Is Your Life." I was really touched by how many people showed up. The ballroom was bursting at the seams.

"At the NARAS event, I sang 'Broken Trust' to her," recalls songwriter Jimbeau Hinson. "And the Oaks backed me up. I con-

sider that to be one of the highlights of my life. She was lip-synching along to me with tears running down her face."

The night ended with me singing a medley of my songs backed by the members of Music Row's A-Team musicians—Harold Bradley, Buddy Harmon, Bob Moore and Owen Bradley. Oversized screens showed historic TV footage from my long career. I became emotional as telegrams of congratulations poured in from Tony Bennett, Dolly Parton, Liza Minnelli, Kenny Rogers, B. B. King, Jimmy Buffett, John Denver, Carole King, Red Skelton and President Ronald Reagan. Fan club members came from as far away as California, Alaska and England.

"There's no one I can think of who's more fitting to receive this tribute," said MCA Records executive Bruce Hinton. "No one is liked or respected more on a personal or a professional level."

"She has withstood every craze, every fad, every musical variation that the world has known for the past thirty years," added Ray Stevens. "The word 'legend' is bandied about a lot. We're talking about a real one here."

I was so moved by those remarks. I thanked everyone by saying, "Nashville and I sort of grew up together. I was given a song and you listened. I grew up on stage and you applauded. I sang all over the world and you welcomed me home here tonight. And I thank you from the bottom of my heart. Of all the audiences I've ever faced, I think this one gathered here is the one that will be etched in my mind. I've heard shouts of approval from all around the world, but to hear this, where it all began, is the highlight of my career."

SIXTEEN

Legendary Lady

I turned forty on December 11, 1984. For many women, this represents a difficult time in life. And for women in entertainment, the rite of passage is virtually a death sentence.

I had been making hit music for thirty years, a practically unheard-of accomplishment. Most music careers sputter and end after a hit or two. Maybe five. If you're very, very lucky, your career on the charts might last for a decade. Somehow I had managed the impossible. My career was still thriving.

Here's what I always say: I don't mind getting older—there's only one alternative, and I don't prefer the alternative.

Still, once a woman enters her forties, her days at the top of the hit parade are usually numbered. My clock may have been ticking, but I wasn't listening.

For one thing, I still had plenty of work as a live performer. For another, Ronnie's cautious socking away of my earnings had long since made us millionaires. The joke around Nashville is, "Poor Brenda and Ronnie. All their money is tied up in cash."

Yet another reason why I felt secure is that my notoriety overseas continued to mushroom. I toured Holland, Germany, Spain, Switzerland, England and Ireland throughout the mid-'80s.

In 1985, I received my fourth Edison Award, which is the Dutch equivalent of the Grammy. In Germany that year, Bear

Family Records reissued my Italian, German and French language recordings on a special commemorative LP. In England, *The Very Best of Brenda Lee* blasted into the top-10 on the pop charts.

In Spain, I learned that the power of rock 'n' roll was still something to be reckoned with. In Barcelona, a riot broke out during my show. I was billed on a package with Jerry Lee Lewis, the Bellamy Brothers, Conway Twitty, Freddy Fender, Tammy Wynette, Boxcar Willie and Rita Coolidge. Bob Moore was in Jerry Lee's band, and they were at each other's throats constantly. Both of them are volatile personalities, and they've been like that with each other for years. Bob's hands are registered weapons, because he's a karate expert. He could tear Jerry Lee apart, and it looked like he was going to. So the atmosphere backstage was tense already.

Meanwhile, out front, there were these Spanish biker gangs in black leather. And they were drinking, getting mean and ready to rumble. It was a big outdoor amphitheater, and they started to rush the stage when I was on doing my rockabilly set. A fight broke out, but I kept on singing. I didn't know what else to do. They had security guards, but not enough. The beer bottles started to fly, right past our heads on stage. I learned later that one of the guys down in front had been stabbed to death during my show.

That's a modern-day nightmare for an entertainer. You always think about the safety of the audience, especially if it's a huge crowd. Anything can happen when thousands of people are crammed together.

Jerry Lee came on after me to close the show, and the riot kept getting bigger and bigger. It was such a melee, you couldn't tell what was happening. They were yelling out things for Jerry Lee to sing, and he wouldn't sing them. Then he went off and wouldn't do an encore, and that's when they really went nuts.

A police guard took us entertainers down into a room below the stage. We had to huddle there, nervous, for two hours or more. You could hear the stomping and screaming up above, and it didn't look like the security force had it under control at all. But we finally got out of there.

Elsewhere, that tour went well. We played Germany, Switzerland and England, and had a ball. It was like the old days when a lot of acts toured together. We all traveled in a chartered plane, and I really felt like I was a rock star.

When I returned from the '85 European tour, the mayor's office proclaimed me Nashville's Ambassador of Goodwill. A brass band from Maplewood High School greeted me at the airport blaring the well-chosen "She Works Hard for the Money." I was delighted, since that was my alma mater.

At the time, I was back on the charts with another big country hit. George Jones and I were on the airwaves as duet partners on the Ray Charles r&b standard "Hallelujah, I Love You So." The single was drawn from George's album *Ladies Choice,* which featured the legendary honky-tonk stylist singing with Emmylou Harris, Janie Fricke, Barbara Mandrell and Loretta Lynn, as well as me.

In mid-1984, my label MCA Records had been completely restructured. My friends Jim Foglesong and Ron Chancey were ousted. Jim moved to Capitol Records, where he signed Garth Brooks. Ron continued to produce both hit records and ad jingles.

My new label boss was my old rockabilly touring partner Jimmy Bowen. After leaving his performing days behind, Jimmy had drifted to Los Angeles. There, he reinvented himself as a record producer, achieving renown as the man behind such smashes as Frank Sinatra's "Strangers in the Night" and Dean Martin's "Everybody Loves Somebody." He then moved to Nashville to become the head of Warner Bros. Records. There,

Jimmy produced a string of No. 1 hits for the likes of Hank Williams Jr., Crystal Gayle, Gary Morris and Conway Twitty.

That brought him to the attention of MCA, which made him the proverbial offer he couldn't refuse. He joined the label in 1984. In addition to cleaning house of the old executive staff, Jimmy quickly took over the record production of up-and-comers George Strait and Reba McEntire. He also hired Bruce Hinton and Tony Brown, the latter of whom signed Vince Gill, Steve Earle, Patty Loveless and Lyle Lovett, among others. Tony was open to new sounds and fresh production approaches. Jimmy Bowen turned thumbs-down on the LP I had recorded with producer Jerry Crutchfield. But my next musical move met with both Tony and Jimmy's approvals.

I was on a *Nashville Now* TV show with Ralph Emery and sang "Kansas City," and not long after that, I sang it again at songwriter Harlan Howard's birthday bash. Emory Gordy Jr., who produced and later married Patty Loveless, heard me singing on one of those occasions. I was already a fan of his. Emory was a Georgia boy who'd written the classic ballad "Traces," and I'd recorded that back on my *Johnny One Time* LP. He was also in Emmylou Harris's Hot Band, and I'd seen them burning up the stage at concerts. So when Emory asked me if I'd be interested in him producing me, I said "Sure!"

"Brenda and I are the same age," says Emory. "I grew up in Atlanta, and I can remember seeing her on TV Ranch on WAGA. I was only eight years old at the time, and I'll never forget my mother saying, 'You ought to marry that girl.' Isn't that something?"

With the label's enthusiastic backing, production began on my *Feels So Right* LP in the spring of '84. Emory Gordy Jr. chose David Hungate as his coproducer on the collection. David had collected buckets full of Grammy Awards as the bass player in the rock band Toto when the group ruled the pop charts in 1982–83 with "Rosanna," "Africa" and other hits.

David and Emory assembled a stellar cast to back me. Former Memphis guitar guru Reggie Young, Elvis Presley's drummer Larrie Londin, new rockabilly guitar hotshot Richard Bennett and background vocalist Nicolette Larson were among those recruited. Nicolette had been big on the pop hit parade with "Lotta Love" in 1978 and was trying to "go country" at the time she was on my sessions in Nashville.

Everybody involved with that record was just first-rate. Richard Bennett was the bandleader for Neil Diamond and made his mark in the studio with everyone from Steve Earle to Mark Knopfler. Reggie Young remains one of the first-call session musicians in Nashville. The same goes for John Jarvis, one of the keyboardists on the record. Sonny Garrish, who played steel guitar, is now in the Grand Ole Opry staff band.

"Brenda's performances with this talented cast were among the best of her career," recalls Diana Reid Haig, who was then working for MCA. "I went to the recording sessions. Brenda was doing live vocals with the band. Over and over and over, she sang her heart out, with each take only improving on perfection. Perfect pitch, impeccable phrasing, tremendous feeling and such a snap and sparkle to her singing. The session players had stars in their eyes. I did, too. I have been at a lot of recording sessions, but I have never heard anything like that before or since. I don't expect to.

"The resulting LP got a lot of critical acclaim when it was released in 1985. The album captures the full range of Brenda's musical tastes. She rocked on tracks like 'Roll Back the Rug,' beautifully explored the deep emotion of country ballads like 'Loving Arms' and waxed soulful on tunes like the Motown classic 'How Sweet It Is.' "

I recorded "How Sweet It Is" as a tribute to my old acquaintance Marvin Gaye, who'd been shot and killed by his father the previous year. Three singles emerged from the *Feels So Right* sessions. "Why You Been Gone So Long" came from the pen of the gifted Mickey Newbury. Josh Leo and his wife Renee Larose cowrote "Two Hearts." The bluesy rocker "I'm Takin' My Time" was cowritten by Pat Alger.

Pat told me that it was his first song to become a country single. And it's his recollection that I was the first Nashville-based artist to be recorded on digital tape, which was a new technology at that time. Anyway, that song was a start for him in Music City. When he did his own album in 1994, I came to sing with him on his version of "I'm Takin' My Time."

Pat Alger soon rose to prominence as the songwriting partner of superstar Garth Brooks on such multimillion-selling hits as "The Thunder Rolls," "Unanswered Prayers," "What She's Doing Now" and "That Summer." But he always reminds me that I was the one who first gave him a break, on that *Feels So Right* album. It's such a pleasure to me to help aspiring songwriters. In Nashville we always say, "It all begins with a song." Like Jerry Reed, Ronnie Self, Jackie DeShannon, Jimbeau Hinson and so many others, Pat was one of my special discoveries.

"The album's spectacular finale was a relentless, pounding treatment of songwriter Paul Kennerley's soul-rocker 'Feels So Right,'" says Haig. "For nearly five minutes, Brenda shouts, growls and wails while the band churns and chimes behind her. Following a choral build over a drum breakdown, she and guitarist Richard Bennett gleefully trade off licks in an obbligato of joyous frenzy. In my opinion, that performance ranks as one of the greatest rockers of her career."

Maybe so, but it turned out to be my parting shot with MCA. Jimmy Bowen soon began dismissing most of the label's veterans as part of his label housecleaning. In '85, he got rid of Don Williams, Gene Watson, John Conlee and Mel Tillis, followed by Barbara Mandrell and me in '86. Loretta Lynn and the Oak Ridge Boys would exit MCA by the end of the decade.

So much for "old time's sake" between Jimmy and me. And so much for "the house that Brenda built." It didn't matter that Jimmy and I went back so many years. And it didn't matter what I'd done for the label in the past. He told me, "Today's the only thing I care about." Well, at least I went out with a bang.

But as good as the record was, the company never promoted *Feels So Right*. MCA had spent more money producing that record than any other album I'd ever done. And then they just let it lie there and die. I'll never understand that.

I've always felt that Jimmy just didn't care about Brenda Lee as an artist. After thirty years with the company, I left with somewhat of a heavy heart.

In 1988, I sued the label for $20 million in unpaid royalties. My lawyers charged that huge amounts remained missing from overseas sales of my records. A complete and exhaustive audit of the label's books resulted in an out-of-court settlement a year later. A gag order was imposed on both parties.

"For a long time I'd had a disgruntled feeling," explains Ronnie. *"I just had this gut feeling that something wasn't right. We'd find out about records that had been put out overseas that we didn't even know about. So that was why we asked for an accounting.*

"The suit wore Brenda out. She cried and cried about it and lost sleep. I would have kept on, but she begged me to call it off."

I can tell you one thing that lawsuit did. To this day, MCA pays me every penny it owes me in royalties. And the checks come like clockwork.

I want to emphasize that the suit was just "taking care of

business." Even now, I have a wonderful working relationship with MCA Records. We collaborate on reissue projects and catalog development all the time.

Well, here I was without a record company for the first time since age eleven. I got over my initial sadness, dusted myself off and marched on. I'm not a quitter.

I joke that I'm indestructible. I hired on to be tough. I've always worked better under pressure. Label or no label, I had a career to maintain. Things were changing so much, and the youth market was coming in so strong that I didn't even know if I wanted to be on the recording scene or not. I had a full workload of shows to play and things to do, so I thought, "Whatever will be, will be." I was actually a little surprised that I wasn't in the depths of depression, but I wasn't.

Most people are shocked to learn that singers do not make the bulk of their money from hit records. Those are merely the calling cards to get bookings as a live attraction. The road is where the real income in the music biz lies. And I toured without a break.

Well, almost. I did take some time off in 1985 to "get a new paint job."

I don't care who knows about it—I'm not ashamed of it—I had a face-lift. It was kind of a "mini" lift, actually. I had my upper eyelids done and a little tuck at the jawline. If I'd known I was going to like the result so much, I'd have had everything done! My daughters sent flowers to the hospital. The note said, "Let's Face It: You look great." I was surprised at how little the procedure hurt. No wonder it's so popular.

And every woman over the age of forty in show business who says she's never had anything done is lying through her capped teeth. Oh, I'm just kidding. But I do know that an awful lot of female performers have had a nip and a tuck here and there. Just ask Dolly. Both she and I could care less who knows.

I figured if I was going to be competing with people half my age, I'd better start looking the part. I was doing so much TV at the time, and the television camera is so unforgiving. After looking at one of my TV appearances, I decided it was time to go under the knife.

This was a period of increasing television opportunities for me. The rapid expansion of cable television throughout the 1980s meant that more and more programming had to be developed. And for many channels, music was a popular option.

The Nashville-headquartered TNN channel was a natural fit for me. I hosted its flagship talk show, *Nashville Now,* a number of times. And in 1985, the channel tapped me to preside over its most ambitious special ever.

That's the year that Willie Nelson staged the first of his famed Farm-Aid benefit concerts. This multiact show was an outgrowth of the "We Are the World" and Live Aid events to raise money for world hunger. On September 22, 1985, Willie mounted a massive show at the University of Illinois football stadium in Champaign, Illinois. Neil Young, Tom Petty, Billy Joel, Kenny Rogers, Alabama, John Cougar Mellencamp, Waylon Jennings, Arlo Guthrie, Johnny Cash, Roy Orbison, Don Henley, B. B. King, Rickie Lee Jones, John Denver, John Fogerty and dozens of other top stars volunteered to come. The lineup was staggering. More than fifty acts performed.

And while 20 million watched, I dutifully hosted the national TV broadcast for twelve hours on TNN. It was all ad-libbed. I repeatedly urged viewers to send in their pledges, and the telecast raised $10 million for the cause. I was probably one of the few entertainers who could equally appreciate both hard rockers and hillbillies. I kept chatting appreciatively no matter what style was being presented.

Sammy Hagar of Van Halen was jumping around on stage,

and I was telling the viewing audience how much energy he had. But I couldn't hear his performance very clearly. It turned out he was talking dirty. TNN pulled the plug and aired a performance that Merle Haggard had done earlier in the day, so I switched gears and talked about that.

A lot of the artists would come up to the broadcast booth between sets, and I'd interview them on the air. I reminded Bob Dylan about that day he walked off *The Ed Sullivan Show* when we were kids. We had a big laugh about it. Carole King gave me her home phone number, and we've stayed in touch. I remember that the Beach Boys' performance was so explosive that I thought the swaying by the 80,000 people would literally topple the stadium.

I got everyone to autograph my program book. It was really great that the country and rock acts were together. Everyone was a fan of everybody else. All in all, it's one of the most historic musical events I've ever been involved with. God bless Willie Nelson.

Two years later, the Cinemax cable channel invited me to participate in a special titled "Legendary Ladies of Rock 'n' Roll." I didn't hesitate for a moment. I flew to Manhattan to appear on the landmark telecast with the Jefferson Airplane's Grace Slick ("White Rabbit"), Lesley Gore ("It's My Party"), Mary Wells ("My Guy"), Martha Reeves ("Heat Wave"), Freda Payne ("Band of Gold"), Shirley Alston Reeves of the Shirelles ("Will You Still Love Me Tomorrow") and Ronnie Spector of the Ronettes ("Be My Baby"). The taping took place at the Latin Quarter, my old stomping grounds as a supper-club singer.

What was so fun about it was that we were all there together. We had a ball. Grace Slick is quite a piece of work. She's a take-charge type of woman and doesn't take any nonsense from anybody. I loved that about her. Lesley and I practically grew up singing together. Mary Wells died of throat cancer just a few years after that in 1992, so I was really glad I got to work with her again. And I'm such a fan of the work of Martha and Ronnie. I mean, how can you top records like "Dancing in the Street" and "Be My Baby"? They've really stood the test of time.

In talking to those ladies, I learned that many of them had had a tough time dealing with this business as women. Almost all of them had been cheated by their record companies. I realized that I've been a lot luckier than most. Part of it had to do with my being in Nashville, where people like Owen Bradley were interested in the artists as people and not just as products. And part of it had to do with Ronnie looking after our finances so meticulously.

Clarence Clemons of Bruce Springsteen's E Street Band came to the taping to blow sax behind me on "That's All You Gotta Do." Big Clarence had such a good time that he stayed for the whole show. Cohost Belinda Carlisle, famed for the all-female rock band the Go-Go's ("We Got the Beat"), told me I was an inspiration to her.

The entire production had the atmosphere of a party, with audience members dancing and jumping around in the nightclub. Celebrities like Carly Simon and Chubby Checker mingled their cheers with the other fans. The finale began with "Da Doo Ron Ron." Then Martha Reeves fronted the ladies on "Dancing in the Street." I led everyone down into the audience where we formed a conga line behind Clarence Clemons.

I told the crowd, "You're witnessing an event tonight that has never happened before, and probably will never happen again. You are witnessing rock 'n' roll! Do you still love it!?" The roar that came back at me was all the answer I needed.

Belinda Carlisle called it a "once-in-a-lifetime experience." And the final product turned out to have quite a long shelf life.

Three years later, "Legendary Ladies of Rock 'n' Roll" became a highly successful home video.

With my TV profile heightened, I was next tapped as a costar of the PBS special "Shake, Rattle and Roll." Taped in Nashville, the 1988 show teamed me with Jerry Lee Lewis, Chubby Checker, the Drifters, the Coasters, Carl Perkins and other founders of rock 'n' roll.

It was like Old Home Week, a big get-together with all my old buddies. Both Chubby and Carl had been my touring partners. The Coasters and I had done the Brooklyn Paramount together. Jerry Lee and I had worked a bunch together, too. People came to the show dressed in poodle skirts and dungarees. They'd get up and do the bop and pretend it was the '50s all over again.

Nostalgia was a prevailing trend of the '80s. Hundreds of radio stations adopted oldies formats to showcase tunes of the previous three decades. Films of the '70s like *American Graffiti* and *Grease* were even more popular ten years after they originally appeared. I don't know; maybe this was a reaction to an onslaught of new technologies and social trends. Homes now featured microwave ovens, telephone answering machines and videocassette players. Ronnie and I were always the first to get the latest modern gizmos.

Also in the '80s, test-tube babies and heart transplants made medical headlines. In science, there was the 1986 explosion of the space shuttle *Challenger* that killed its astronauts. The big financial news was that a year later came the worst crash in the history of the New York Stock Exchange.

In youth culture, increasingly sophisticated sound systems blasted the new pop music styles of rap, grunge rock and speed metal. As always, I kept my ears tuned to whatever was happening musically.

At a show at the Omni in Atlanta, I became reacquainted

with Paul Simon, then on a roll with his million-selling world music explorations *Graceland* and *Rhythm of the Saints*. We talked about knowing each other way back when and laughed about the fact that we were both still around. I asked him about his old hits.

"I'm still doing them," Paul replied with a chuckle. "But you might not recognize them. I've changed them somewhat." And he had—they were radically different, but still just as great.

In 1987, *Life* magazine called me to Memphis for a photo spread to mark the tenth anniversary of Elvis Presley's death. Among the others who participated were Joan Jett, Robert Plant, Roy Orbison, Billy Joel and the Beastie Boys.

The roadwork continued. Even without new records to promote, I performed constantly as the 1980s wound down. My international concert bookings remained steady, too. But following my twentieth tour of Japan, I decided to take time off from the rigors of constant travel.

I accepted the lead role in a stage production called *Music, Music, Music*. Staged in the Roy Acuff Theater at the Opryland theme park in Nashville, the musical drew sell-out crowds of 1,600 patrons per show, two shows a day, six days a week. I kept up this pace for three seasons in 1988–90. That's something like 1,212 shows, and I'm proud to say I never missed a performance.

The show was like a Broadway revue, spanning music from the '20s to the '90s. We had a sixteen-piece orchestra and a cast of twenty-two singers and dancers. The sets were real elaborate. It opened with a circus with dancers dressed like animals going through the audience. There was a railroad set, a mechanical dragon and a big production number involving a beach party. There was a mechanical Statue of Liberty for the patriotic finale.

I changed clothes seven times in each performance, wearing everything from a hobo outfit to an antebellum gown.

I did tributes to Sophie Tucker, Elvis Presley and Judy Garland. *Music, Music, Music* was a real cornucopia of songs.

One of the reasons I did it was that I hoped to get Broadway producers to come to Nashville to see me. I've always loved doing musical theater. And it's still one of my dreams to star on the Great White Way. A few years later I was offered the lead role in the touring company of *Nunsense*. But that was a show I didn't feel I could fit in. Me as a nun? I don't think so. The cornette would never fit over my hair!

Another reason I wanted to do *Music, Music, Music* was that I could sleep in my own bed every night for a change. And I loved going to perform every day with all these young people in the cast who had stars in their eyes. They'd all gather in my dressing room after the performances, and I'd give them advice, or we'd all just tell jokes and have a ball.

The *Tennessean* praised the production. And it really was a treat to read the very first concert review I ever got in my hometown paper:

During the course of the *Music, Music, Music* revue, enduring superstar Brenda Lee belts out rockers, joyfully swings through show tunes, recreates golden Hollywood moments, performs spine-tingling patriotic numbers, romps through hoedowns and burns through ballads with torchy passion.

There are few . . . artists with as much stylistic range. There are fewer who can match her record sales. And even fewer with the professionalism, stamina and moxie to rip through 16 songs, 15 production numbers and seven costume changes twice a day, six days a week for eight months.

... When they stumble into the air-conditioned Acuff Theater out of the broiling Tennessee sun, most of the Opryland tourists don't know there's an American music legend inside. But by the time they walk out an hour-and-a-half later, they do.

SEVENTEEN

Your One and Only

The Calgary Stampede is a big, huge rodeo-type thing that's famous throughout Canada and the western United States. It's an annual event that draws tens of thousands to the province of Alberta. They book dozens of entertainers to perform during the ten-day festival, so that's what I was doing there in the summer of 1984.

The Stampede's show was a big production with dancers, baton twirlers and anything else you can think of. Some of the kids in the show would go out on the town after we finished our performance. They came back one night and told me there was a girl I'd really like who was playing at one of the local dance halls. I'm not much of a club-goer, but I do love other entertainers, and the kids in my show were so insistent.

So some of my band members and I went over to this big barn of a place. And there on stage was this spiky-haired young gal wearing cutoff cowboy boots, a gypsy-looking prairie skirt, a short rhinestoned jacket and Buddy Holly glasses. I had never seen anything like this woman in my life. She was the epitome of a whirling dervish in her stage movements. The whole persona was kind of kooky, so I didn't expect that kind of a voice to come out of her. But her voice was simply glorious; it was extraordinary. She had a huge range and could leap from one musical style to another so easily. You could tell she was a huge Patsy Cline fan, because she was doing some of Patsy's numbers. But unlike most singers, she didn't try to copy Patsy. She had her own style. She was also singing "Bop-a-Lena," Ronnie Self's old rockabilly hit. In fact, it was her first music video in Canada and the opening track on her debut LP up there.

I was blown away by her energy, her talent and her complete devotion to what she was doing. She had such confidence. That was my first experience of k.d. lang.

I asked if I could go backstage and meet her. Her mother was back there with her. Unlike her stage character, k. d. in person was very quiet and reserved, I thought. But she couldn't have been nicer and seemed thrilled to meet me. And she immediately began to ask me about Owen Bradley. She was a huge fan of Owen's because of his work with Patsy Cline. I told her that he had semiretired, but that he was doing some special projects.

"Do you think there's a chance that he would produce me?" asked k.d. earnestly.

"I don't see why not," I replied. "Owen loves talented people, and he's always up for a new challenge. Give me your name and telephone number, and I'll take it back to him and tell him how great I think you are."

At the time, k.d. lang had only a locally produced Canadian LP. But in 1986, she was signed by Warner Bros. Records, and the following year she showcased her debut U.S. collection for the label at Nashville's Exit/In nightclub. The singer continued to pursue Owen Bradley, enlisting him to produce her Nashville Sound homage album, *Shadowland,* later that year.

The next thing I know, Owen is on the phone asking me if I want to be a part of k.d.'s record. It was a medley they were putting together called "Honky Tonk Angels," and the cast was going to be comprised of "Owen's girls," Loretta Lynn, Kitty Wells, k.d. lang and me. I said, "Great!" Any chance to work with Owen was something I jumped at. Plus, to sing with somebody who I was convinced was going to be a superstar sounded like a lot of fun. I was, and am, a great admirer of k.d.'s talent.

The young Canadian admitted to being intimidated by the prospect of singing with Kitty and Loretta and me: "Of course I was nervous," k.d. recounted in the *Shadowland* press kit. "I'd listened to these girls my whole life, and so much of what I love about country music is wrapped up in their voices. But they made it easy and, to tell you the truth, just being in the studio with them gave me a feeling of being loved and accepted.

". . . Thank you, Brenda, Kitty and Loretta for embracing this young upstart with gentle and loving arms."

I was just as thrilled to be singing with her. When you've been around awhile like I have, you pick up on that special quality that separates the best from the rest. k.d. is one of the best.

The recording session was a breeze. I'd already met k.d., so we renewed our friendship. We had a few drinks and said hello for an hour, cut the record in an hour and listened back, laughed, chatted and listened again for another hour. Owen said, "That's the union way of making a record for three hours." It felt like the old days to me.

"Honky Tonk Angels Medley" became a much-aired music video. It also netted k.d., Loretta, Kitty and me a Grammy Award nomination. It was my fourth chance to earn the music world's highest honor. But our collaboration lost out to the highly publicized electronic "duet" between Hank Williams Jr. and his late father, my childhood musical idol. "Owen's girls" did get the opportunity to perform our historic quartet on the nationally telecast Country Music Association Awards show of 1988.

It turned out that the collaboration with k.d. lang also led to renewed interest in my recording career. I hadn't been in the studio as a solo since being dropped by MCA in 1986. Warner Bros.

Records executive Carl Scott told me that he thought it was a shame that a still vibrant vocalist was going to waste without a recording outlet. He took me under his wing.

Carl was on the West Coast in the pop division, so that made me happy. He's an old hippie who knew my music. I wasn't sure Nashville knew what to do with me, and I hoped he would. He came to see me after k.d.'s album was finished and asked me if I'd be interested in recording an album for Warner Bros.

To be perfectly honest, I had to think about it. I didn't know if I wanted to be back in that competitive popularity war or not. I didn't want to record just for the sake of recording. I wanted a company that would take an interest in me as I was, and that wouldn't try to make me into something I wasn't. But I decided that I really did miss being in the recording studio, so I said yes.

Carl suggested a makeover, some changes in wardrobe and hair. I said, "I'll not only lose the bouffant, I'll shave my head if you need me to."

You have to understand, I haven't slept in forty years because I've been maintaining this "do." My daughters say I look like I'm in my coffin when I'm in bed. So I don't muss my hair, I sleep on my back with a little pillow at the nape of my neck. Like a mummy. I never move in the night. It comes from years of practice. It drives Ronnie crazy. Julie and Jolie are always pestering me to get rid of the bouffant. At one point I did, and all I got was letters from the fans saying how much they hated my getting rid of it. To them, the bouffant is a part of me, and they expect to see it every time I'm in public.

I told my daughters, "I'll have you both know that my bouffant was chosen by *Vogue* magazine as the icon of the '60s in its 'History of Hair' article in 1990." I was in good company, too— Priscilla Presley's cascading beehive, Cher's Mohawk, Farrah Fawcett's long shag, Nancy Reagan's bubble, Twiggy's pixie

cut, the Rolling Stones' mops and Clarence Williams's Afro on
The Mod Squad were the other icons. So there.

At any rate, Warner Bros. flew me out to L.A. and restyled
me. I went blonde after years of being a redhead. I lost a bunch of
weight so I could get into their new slinky gowns. They re-
vamped my makeup to go with the softer hairstyle. I liked most
of the changes, and I've kept the blonde hair.

My first recording for Warner Bros. Records was "You're in
the Doghouse Now," which appeared on the soundtrack album
for the 1990 Warren Beatty/Madonna film *Dick Tracy*. This was
one of many movie tie-ins for me during this decade. Just as had
been the case in the 1980s, Hollywood turned to my sound time
and again in the 1990s.

I have to thank John Smith, a past president of my fan club.
He's the one who compiled all the information for me about the
films that have included my songs on their soundtracks. And
didn't I have a ball renting these and listening for my tunes?

In 1990, the same year as *Dick Tracy*, the blockbuster *Home
Alone* featured "Rockin' around the Christmas Tree." "I'm
Sorry" was used throughout the decade, appearing on the sound-
track of the Robin Williams film *The Fisher King* (1991), in *This
Boy's Life* (1993) starring Robert De Niro and Leonardo Di-
Caprio, in *Casino* (1995) also starring De Niro, in the Chris Far-
ley/David Spade/Dan Aykroyd comedy *Tommy Boy* (1995) and
in the Vietnam war saga *A Bright Shining Lie* (1998).

Other Brenda Lee classics were on screen as well. The 1996
Steve Buscemi drama *Trees Lounge* featured "Break It to Me
Gently." In 2000, Ben Affleck's suspense-filled *Reindeer Games*
incorporated "Rockin' around the Christmas Tree" into its soundtrack. The gothic drama *The Locusts* (1998) opens with "Sweet
Nothin's," features "As Usual" in a key coming-of-age scene
with Ashley Judd and employs me as an icon of the '60s in its di-

alogue. "Do you think I look like Brenda Lee?" asks a Tastee Freeze waitress. "Everybody says so."

My name was also bandied about in *Throw Momma from the Train* (1987). In that black comedy, Billy Crystal is teaching a creative writing class to a group of losers including Danny DeVito. The magnum opus of one of the students is *100 Girls I'd Like to Pork*. It begins, "Chapter One: Kathleen Turner; Chapter Two: Cybill Shepherd; Chapter Three: Suzanne Pleshette." "How about Brenda Lee?" asks a helpful classmate. "Do you like Brenda Lee?"

That's so hilarious. But that's not the worst of it. This one takes the cake: There's a German movie called *Killer Kondom* that has me singing "I'm Sorry" on its soundtrack.

At first, I was disappointed when Boy George got to sing my song "The Crying Game" in the movie with that title instead of me—that is until I found out that it was about a terrorist. Maybe that one was for the best.

On TV, the off-center *Northern Exposure* used "As Usual," "Emotions" and "A Little Unfair" on various soundtracks during its run in the '90s. *Sabrina the Teenage Witch* showcased "Rockin' around the Christmas Tree."

That's probably my most famous song now. And I guess that's why Ronnie suggested to Warner Bros. Records that I record a second Christmas album. The one I'd recorded for Decca back in 1964 was still selling, so it seemed like a good idea.

The Warner executives agreed. But first they put me in the studio with Nashville producers Jim Ed Norman and Eric Prestidge to create my debut album for the label, the simply titled *Brenda Lee*. In 1991, it became my first release on compact disc.

The album included "A Little Unfair," which is the number they used on *Northern Exposure*. The best song on the album is "Your One and Only." Dolly Parton's producer Steve Buckingham worked on that one, and it's the track they chose for the first single.

The crackling country-rocker "Your One and Only" got a moderate amount of airplay, as did the yearning follow-up ballad single "A Little Unfair." But most of the production on the *Brenda Lee* CD had neither the blue-velvet shades of Owen Bradley's arrangements nor the fiery red energy of Ron Chancey's style. Instead, I felt like I was surrounded by bland beige. The Warner Bros. album climbed only to a lackluster No. 67 on the country album charts. Meanwhile, my old label, MCA, made hay with its *Brenda Lee Anthology* package of forty earlier hits (country as well as pop) and reissued 1973's *The Brenda Lee Story* on CD. Maybe my giant catalog of oldies worked against the Warner comeback record.

I really wanted my Warner Bros. album to be handled by the L.A. office. After all, that's who signed me. But that didn't turn out to be. I was forty-five when I recorded that album, and I was realistic enough to know that the business belonged to younger people. Still, it would have been nice if all the promises that were made up front had been kept.

Being forty-five years old wasn't a plus in an increasingly youth-oriented marketplace. But you know what? Other women have overcome the obstacle, as illustrated by the comebacks of Cher at age fifty-three and Tina Turner at age forty-six. In country, K.T. Oslin didn't have her first hit until age forty-five. But with me, the issue went deeper. Because I'd started out so young, the public perception was that I was sixty-five or more. I battle that to this day.

Another factor was that the early '90s was a time of intense turnover in country music. A stampede of cowboy-hatted hunks in tight jeans with rodeo belt buckles mowed down an entire generation of established stars. Even icons like Dolly Parton, George Jones, Merle Haggard, Tammy Wynette and Johnny Cash lost their status as chart regulars. The country genre took aim at the vast youth marketplace and hit a bull's-eye when annual sales quadrupled between 1989 and 1995—from $500 million to $2 billion.

But this explosive growth came at the expense of country's female performers, as well as its veteran stars. In the early '90s, country was overwhelmingly male-dominated—Garth Brooks, Alan Jackson, George Strait, Vince Gill, Brooks & Dunn, Billy Ray Cyrus, Clint Black, Tim McGraw and their peers ruled the hit parade. Women's share of the charts fell to its lowest percentage since the heyday of Patsy Cline. It was not until the advent of performers such as Shania Twain, Faith Hill, the Dixie Chicks and their contemporaries in the late '90s that country became female-driven.

So it wasn't just that I was forty-five. It was that I was wrongly perceived to be much older. It was that I was lumped with a generation of acts that were being exiled from the charts. And the final card in the deck stacked against me was that I was attempting a comeback at a time when female country acts were in eclipse.

In hindsight, it was foolish of me to even hope that I could prevail in the climate of that time. I was under the misconception that the record business was as it used to be, that great songs and a great performance would carry you through. It wasn't. The business is almost completely driven by marketing and promotion staffs. Music seems to be the last thing on their minds. And heaven knows I wasn't the sex symbol or the beauty queen. I never had been. I wasn't marketable, apparently.

Despite country radio's indifference, Carl Scott and Warner Bros. kept trying. Due to the flurry of media surrounding the new album and to Carl's lobbying in New York, I won a nomination to the Rock 'n' Roll Hall of Fame in 1991.

That was overwhelming. I always felt that I was one of the

women who helped lay the foundation for rock 'n' roll. But I'd always been overlooked by the Hall. At the time, people were commenting about women being excluded from the Hall of Fame, so I didn't think I had a chance. It turned out I was right. Even today, there are only a handful of solo women in there. And if you take out the r&b female stars there are even fewer—Dusty Springfield, Carole King, Joni Mitchell, Janis Joplin—and I've cheered for every one of them.

I was nominated again in 2000 and 2001, so I guess they're still thinking of me. I don't want to sound bitter. I'm truly not. I really do respect the Hall, and I want to be in there one day. I've made it into England's version of the Rock 'n' Roll Hall of Fame and into the Rockabilly Hall of Fame. So maybe someday I'll get to go to the Big Show.

Carl Scott also engineered a major performance coup for me in 1991. He arranged for me to be a showcase artist at the prestigious Montreux Jazz Festival in Switzerland. This annual extravaganza is one of the premier events on the international music calendar. The year I was chosen to perform, Montreux also featured such greats as Ray Charles, Anita Baker, Miles Davis, Tori Amos, Elvis Costello, George Clinton, Roberta Flack, Ice-T, Al Jarreau, David Sanborn and the Texas Tornados.

I was introduced at the evening show by legendary producer Quincy Jones. The multiple Grammy winner had been behind the control board for Michael Jackson's phenomenally successful *Thriller,* among many other discs.

Said Quincy, "When I was making records with Lesley Gore, we always used to wonder if they were good enough to come out next to this lady's, Miss Brenda Lee." I was a nervous wreck.

"I've watched the videotape of that performance," says Mary Bufwack. "Brenda's rockers simply sizzled. The ballads were as torchy as I've ever heard them performed. One minute it

*was rough r&b and the next smooth jazz. All in all, it's a stunning
set, proof that she was still an amazing singer.*

*"By the time Brenda finished, the audience was in a frenzy.
It's clear that her European fans were still in thrall of Little Miss
Dynamite. After repeated ovations, Brenda returned to encore
with John Fogerty's appropriate 'Rockin' All Over the World.'
The audience still wouldn't let her go. For a second encore, she
shouted 'Kansas City!' to the band, and at its conclusion, the
crowd clapped and cheered for five more minutes."*

I was completely unprepared for that reception. The band and
I hadn't even rehearsed enough encores. I'd been so worried
about sharing a stage with all those superstars and in front of that
sophisticated musical audience. But after that show, I stayed on
an emotional high for weeks. It was just breathtaking.

Back in the States, pushing ahead, Warner issued *A Brenda
Lee Christmas: In the New Old-Fashioned Way* in late '91. The
holiday collection contained new versions of "Silver Bells,"
"Santa Claus Is Coming to Town" and "Rockin' around the
Christmas Tree," all of which were on my earlier Yule disc. The
rest of the new collection was composed of standards. I think the
black spiritual "Go Tell It on the Mountain" and my reworking of
Judy Garland's "Have Yourself a Merry Little Christmas" are
particular highlights.

As part of my reemergence, I agreed to perform with a
Nashville orchestra at the massive 1991 downtown arts festival
Summer Lights. My appearance capped a four-day cornucopia of
music that showcased more than 125 performers, including Bill
Monroe, Emmylou Harris, Take 6, Bobby Jones, the Fairfield
Four and Lyle Lovett. The organizers told me that my perfor-
mance was the most attended of the festival.

I usually make it a point to never perform in Nashville.
You're just never as "new" as you are somewhere else. Your

hometown can sometimes take you for granted. After all, they see you at the grocery store. I am pretty high-profile with charity work and public appearances for music industry functions. However, I seldom do concerts in town. But since I'd done the three seasons at Opryland for our visitors, I thought I should do a show for the natives, too.

I was nervous. I remember thinking, "Oh please, let there be people there." I was worried that no one would show up. It turned out that the Legislative Plaza was so packed you could hardly breathe. It was a hot evening, but it was beautiful. And the hometown applause was even more beautiful. It's nice to be so appreciated where you live.

Getting me to sing in Nashville would ordinarily be a tough sell. But there was one man I would never deny. In 1994, the Recording Academy selected pioneering producers Owen Bradley and Chet Atkins as the co-recipients of its Governors Award. Would I sing for Owen? You bet. Furthermore, would I talk the publicity-shy pair into participating in the gala?

Everybody was afraid to ask Owen and Chet if they'd agree to be honored. Neither one of them liked "blowing their own horn" or seeking publicity. Various organizations had been asking to honor them for years, and both had always turned them down. So the Recording Academy begged me to make the request. I called Owen and explained the whole idea to him. He said that if Chet would do it, he would do it. Then I called Chet and gave him the same speech. He said he'd do it if Owen would do it.

I said, "Done!" And fooled them both into it.

I also recruited Kitty Wells and Loretta Lynn to participate. And as the icing on the cake, I called my old buddy k. d. lang. So the "Honky Tonk Angels" reunited as "Owen's girls" one more time.

The evening was the first Nashville event to raise money for

MusiCares. The gala netted more than $200,000 for the Recording Academy's human resources, health and welfare arm. MusiCares offers assistance to people who've given their lives to music but who find themselves in financial straits due to catastrophic illness, substance abuse problems or other difficulties. Unfortunately, that's a lot of people. The music business can be very cold. And it doesn't honor its elders. I was proud to be there to help.

Owen loved that night. And I think it's the best thing I've ever done as an organizer. Whenever I was asked, I wouldn't hesitate to pay homage to the man who'd meant so much to me. In 1997, the organizers of the Nashville Music Awards show asked me to present Owen with its Heritage Award. The final "honor" came just a year later. In early 1998, Owen's son, producer/publisher Jerry Bradley, called Ronnie. Owen was dead at age eighty-two. Jerry told Ronnie that one of his father's last requests was that I sing "Peace in the Valley" at his funeral.

I had spent a lot of quality time with Owen during the last years of his life. I got this idea that I'd like to own my catalog of hits. The only way I could do that was to rerecord them. And who better to do them than the original producer and the original players? Plus, it gave me an excuse to spend time with Owen. I loved him so much. We spent months working on the project. We could have done it quicker, but I was having so much fun just being with him again. I didn't want it to ever end. I wanted us to just be there together always in that studio. And I think I knew that this would be the last time. So I strung it out as long as I could. And I should point out that Owen was as much of a genius producer at age eighty as he had been thirty years before.

Even when I was on the road, I talked to Owen a lot on the phone. When I got back around Christmastime that year, I found out that he was sick. It didn't dawn on me that there was anything terribly wrong, because everyone thought he just had the flu or something. So I didn't want to bother him with a visit. When Ronnie told me that Owen had died, I was just devastated. I cried like a baby for days. One of my great regrets is that I never got to say goodbye.

Singing at his funeral was one of the hardest things I've ever had to do. I could barely get through it for crying. I wanted it to be so good for him, so I made myself as strong as I possibly could and did my best. It was the last thing I could do for him—he had done so much for me. It was like a dream. I can't even remember singing the song. Later, people told me it was beautiful, but I honestly can't recall.

A who's who of the Nashville entertainment world gathered in the Ryman Auditorium to pay last respects to Music Row's founder. I was trembling as I began to sing for Vince Gill, Charley Pride, Eddy Arnold, Mandy Barnett, Ray Stevens, Ricky Skaggs, Bill Anderson, Ralph Emery, Loretta Lynn, Frances Preston and 2,000 other Nashville music industry personalities. They all knew my heart was breaking, and that's what made the performance all the more poignant.

One by one, it seemed as though "the founders" were passing on during these years. Roy Orbison was felled by a heart attack in 1988. Tennessee Ernie Ford, who'd featured me as a child on his national TV show, died of liver failure in 1991. Roger Miller died of cancer a year later. Conway Twitty, a fellow *American Bandstand* alumnus, died of a stomach aneurysm in 1993. The Grand Ole Opry's Minnie Pearl, one of my first big boosters, died in 1996. Floyd Cramer, the "Last Date" pianist who'd been a key player in Music Row's A-Team on my records, followed in 1997. Carl Perkins, who'd spent so much time on the road with me in the rockabilly days, died twelve days after Owen Bradley in 1998.

Throughout the early months of '98, I substituted for Tammy Wynette at show dates when the country queen was too ill to perform. Tammy's name was another added to the obituary list that year. Buddy Knox, my "Party Doll" rockabilly touring partner, died in 1999. Then, without warning, came the passing of Shel Silverstein, the songwriter who'd given my country career such a boost with "Big Four Poster Bed" and "Wrong Ideas." Shel died of a heart attack at his home in Key West, Florida, at age sixty-six in the spring of 1999.

That one took me completely by surprise. I had just spoken with Shel a few weeks before that, and he was fine. I'm not the only one who misses Shel Silverstein. When you think about him writing "A Boy Named Sue" for Johnny Cash, "One's on the Way" for Loretta Lynn, "Cover of the Rolling Stone" and "Sylvia's Mother" for Dr. Hook, "Queen of the Silver Dollar" for Emmylou Harris and Dave & Sugar, plus songs for Bobby Bare, Waylon Jennings, Jerry Reed and Mel Tillis, he left an awful big hole when he left us.

I know one thing, his children's books will live forever. Shel had just autographed copies of his latest book, *Falling Up,* for my daughters. We also have copies of *Where the Sidewalk Ends* and *The Giving Tree,* and they're among my family's most treasured possessions. I still think about him to this day.

The most personal loss of all, however, was the death of Ronnie's father, Earl Shacklett, in the summer of 1995. The legendary Nashville councilman was being treated for arthritis throughout the early '90s. Then doctors suddenly discovered that he was suffering from bone cancer. Two weeks later he was dead.

"I've never gotten over it," says Ronnie. "I think I've been depressed ever since. Maybe we were too close. My dad was the role model for my life and the rock of our family. No matter what was going on in my life, I could go to him and talk. He was like my shrink. He was more of a listener than anything else. If I was having trouble with anything in the music business I could go

next door, and he would listen. Then he'd say, 'You know right from wrong. Do what you think is right.' And that was all I needed to hear."

"Work hard; tell the truth; pay your bills," "Pop" Shacklett would say. "And if you do that long enough, people will respect you." That was the motto that Ronnie used to manage my career. And Earl Shacklett's memory has still never left him.

Dub Allbritten had died. Charlie Mosley had died. Ronnie had depended on them for advice as father figures. And now his most trusted advisor was gone, too. He's never been the same since then. His personality changed and became gloomier. To this day, you can't get into a discussion with Ronnie about his dad without him crying.

The Nashville that Earl Shacklett knew had all but faded away by the time of his death. The old Southern families who'd controlled the town for generations were no longer in charge. The city even elected a Northerner as its mayor, and under his regime Nashville became the home of the professional football team the Tennessee Titans and the professional ice hockey team the Nashville Predators. Downtown, an art museum, an arena, a central library and a convention center became new civic monuments. Factories for Saturn cars, Bridgestone tires and Dell computers now loom where farms once stood on the outskirts of town. And those outskirts are pushing steadily outward—Ronnie's liquor store on Nolensville Road used to be on the farthest edge of development. Now it is surrounded by bustling strip malls and apartment complexes.

By 1996, Nashville's population had tripled from the size it was when I recorded "I'm Sorry" in 1960. And its music business had ballooned even more dramatically. There were two recording studios when I arrived. Now there were more than a hundred. There were five major record labels back then and more than five

times that many by 1998. On Music Row, office buildings have
replaced many of the old homes that used to contain the music industry's booking agencies, publishing companies and management firms.

Attracted by the glamour of show business, tourists poured
into Nashville in the 1970s and 1980s. By the 1990s, more than 7
million visitors a year were beefing up Music City's economy. In
May 2001, Charley Pride, Kitty Wells and I cut the ribbon at the
grand opening of a massive new Country Music Hall of Fame
downtown. That awesome building is truly a testament to the
power of tourism in Nashville.

♪

The economic boom that tourism represented to Nashville did not
go unnoticed by other communities. With its cross-generational
appeal and family orientation, country music was clearly a
tourism winner. Dolly Parton, Louise Mandrell, Lee Greenwood,
T. G. Sheppard and other stars built attractions in the Smoky
Mountains of East Tennessee. That made the town of Pigeon
Forge a country music lover's mecca. The country band Alabama
led a similar trend to turn Myrtle Beach, South Carolina, into a
country tourism capital.

But no town was more aggressive in reaching for country's
tourism dollar than Branson, Missouri. Located just south of
Springfield in the Ozark Mountains, Branson already had lakes
and scenery in its favor. But the city wanted more than campers
and recreation seekers. Two groups of locals began staging
nightly country shows for visitors there in the 1960s. They were
joined by five other acts during the following decade. In 1983,
Roy Clark became the first national country star to open his own
theater in the town. By the 1990s, he'd been joined by Mickey
Gilley, Boxcar Willie, Glen Campbell, Moe Bandy, Ray Stevens

and others. In 1992, there were twenty-nine country music theaters on the Branson strip, leading to its billing as "The Las Vegas of Country Music."

One of the main theaters there belongs to Mel Tillis, one of my oldest friends. Mel called me in 1996 and asked if I would be interested in coming up to the Ozarks to be co-billed with him for the '97 season. I had played Branson since the early 1980s, but only a day here and a day there. Never for any length of time. So I had no idea what I was getting into.

Mel basically made me an offer I couldn't refuse, so we packed our bags and moved to Branson. It seemed kind of fitting to go, since it was taking me full circle, back to the Ozarks, back toward Springfield, Missouri, the site of the old *Ozark Jubilee*, where I'd first become noticed nationally. I got a friend to house-sit in Nashville, left our office staff intact and rented a condo behind the Grand Palace on the Branson strip.

It was exciting at first, because it was like a new adventure. The countryside up there is beautiful. And I felt like I was setting up housekeeping in a new house. And for the first time in my life there was no housekeeper, no cook, no one to look after us but me. It was the first time that Ronnie and I were living alone together since we were newlyweds, and that was great. By this time, of course, I'd learned to cook. But what I had never done was laundry. I discovered the Downy Ball, and I loved it! I washed every day. Ronnie had to explain to me that you were supposed to wait until you had a load of laundry to do before you washed. I was doing an article of clothing at a time.

Everything was pretty much fun and games until it hit me that I was going to be doing 378 shows—two shows a day, six days a week. I thought, "What have I got myself into?" Even *Music, Music, Music* at Opryland wasn't that grueling. In Branson, you literally live at the theater. You only go home to sleep at night.

Mel didn't spend much time with the fans, but I did. I autographed after every show. The fans would say the funniest things. One lady demanded to know when my publicity photo had been taken. When Ronnie told her it was brand new she snarled, "Yeah, I'll bet!" One couple got into an argument at the box office. The husband swore I was dead, and the wife argued that I wasn't. I don't know what they thought they were buying tickets for if I was in the ground. The audience was often composed of retirees on bus tours. Some of the older people would just steal the albums from the concession stand, and Ronnie didn't have the heart to stop them.

One benefit of the whole experience was that I knew I had to get in shape in order to survive the show schedule. I was on that treadmill every single day.

In the middle of all this came a call from Nashville in the summer of 1997. It was Ed Benson, the executive director of the Country Music Association.

"Brenda, I just wanted to tell you that you are going into the Country Music Hall of Fame," said Ed. "Congratulations!"

"Is this a joke?" I asked. "Are you truly serious?"

And then I started crying. Ronnie was right there beside me, and he started whooping and hollering.

Then my heart sank. I thought, "Oh my gosh, I'm booked here in Branson. I can't even go to Nashville to be inducted."

Ronnie laughed at me. He said, "Are you kidding? You're going! Just tell Mel you're not going to be at work that day." I said, "I can do that?" It's crazy the things you think about. Mel was so happy for me. He said, "Don't be silly. Take the day off and go. This doesn't happen but once in your life." So on the day of the CMA Awards, Tennessee's governor, Don Sundquist, sent a private plane to Missouri and flew me to the show.

The big night of my induction was on September 23, 1997. I

arrived at the Opry House and was immediately consumed with media interviews. Backstage at the national TV broadcast, super-stars were milling around and production people were scurrying. The show was running late. Director Walter Miller approached me in the wings as Mindy McCready, Lorrie Morgan and Michael Peterson sang a medley of my hits.

Walter told me the show was running long, and that I was to keep my acceptance speech short. I didn't answer him, but I thought, "Baby, I'm sayin' what I'm sayin' when I get out there. It's live TV, and there's nothin' you can do about it."

As it turned out, I was so moved when I got out there that I forgot I had my acceptance speech in my hand. I just started talk-ing. I thanked Red Foley, Dub Allbritten, Owen Bradley, my mother, Ronnie, my family and others who had helped along the way. Then I addressed the millions who were watching:

"God gave me a voice, and my audience gave me a career. And for that I am eternally grateful. All of you have given me the greatest gift of all. I thank you from the bottom of my heart. And I love you for letting me sing."

Owen Bradley, then only three months away from death, was watching at home. "Now all my girls are in there," he wept softly to me on the phone after the telecast. Patsy Cline, Kitty Wells and Loretta Lynn had all preceded me into the Country Music Hall of Fame, as had Owen himself.

I never thought my accomplishments in country music meas-ured up to theirs. In fact, until they inducted me, I didn't realize I'd had as big a country career as I actually have had. One of the best things about it is that it opened the door for other rockabilly artists to be recognized by the Hall. The next year, Elvis was voted in. The year after that they admitted Conway Twitty. The Everly Brothers got their due in 2001.

I'm still overwhelmed by that honor to this day. When people come to visit me in Nashville and ask to go see my plaque in the Hall of Fame, it still takes me a minute for it to register. I'd never even been nominated before the year they inducted me. I've never won a CMA Award. I never guessed that the industry thought that highly of me.

The rock star Sting was sitting in the audience that night, right in front of me. Upon meeting me, he bowed to the floor and exclaimed, "I love you, Brenda Lee." I must have talked to a hundred artists that night. Everybody was just so loving.

When the show was over and the dust had settled, I went back out to the airport, got on the plane and went right back to Branson. The next day, I was back on stage doing my two shows a day, six days a week.

The only major Brenda Lee record release during the late '90s was a lavish boxed set issued in Germany of every note I recorded between 1956 and 1962. Spanning four CDs and incorporating a full-color hardback oversized book, this is the most exhaustive overview of my music to date. It is titled, of course, *Little Miss Dynamite*.

For the Branson fans, I recorded my first gospel collection in 1997. Ever since my youth as an admirer of Mahalia Jackson, I had yearned to record the songs I sang as a child in Georgia. Now that I had no major label to tell me I couldn't, I did. The *Precious Memories* CD includes such standards as "Just a Closer Walk with Thee" and "In the Garden."

The other item that Ronnie dutifully sold at the Branson concession stand was *Brenda's Cookbook: Hits from the Kitchen*. I compiled it with the help of my daughters Julie and Jolie, my mother, my mother-in-law Helen Shacklett, my housekeeper Annie Esmond, my sister-in-law Pat Shacklett and family friends.

It's kind of ironic, considering what a terrible cook I was in the early days. But I have improved a lot since then. I'm still no gourmet, but that's not the kind of recipes these are. This is just good, healthy Southern fare and how to prepare it. And unlike me, both of my girls are excellent chefs.

Julie married her childhood sweetheart. They made me a grandma, "Meemaw," in 1988 with their daughter Taylor. Julie published *The Stars That Shine* as her first book in 2000. It's a neat inspirational series of stories about country singers and their humble beginnings that's designed for young readers. She lives just a few miles from me in Nashville.

Jolie went to Southern Methodist University, remained in Dallas after her graduation and later married. She works for the state's criminal justice division there. Jolie made me a grandma again in 1996 when her daughter Jordan was born—on the same day that Taylor was born eight years earlier.

Both of my granddaughters are born hams. I incorporated Jolie's baby Jordan into my Christmas show in Branson. As a child, Julie's daughter Taylor became enthralled with the music of Britney Spears and other teen-pop divas. She would bounce around the house, singing their songs by heart at age ten.

Looking at Britney and her peers, it looks to me like pop music history is repeating itself. My successors as teen stars of the '70s included Marie Osmond and Tanya Tucker. In the '80s, it was Tiffany and Debbie Gibson. In the late '90s, teen sensations were everywhere. The latest incarnations of "the little girl with the great big voice" were Britney, Christina Aguilera, Brandy and Jessica Simpson.

Even more surprising was the wholesale embrace of teen girls by the country music industry. The field was always previously noted for its adult topics and audience. But the youthful Alecia Elliott, Amanda Wilkinson, Lila McCann, Jessica Andrews and, especially, LeAnn Rimes were changing the face of Nashville.

I wish I could take them all aside and tell them what's in

store. Bless their hearts, they're going to go through even more stuff than I did. The business demands so much more of you today. The industry works them even harder than I was worked and with no thought of having any longevity. My heart goes out to them, especially to the ones who were truly born to sing and who truly love this business. They won't be as protected as I was. And, like me, they'll have to grow up awfully fast.

Many of them have sought my advice. Alecia Elliott met me and quizzed me at length when we were both booked for Don Sundquist's inauguration as Tennessee's governor. Jessica Andrews took me to lunch and picked my brain. I was booked in concert alongside the precocious LeAnn Rimes when the youngster exploded on the charts with her breakthrough hit, "Blue." I recall that LeAnn was so overworked at the time that she was practically in tears when we chatted between shows. I've been there, so I knew exactly how she felt.

Thanks to steady exposure on television, if not on the charts, I think I became familiar to many of the singing youngsters. The outlines of my saga aired in a TNN special titled "The Life and Times of Brenda Lee." Following its premiere in 1996, I hear that it became the highest rated biography the cable channel has ever aired. Thus, it was retelecast throughout the remainder of the decade.

The prominence of cable television was one of many characteristics of the 1990s. This was never more evident than in 1991 when millions were glued to CNN's twenty-four-hour, live coverage of the Persian Gulf War. When O. J. Simpson went on trial for murder in 1994, people watched cable's coverage even while at work. Heck, I was one of them. In 1995, the nation was horrified by the bombing of the federal building in Oklahoma City. The death of Britain's Princess Diana caused another outpouring of media attention in 1997.

An information explosion occurred. By mid-decade, millions of Americans were "wired" as the Internet came into their homes. Sales of computers, cell phones and electronic organizers multiplied astronomically. The U.S. economy boomed. Naturally, Ronnie and I did our part—I've already gone through six cell phones.

At the movies, *Titanic* became the highest grossing movie of all time in 1997. As the decade closed, Latin music enjoyed an upsurge in popularity, reflecting a shift in the nation's population makeup. The '90s were the '60s turned upside down in fashion as mood rings, lava lamps and miniskirts were revived.

Don't think for a minute that I'm a relic of the '60s. I'm up to date. I've got my computer. Ronnie and I always rush to get the latest electronics. I bought a DVD player right when they came out. I email my friends. I've had my own web site for years—www.brendalee.com.

The site stays busy with updates of my awards and honors. "I'm Sorry" was inducted into the Grammy Hall of Fame in 1999. In 2001, the song was selected by the National Endowment for the Arts and the Recording Industry Association of America as one of the 365 Songs of the Century. The Rockabilly Foundation announced me as its Lifetime Achievement winner in 2001. And production began that year on a Biography special devoted to my career on the A&E cable channel.

In 2001, I went back to the recording studio on a lark. Jimmy Sturr, the multiple Grammy Award–winning polka music king, called me in Nashville with an unusual request. Would I be interested in being the guest vocalist on his next polka recording?

Well, why not? I'm free to do whatever I want. And polka was something I definitely hadn't done in my career. I'd never met Jimmy, but everyone said what a nice guy he was. And it turned out to be true. He wanted me to sing the old Teresa Brewer hit "Ricochet Romance," which I already knew. Once I got into the studio with him, it went so well that we decided to do "Music, Music, Music," too.

Jimmy Sturr just about owns the polka Grammy Award. So maybe finally I'll be on a Grammy-winner. At any rate, I have no intention of quitting singing any time soon. I've been at it too long to stop now.

Plus, the power of music has come to me like never before. Like all Americans I ached inside as the events of September 11, 2001, unfolded. I cried every time I watched the footage of the World Trade Center on TV. I felt helpless and completely violated. I wished there were something I could do. It turned out that I already had.

The previous summer, TV producer Norman Lear recorded a group of us doing "America the Beautiful" for an Independence Day special. I sang with Kenny Rogers, Amy Grant, Lyle Lovett, Alabama, Toby Keith, Vince Gill, the Oak Ridge Boys and others. I didn't think anything more about it, but after the attack on America, CMT began airing the song as a music video, and it came onto the charts as one of the "healing" records in the fall of 2001. Six decades after I was first on the radio, I was on it again. But I would have given anything for it to be under other circumstances.

I've sung patriotic music all my life, but the words have never meant as much to me as they do today.

EIGHTEEN

Are We There Yet?

The day I finished writing this book, I cried. I didn't want it to end. For years other entertainers have told me how "painful" and awful writing their autobiographies was. Maybe that's why I waited so long. I thought it would be a bad experience. But I loved writing mine.

Plus, it always seemed so final to me to be writing your life story. Heck, I'm not dead yet. I also didn't want to write it because, believe it or not, I didn't think my life had been interesting enough. It wasn't until I put it all down on paper that I realized all the experiences I've been through. I guess you know by now that my story isn't a sensational, sexy "tell-all." There's no scandal. Maybe it all sounds too good to be true, but that's the way it happened. The bad might have been there, but I don't dwell on it. I'm just not that kind of person.

I never really stood back and looked at my life and career. It's been an extraordinary trip, don't you think? And instead of feeling "final," the whole process of writing *Little Miss Dynamite* has been a series of beginnings. I had fun doing it. It was such a journey of discovery. This has been a healing process, too. I reconnected with my family. I think I came to understand Dub Allbritten better. I visited with old friends, and what a pleasure it was to catch up with all my buddies in the music business.

I'm not saying this was easy. Writing, I've learned, is hard work. And at the beginning, I found it almost impossible to articulate my deepest emotions. I'm not used to introspection. I've never lingered on my feelings. The show must go on.

I've always thought that philosophy hurt those closest to me. Julie and Jolie used to cry when I'd leave them. I carried a guilt trip around about that for decades. Now both of them insist that my separations didn't leave bad memories at all. At any rate, I've tried to make it up to both of them by becoming their friend as an adult. We laugh together so much now, and we're closer than ever. Maybe it's because I never really was the stereotypical "Mommy" to them that I can be their buddy today.

My kids say I'm eccentric, and I guess I am. Doesn't everyone stay up all night watching old movies on cable TV, eating sardines and crackers?

You wouldn't believe my attic. I'm a hopeless pack rat. I save everything. I have every outfit I've ever worn on stage. Because I'm so short, my clothes have been custom-made throughout my career. I wear a size 2 children's shoe, and my 800-square-foot closet is a shoe fetishist's dream. I also have a jewelry fixation, keeping mountains of gems that I never wear in a safe at the bank. But I just love to go and take them out and look at them.

The career memorabilia is another thing. I've got tons of that stuff, mostly at the office. Since I'm an inveterate autograph collector, I have drawer after drawer containing photos of me with everyone from Liberace to Colonel Sanders, not to mention every music star you've ever heard of. Most recently I called Aerosmith to get their autographs, because they're my favorite band. Then there are the fifteen volumes of Brenda Lee scrapbooks. These aren't your regular-sized tomes, either. They are leather-bound volumes four feet tall and three feet wide. And each one of them is full of all the thousands of clippings, pictures, reviews, promotions and everything relating to my career. Dub Allbritten was obsessive about saving all that. And I'm glad he did. They helped me write this book.

I collect clowns, miniatures, dollhouses, crystal, books, silver, clocks and china. I have souvenirs from more than fifty countries. Ronnie says if I hang one more thing on the walls at home, they're going to fall in.

These days, Ronnie goes with me to almost all my concerts on the road. He's still managing the finances, which is a good thing. It's still just like when I was a kid—my job is to sing, and I don't worry about the rest.

I don't have to work. We live more than comfortably on the interest our savings earns us each year. I sing because I still love the sound of applause, because it's who I am, and because I still can. I love this business. I don't think I ever want to work as hard as I have in the past. But I do want to be a part of it as long as I'm able and as long as the fans allow me to sing.

This is what I joke: "I still get butterflies, but now they fly in formation." One of my greatest fears has always been that I'd fall off the stage. It finally happened last year. I was bopping along with the lights in my eyes, and I went right over the edge into the orchestra pit. I still had the microphone, so I just kept singing.

As you might imagine, Christmas is a pretty busy time of year for me. Every year, I get so many requests from fans and concert promoters to come sing "Rockin' around the Christmas Tree." As recently as 1997 it was a big hit on the A/C charts, once again. That's the same year that singer Bobby Helms died. He had originated the evergreen holiday favorite "Jingle Bell Rock," but we both had hit singles with it. So after Bobby died, I kind of inherited that song as my other holiday standard. It keeps coming back every year, too. I guess those two songs will still be here, even after I'm gone.

One of the greatest joys I have today is that my hometown still embraces me so warmly. I often take part in the annual Nashville Music Awards gala. In 2000, MCA Records gathered all the Brenda Lee Christmas recordings in its vaults, including my kiddie records "I'm Gonna Lasso Santa Claus" and "Christy Christmas" from 1956. The resulting disc won a Nashville Music Award as Reissue Recording of the Year in 2001.

But the most fun I ever had at one of those ceremonies was in 1996. On that occasion, I was at the Ryman Auditorium as the presenter of the Nashville Music Awards' Female Vocalist of the Year trophy to Trisha Yearwood.

Michael McDonald, who also lives in Nashville, was on the show that night. I am a huge, huge fan of his work both in the Doobie Brothers and on his own. You know me, I had to meet him. I told him I'd just started writing lyrics and asked him if he'd like to write with me. Wasn't that brazen?

I gave him my phone number, and to my surprise he called a few days later. We got together in my living room with my guitar player, Dave Powelson. Michael brought an idea for a song, and the three of us put it together. Just a few weeks later I found out that Wynonna was going to record it.

Wynonna Judd included the song, "The Kind of Fool Love Makes," on her 1997 CD *The Other Side*. The album became a Gold Record. Then, in 2000, Kenny Rogers recorded "The Kind of Fool Love Makes" for his CD *She Rides Wild Horses*. That collection became a Platinum Record. All of a sudden, I've got songwriting royalties rolling in. RonBre, the company that Dub said was worthless in his will, is turning a profit at last.

Isn't that something? Me, who's never seriously written a

song before. And here the first time I do, it winds up as a huge success right out of the chute. So now I'm bound and determined I'm going to write some more. I'm motivated. I've got a whole new career in front of me. I must be the cat with nine lives.

Let's see, the first one would have been as "TV's Biggest Little Star." Then came my adventure as an overseas child sensation. Next, "Little Miss Dynamite" was a rockabilly teen queen. Then I headlined as a supper-club chanteuse. When that ended, I reinvented myself as a country entertainer. And now I'm a successful songwriter.

That's only six lives, so I've got a few left. I'm only in my fifties. I still care about music to the depths of my soul. The facelift is sagging a little, but I can get that fixed. I can still rock with the best of 'em, and I'm hitting the road again.

So here I am. I have my battle scars, both professional and personal. I fought my way out of childhood poverty. I lost my father. I went to work at age eight. I was forced to perform to the point of exhaustion. I gave up my childhood for a career. I married young and faced the struggles of a wife and mother who lived as a gypsy. I survived a career that collapsed on more than one occasion. I picked myself up after drastic health problems knocked me down.

I've faced a lot of hardships, but I refuse to be melodramatic or self-pitying. There are so many people who have gone through much worse than I have. When you look at the big picture, I've had a blessed life. If perseverance counts, put me on that TV show *Survivor*.

How did I survive when so many others do not? I think a lot of it has to do with attitude. I've always had a thankful heart, I've held on to my sense of humor and I still don't look at myself as a "star."

I hope that in some small way, people might find inspiration from the story of my life. It has been an amazing journey. My voice was a gift, but I've never taken it for granted. And I worked with stamina and guts to make something of myself. When I talk about my dad and mom being tough, I see those same qualities in myself. More important, I've always looked forward with a positive, hopeful outlook.

I think the amazing thing is that I'm sane. I'm not bitter. I'm not drugged out. I'm not broke. I'm still married to the same guy. My children don't hate me. And I still have my voice.

Am I "there" yet? I don't have an answer for that question. I'm still on my way.

Discography

BRENDA LEE—THE SONGS*

1956: "Jambalaya"/
   "Bigelow 6-200"
   "I'm Gonna Lasso Santa Claus"/
   "Christy Christmas"
1957: **"One Step at a Time"**/   #15 country/#43 pop
   "Fairyland"
   "Dynamite"/   #72 pop
   "Love You 'Til I Die"
   "One Teenager to Another"/
   "Ain't That Love"
1958: "Rock the Bop"/
   "Rock-a-Bye Baby Blues"
   "Ring-a-My Phone"/
   "Little Jonah (Rock on Your
   Steel Guitar)"
   "Rockin' around the Christmas
   Tree"/
   "Papa Noel"

*Boldfaced singles titles became top-20 hits on various charts.
Dates for international releases are approximate.
Discography compiled by Jon Nickell, Pat O'Leary, Bob Borum and
Robert K. Oermann.

1959:	"The Stroll"/	France
	"Baby Face"	
	"Dynamite"/	France
	"Love You 'Til I Die"	
	"Rock the Bop"/	France
	"Rock-a-Bye Baby Blues"	
	"Bill Bailey Won't You Please Come Home"/	
	"Hummin' the Blues Over You"	
	"Let's Jump the Broomstick"/	
	"Some of These Days"	
	"Jambalaya"/	Brazilian, French,
	"Bigelow 6-200"	German release
	"Dynamite"/	
	"Jambalaya"	Polish release
	"Sweet Nothin's"/	#4 pop/#12 r&b/
	"Weep No More, My Baby"	#4 England/#34 Germany
1960:	**"I'm Sorry"/**	#1 pop/#4 r&b/ #12 England
	"That's All You Gotta Do"	#6 pop/#19 r&b
	"I Want to Be Wanted"/	#1 pop/#7 r&b/
	"Just a Little"	#40 pop #31 England
	"Rockin' around the Christmas Tree"/	#6 England/#14 pop
	"Papa Noel"	
1961:	**"Let's Jump the Broomstick"/**	#12 England
	"Rock-a-Bye Baby Blues"	
	"Emotions"/	#7 pop/#45 England
	"I'm Learning about Love"	#33 pop
	"You Can Depend On Me"/	#6 pop/#25 r&b
	"It's Never Too Late"	#101 pop
	"Dum Dum"/	#4 pop/#22 England
	"Eventually"	#56 pop
	"Fool #1"/	#3 pop/#38 England
	"Anybody but Me"	#31 pop

"Rockin' around the Christmas Tree"/	#50 pop
"Papa Noel"	
1962: "Geh am Gluck Nicht Vorbei"/	Germany, Canada
"Darling Bye Bye"	
"La Premiere Fool"/	France, Canada
"Pourquoi Jamais Moi"	
"Sono Sciocca"/	Italy
"Nulla di Mi"	
"Break It to Me Gently"/	#4 pop/#46 England
"So Deep"	#52 pop
"Speak to Me Pretty"/	#4 England
"Lover Come Back to Me"	
"Everybody Loves Me but You"/	#2 AC/#6 pop
"Here Comes That Feelin'"	#5 England/#89 pop
"Heart in Hand"/	#4 AC/#15 pop
"It Started All Over Again"	#15 England/#29 pop
"All Alone Am I"/	#1 AC/#3 pop/#7 England
"Save All Your Lovin' for Me"	#53 pop
"Rockin' around the Christmas Tree"/	#59 pop
"Papa Noel"	
1963: **"Your Used to Be"/**	#12 AC/#32 pop
"She'll Never Know"	#15 AC/#47 pop
"Losing You"/	#2 AC/#6 pop/#13 r&b/ #10 England
"He's So Heavenly"	#73 pop
"Darling Was Is Los Mit Dir"/	Germany
"In Meinen Traumen"	
"My Whole World Is Falling Down"/	#8 AC/#24 pop
"I Wonder"	#9 AC/#25 pop/ #14 England
"The Grass Is Greener"/	#7 AC/#17 pop
"Sweet Impossible You"	#28 England/#70 pop

	"Rockin' around the Christmas Tree"/	#12 Xmas chart
	"Papa Noel"	
1964:	**"As Usual"**/	#5 AC/#12 pop/
		#5 England
	"Lonely, Lonely, Lonely Me"	
	"Think"/	#4 AC/#25 pop/
		#26 England
	"The Waiting Game"	#101 pop
	"Alone with You"/	#8 AC/#48 pop
	"My Dreams"	#85 pop
	"Weidersehn Ist Wunderschon"/	Germany
	"Kansas City"	
	"When You Loved Me"/	#8 AC/#47 pop
	"He's Sure to Remember Me"	#135 pop
	"No My Boy"/	Germany
	"Drei Rote Rosen Bluhn"	
	"Ich Will Immer auf Dich Warten"/	#13 Germany
	"Ohne Dich"	
	"Jingle Bell Rock"/	#1 Germany/#10 Xmas chart
	"Winter Wonderland"	
	"This Time of Year"/	#12 Xmas chart
	"Christmas Will Be Just Another Lonely Day"	#24 Xmas chart/ #29 England
	"Rockin' around the Christmas Tree"/	#4 Xmas chart
	"Papa Noel"	
	"Is It True"/	#17 England
	"What'd I Say"	
	"Is It True"/	#17 pop
	"Just behind the Rainbow"	
1965:	"Thanks a Lot"/	#45 pop
	"The Crying Game"	#87 pop
	"Thanks a Lot"/	#41 England
	"Just behind the Rainbow"	

"Truly Truly True"/	#9 AC/#54 pop
"I Still Miss Someone"	
"Too Many Rivers"/	#2 AC/#12 pop/
	#22 England
"No One"	#25 AC/#98 pop
"One Rainy Night in Tokyo" (in Japanese)/	#1 Japan
"One Rainy Night in Tokyo" (in English)	
"La Vie en Rose" (in Japanese)/	Japan
"La Vie en Rose" (in English)	
"If You Love Me"/	#1 Japan
"Side by Side"	
"Rusty Bells"/	#3 AC/#33 pop
"If You Don't"	
"Rockin' around the Christmas	
Tree"/	#3 Xmas chart
"Papa Noel"	

1966: "Too Little Time"/ #123 pop
"Time and Again" #126 pop

"Ain't Gonna Cry No More"/ #77 pop
"It Takes One to Know One"

"Walk Away"/ Japan
"Beautiful Dreamer"

"Coming On Strong"/ #11 pop
"You Keep Coming Back to Me"

**"Rockin' around the Christmas
Tree"/** #4 Xmas chart
"Papa Noel"

"White Christmas"/ Japan
"Jingle Bells"

1967: "Ride, Ride, Ride"/ #37 pop
"Lonely People Do Foolish
Things"

"Take Me"/ #126 pop
"Born to Be by Your Side"

"Where Love Is"/ #134 pop
"My Heart Keeps Hangin' On"

"Where's the Melody"/	#105 pop
"Save Me for a Rainy Day"	
"Rockin' around the Christmas Tree"/	#8 Xmas chart
"Papa Noel"	
"Jingle Bell Rock"/	#8 Xmas chart
"Winter Wonderland"	
1968: "That's All Right"/	#118 pop
"Fantasy"	
"Cabaret" (w Pete Fountain)/	
"Mood Indigo"	
"Kansas City"/	
"Each Day Is a Rainbow"	
"Rockin' around the Christmas Tree"/	#14 Xmas chart
"Papa Noel"	
1969: **"Johnny One Time"/**	#3 AC/#41 pop/ #50 country
"I Must Have Been Out of My Mind"	
"You Don't Need Me Anymore"/	#32 AC/#84 pop
"Bring Me Sunshine"	
"Let It Be Me"/	
"You Better Move On"	
"Rockin' around the Christmas Tree"/	#4 Xmas chart
"Papa Noel"	
1970: "I Think I Love You Again"/	#37 AC/#94 pop
"Hello Love"	
"Sisters in Sorrow"/	
"Do Right Woman, Do Right Man"	
"Proud Mary"	Turkey
1971: "If This Is Our Last Time"/	#30 country
"Everybody's Reaching Out for Someone"	

"Omoide No Bara"/	Japan
"Everybody's Reaching Out for Someone"	
"Hiosobi"/	Japan
"Help Me Make It through the Night"	
1972: "Misty Memories"/	#37 country
"I'm a Memory"	
"Always on My Mind"/	#45 country
"That Ain't Right"	
1973: **"Nobody Wins"**/	#5 country/#70 pop
"We Had a Good Thing Goin'"	
"Sunday Sunrise"/	#6 country
"Must I Believe"	
"Densetsu No Mizuumi"/	Japan
"Gomennasaine"	
"Gogatu No Bara"/	Japan
"Return to Me"	
"Omoidasanaide"/	Japan
"You Are the Sunshine of My Life"	
"Rockin' around the Christmas Tree"/	#16 Xmas chart
"Papa Noel"	
"Jingle Bell Rock"/	
"Winter Wonderland"	
1974: **"Wrong Ideas"**/	#6 country
"Something for a Rainy Day"	
"Big Four Poster Bed"/	#4 country
"Castles in the Sand"	
"Rock On Baby"/	#6 country
"More Than a Memory"	
1975: **"He's My Rock"**/	#8 country
"Feel Free"	
"Bringing It Back"/	#23 country
"Papa's Knee"	

1976:	"Find Yourself Another Puppet"/	#38 country
	"What I Had with You"	
	"Brother Shelton"/	#77 country
	"Now He's Coming Home"	
	"Takin' What I Can Get"/	#41 country
	"Your Favorite Wornout	
	Nightmare's Coming Home"	
1977:	"Ruby's Lounge"/	#78 country
	"Oklahoma Superstar"	
	"Dare"/	Japan
	"Tie a Yellow Ribbon 'round	
	the Old Oak Tree"	
	"Arukigeki"/	Japan
	"Dare"	
	"Take Me Home, Country Roads"/	Japan
	"My Way"	
1978:	"Left-Over Love"/	#62 country
	"Could It Be I Found Love	
	Tonight"	
	"I'm Sorry"/	#1 France
	"That's All You Gotta Do"	
1979:	**"Tell Me What It's Like"**/	#8 country
	"Let Your Love Fall Back	
	on Me"	
1980:	**"The Cowgirl and the Dandy"**/	#10 country
	"Do You Wanna Spend the	
	Night"	
	"Keeping Me Warm for You"/	
	"At the Moonlight"	
	"Don't Promise Me Anything	
	(Do It)"/	#49 country
	"You Only Broke My Heart"	
	"Broken Trust" (w Oak Ridge	
	Boys)/	#9 country
	"Right behind the Rain"	
	"Again and Again"	soundtrack release

"Rockin' around the Christmas
Tree"/
  "Papa Noel"
"Jingle Bell Rock"/
  "Winter Wonderland"

1981: "Every Now and Then"/   #26 country
  "He'll Play the Music"
"Fool, Fool"/   #67 country
  "Right behind the Rain"
"Enough for You"/   #75 country
  "What Am I Gonna Do"
"Only When I Laugh"/   #32 country
  "Too Many Nights Alone"

1982: "From Levi's to Calvin Klein
Jeans"/   #33 country
  "I Know a Lot about Love"
"Keeping Me Warm for You"/   #70 country
  "There's More to Me Than You Can See"
"Just for the Moment" (w Oak
Ridge Boys)/   #78 country
  "Love Letters"
"Where Were You"/
  "Lay Away Your Heart"

1983: "You're Gonna Love Yourself in   #43 country
the Morning" (w Willie Nelson)/
  "What Do You Think about
  Lovin'" (w Dolly Parton)
"Didn't We Do It Good"/   #75 country
  "We're So Close"
**"Rockin' around the Christmas
Tree"/**   #9 Xmas chart
  "Papa Noel"

1984: "A Sweeter Love (I'll Never
Know)"/   #22 country
  "A Woman's Mind"
"Rockin' around the Christmas

	Tree"/	#5 Xmas chart
	"Papa Noel"	
1985:	**"Hallelujah, I Love You So"**	
	(w George Jones)/	#15 country
	"The Second Time Around"	
	"I'm Takin' My Time"/	#54 country
	"That's the Way It Was Then"	
1986:	"Why You Been Gone So Long"/	#50 country
	"He Can't Make Your Kind of Love"	
	"Two Hearts"/	
	"Loving Arms"	
1987:	"Dynamite"/	Holland
	"I'm Sorry"	
	"Sweet Nothin's"/	Holland
	"Emotions"	
	"I'm Sorry"/	Italy
	"Dum Dum"	
1989:	"Honky Tonk Angels Medley" (w k.d. lang, Loretta Lynn, Kitty Wells)	
1990:	"You're in the Doghouse Now"/	soundtrack release
	"Sweet Memories" (w Ricky Van Shelton)	
1991:	"Your One and Only"/	
	"You Better Do Better"	
	"A Little Unfair"/	
	"One of These Days"	
1997:	"Precious Memories"	gospel release
	"Rockin' around the Christmas Tree"/	#16 AC/#62 country
	"Papa Noel"	
2001:	"Ricochet Romance" (w Jimmy Sturr)	polka release
	"Music, Music, Music" (w Jimmy Sturr)	polka release

"America the Beautiful . . ."
(w various artists)   #58 country

BRENDA LEE—HER ALBUM CAREER

1959: *Grandma What Great Songs*
    You Sang   Decca
1960: *Brenda Lee*   Decca
    This Is Brenda   Decca
1961: *Emotions*   Decca
    Brenda Lee Sings Songs
      Everybody Knows   Decca
    All the Way   Decca
1962: *Sincerely, Brenda Lee*   Decca
    Brenda, That's All   Decca
1963: *All Alone Am I*   Decca
    Let Me Sing   Decca
1964: *By Request*   Decca
    Merry Christmas from Brenda Lee   Decca
1965: *Top Teen Hits*   Decca
    The Versatile Brenda Lee   Decca
    Too Many Rivers   Decca
    Brenda Lee in Tokyo (live)   Decca (Japan)
1966: *Bye Bye Blues*   Decca
    Ten Golden Years   Decca
    Coming On Strong   Decca
1967: *Reflections in Blue*   Decca
    Here's Brenda Lee   Vocalion
1968: *For the First Time*
    (w Pete Fountain)   Decca
1969: *Johnny One Time*   Decca
1970: *Memphis Portrait*   Decca
    Let It Be Me   Vocalion
1973: *Brenda*   MCA
    New Sunrise   MCA

	The Brenda Lee Story (double LP)	MCA
1974:	*Brenda Lee Now*	MCA
1975:	*Sincerely*	MCA
	Let It Be Me	Coral
	Live in Japan	Victor/MCA (Japan)
1976:	*The L.A. Sessions*	MCA
1977:	*Just for You, Something Nice*	Victor/MCA (Japan)
1978:	*The Best of Brenda Lee*	Tee Vee
1979:	*More American Graffiti*— soundtrack (1 song)	MCA
1980:	*Even Better*	MCA
	Smokey and the Bandit II— soundtrack (1 song)	MCA
1981:	*Take Me Back*	MCA
	Urban Chipmunk—The Chipmunks (1 song)	RCA
1982:	*Only When I Laugh*	MCA
	Greatest Country Hits	MCA
1983:	*The Winning Hand* (w Kris Kristofferson, Willie Nelson, Dolly Parton)	Monument
1984:	*Ladies Choice*—George Jones (1 song)	Epic
1985:	*Feels So Right*	MCA
	Rockin' around the Christmas Tree	MCA
	Tennessee Christmas (1 song)	MCA
	Wiedersen Ist Wunderschon	Bear Family (Germany)
1988:	*Shadowland*—k.d. lang (1 song)	Sire
1989:	*In Concert*	(U.K., Australia)
1990:	*Dick Tracy*—soundtrack (1 song)	Sire
	RVS III—Ricky Van Shelton (1 song)	Columbia
1991:	*Brenda Lee*	Warner Bros.
	A Brenda Lee Christmas	Warner Bros.
	Anthology (double CD)	MCA
	The Brenda Lee Story (reissue)	

(double CD)	MCA
The Fisher King—soundtrack	
(1 song)	MCA
1992: *Greatest Hits Live*	K-tel
1995: *Casino*—soundtrack (1 song)	MCA
Little Miss Dynamite	
(four-CD box set)	Bear Family (Germany)
EP Collection	See for Miles (U.K.)
1996: *21 All-Time Greatest Hits*	
(double CD)	Brenda Lee Productions
Trees Lounge—soundtrack	
(2 songs)	MCA
1997: *Precious Memories: Favorite*	
Gospel Songs	Brenda Lee Productions
1998: *In the Mood for Love*	Uni/Hip-O
1999: *Best of Brenda Lee: 20th Century*	
Masters, Millennium Collection	MCA/Decca
Rockin' around the Christmas Tree:	
Decca Christmas Recordings	MCA/Decca
2001: *Gone Polka*—Jimmy Sturr (2 songs)	Rounder

BRENDA LEE—SELECTED FOREIGN SINGLES*

1956: "Jambalaya"/	
"Bigelow 6-200"	Canada
"I'm Gonna Lasso Santa Claus"/	Canada
"Christy Christmas"	
1957: "Ain't That Love" /	Canada
"One Teenager to Another"	
1959: "The Stroll"/	France
"Baby Face"	

*Dates for international releases are approximate.
 International release list is incomplete; many of the overseas discs are still being discovered.

"Dynamite"/	France
"Love You 'Til I Die"	
"Rock the Bop"/	France
"Rock-a-Bye Baby Blues"	
"Jambalaya"/	Brazil, France,
	Germany
"Bigelow 6-200"	
"Dynamite"/	Poland
"Jambalaya"	
"Sweet Nothin's"/	U.K., Germany, Canada
"Weep No More, My Baby"	
1960: "I'm Sorry"/	U.K., Germany, France,
"That's All You Gotta Do"	Canada
"I Want to Be Wanted"/	U.K., Germany, France,
"Just a Little"	Canada
"Rockin' around the Christmas	
Tree"/	U.K.
"Papa Noel"	
1961: "Let's Jump the Broomstick"/	U.K.
"Rock-a-Bye Baby Blues"	
"Emotions"/	U.K., Canada
"I'm Learning about Love"	
"Dum Dum"/	U.K., Germany, France,
"Eventually"	Spain, South America
"Fool #1"/	U.K., Germany, France,
"Anybody but Me"	Spain
1962: "Geh am Gluck Nicht Vorbei"/	Germany, Canada
"Darling Bye Bye"	
"La Premiere Fool"/	France, Canada
"Pourquoi Jamais Moi"	
"Sono Sciocca"/	Italy
"Nulla di Mi"	
"Break It to Me Gently"/	U.K., Germany, France
"So Deep"	
"Speak to Me Pretty"/	U.K.
"Lover Come Back to Me"	

"Everybody Loves Me but You"/ "Here Comes That Feelin' "	U.K.
"Heart in Hand"/ "It Started All Over Again"	U.K., Germany, France, South America
"All Alone Am I"/ "Save All Your Lovin' for Me"	U.K., Germany, France
"Rockin' around the Christmas Tree"/ "Papa Noel"	Spain, France, Germany
1963: "Your Used to Be"/ "She'll Never Know"	Spain, France, Germany, Canada
"Losing You"/ "He's So Heavenly"	U.K., Germany, France, Spain, Canada
"Darling Was Is Los Mit Dir"/ "In Meinen Traumen"	Germany
"My Whole World Is Falling Down"/ "I Wonder"	U.K., Germany, France, Canada
"The Grass Is Greener"/ "Sweet Impossible You"	U.K., Germany, France, Japan, Mexico, South America
1964: "As Usual"/ "Lonely, Lonely, Lonely Me"	U.K., Germany, France
"Think"/ "The Waiting Game"	U.K., Germany, France, Spain, Canada, Japan
"Weidersehn Ist Wunderschon"/ "Kansas City"	Germany
"When You Loved Me"/ "He's Sure to Remember Me"	Japan, France, Germany
"No My Boy"/ "Drei Rote Rosen Bluhn"	Germany
"Ich Will Immer auf Dich Warten"/ "Ohne Dich"	Germany
"Jingle Bell Rock"/ "Winter Wonderland"	Germany
"This Time of Year"/	U.K.

"Christmas Will Be Just Another
Lonely Day"

"Is It True"/ "What'd I Say"	U.K., Germany, France, Spain, Canada, Sweden, South America
"Is It True"/ "Just behind the Rainbow"	Japan
"I'm Sorry" / "That's All You Gotta Do"	South Africa
"I Want to Be Wanted"/ "Just a Little"	South Africa
1965: "Thanks a Lot"/ "The Crying Game"	Japan, France, Germany, Spain, Canada, Mexico, South America
"Thanks a Lot"/ "Just behind the Rainbow"	U.K.
"Too Many Rivers"/ "No One"	U.K.
"One Rainy Night in Tokyo" (Japanese)/ "One Rainy Night in Tokyo"	Japan
"La Vie en Rose" (in Japanese)/ "La Vie en Rose" (in English)	Japan
"Emotions"/ "I'm Learning about Love"	Japan, South Africa
"Here Comes That Feeling"/ "Everybody Loves Me but You"	Japan

"Only You"/
  "You Always Hurt the One
  You Love"
	Japan

"If You Love Me"/ "Side by Side"	Japan
"Rusty Bells"/ "If You Don't"	Japan, France, Germany, Spain, Canada
"All Alone Am I"/ "Save All Your Lovin' for Me"	Japan

"The End of the World"/ "Night and Day"	Japan
"When Your Lover Has Gone"/ "Our Day Will Come"	Japan
"Danke Schoen"/ "Blue Velvet"	Japan
"Jambalaya"/"Bigelow 6-200"	South Africa
"Ain't That Love"/ "One Teenager to Another"	South Africa
"Sweet Nothin's"/ "Weep No More My Baby"	South Africa
"Fool #1"/ "Anybody but Me"	South Africa
"All Alone Am I"/ "Save All Your Lovin' for Me"	South Africa
1966: "Too Little Time"/ "Time and Again"	Japan
"Ain't Gonna Cry No More"/ "It Takes One to Know One"	Japan
"Walk Away"/"Beautiful Dreamer"	Japan
"Coming On Strong"/ "You Keep Coming Back to Me"	Japan, France, Germany, Spain, Sweden, South America
"Yesterday's Gone"/ "Love Letters"	Japan
"A Taste of Honey"/ "Bye Bye Blues"	Japan
"Flowers on the Wall"/ "Yesterday"	Japan
"September in the Rain"/ "The Shadow of Your Smile"	Japan
"Akasaka after Dark"/ "Endless Love"	Japan
"Uptight"/ "Summer Wind"	Japan

"White Christmas"/	Japan
"Jingle Bells"	
1967: "Take Me"/	Japan
"Born to Be by Your Side"	
"Pennies from Heaven"/	Japan
"Pretty Baby"	
"Where's the Melody"/	Japan, Germany, Spain,
"Save Me for a Rainy Day"	Sweden
"Where's the Melody"/	U.K., France
"Born to Be by Your Side"	
1968: "Since There's No You"/	Japan
"Fantasy"	
"More"/	Japan
"Fool #1"	
"Jambalaya"/	Japan
"Lover Come Back to Me"	
"You Don't Have to Say You Love Me"/	Japan
"Strangers in the Night"	
"That's All Right"/	U.K.
"Baby Won't You Please Come Home"	
1969: "Johnny One Time"/	U.K., Japan, France,
"I Must Have Been Out of My Mind"	Germany, Spain, South America, Mexico
"A Taste of Honey"/	Russia
"The Shadow of Your Smile"	
1970: "I Think I Love You Again"/	Japan
"Hello Love"	
"Sisters in Sorrow"/	Japan
"Do Right Woman, Do Right Man"	
"Proud Mary"	Turkey
1971: "If This Is Our Last Time"/	Japan
"Everybody's Reaching Out for Someone"	

"Omoide No Bara"/ "Everybody's Reaching Out for Someone"	Japan
"Hiosobi"/ "Help Me Make It through the Night"	Japan
1973: "Nobody Wins"/ "We Had a Good Thing Goin'"	Japan
"Densetsu No Mizuumi"/ "Gomennasaine"	Japan
"Gogatu No Bara"/"Return to Me"	Japan
"Omoidasanaide"/ "You Are the Sunshine of My Life"	Japan
1974: "Rock On Baby"/ "More Than a Memory"	Japan
1975: "He's My Rock"/ "Feel Free"	Japan
"Nobody Wins/ "We Had a Good Thing Goin'"	Russia
1976: "Find Yourself Another Puppet"/ "What I Had with You"	Japan
1977: "Ruby's Lounge"/ "Oklahoma Superstar"	Japan
"Dare"/ "Tie a Yellow Ribbon 'round the Old Oak Tree"	Japan
"Arukigeki"/ "Dare"	Japan
"Take Me Home, Country Roads"/ "My Way"	Japan
1978: "I'm Sorry"/ "That's All You Gotta Do"	France
1979: "Tell Me What It's Like"/ "Let Your Love Fall Back on Me"	Japan
1987: "Dynamite"/	Holland

"I'm Sorry"
"Sweet Nothin's"/   Holland
   "Emotions"
"I'm Sorry"/   Italy
   "Dum Dum"

BRENDA LEE—SELECTED FOREIGN ALBUMS

1960:	*Brenda Lee*	Germany
	This Is Brenda	South America
	Brenda Lee Rock	South America
	Miss Dynamite	U.K., Germany
	Grandma What Great Songs You Sang	U.K.
1961:	*Emotions*	U.K., Germany, France
	All the Way	U.K., South America
	This Is Brenda Lee	U.K., Germany, France
1962:	*Sincerely, Brenda Lee*	U.K., Germany, France, South America
	Brenda, That's All	U.K., Germany, France, South America
	Abuelita, Que Hermosas Canciones Cantabas!	South America
1963:	*All Alone Am I*	U.K., Germany, France, South America
	Let Me Sing	South America, Germany, France
	Love You	U.K.
	Canciones que Todos Conocen	South America
	Esta Es Brenda	South America
1964:	*By Request*	U.K., South America
	Merry Christmas from Brenda Lee	U.K.
	Favorite Songs	Japan
	Dejenme Cantar	South America

Dejenme Cantara	Mexico
Losing You	Australia/NewZealand
My Whole World Is Falling Down	Australia/New Zealand
It Started All Over Again	Australia/New Zealand
1965: *Top Teen Hits*	U.K., Germany, France, South America
The Versatile Brenda Lee	U.K., Germany, France
Too Many Rivers	U.K., Germany, France
Coletanea de Ouro	South America
Brenda Lee in Tokyo (live)	Japan
Merry Christmas from Brenda Lee	Japan
One Rainy Night in Tokyo	Japan
Brenda Lee	Japan
This Is Brenda	Japan
If You Love Me	Japan
All Alone Am I	Japan
Brenda, That's All	Japan
Brenda at Hitsville	Australia/New Zealand
1966: *Bye Bye Blues*	U.K., Germany, France, Japan
Coming On Strong	U.K.
Walk Away	Japan
Best Of	Japan
The Versatile Brenda Lee	Japan
Musical Autobiography	Japan
A Dozen Golden Years	Germany
Brenda Lee Las Diez Millionaria's	South America
10 Golden Years	Australia
1967: *Reflections in Blue*	U.K., Japan
Call Me Brenda	U.K.
Good Life	U.K.
My Greatest Songs	Japan
Sa Releases/Y Sus Exitos	South America
Vindo Com Mais Forca	South America
Dez Anos De Curo	South America
Will You Love Me Tomorrow	Australia/NewZealand

1968:	*For the First Time* (w Pete Fountain)	U.K., Germany, France
1969:	*Johnny One Time*	U.K., South America
1971:	*Brenda Lee by Request*	Italy
	Memphis Portrait	U.K.
	He's Sure to Remember Me	China
	All-Time Greatest Hits (double LP)	Holland
1972:	*A Whole Lotta*	U.K.
	Saltemos El Palo de la Escoba	Argentina
1973:	*Brenda*	U.K., Germany, Japan, South America
	New Sunrise	U.K., Japan
	Brenda Lee: The Legends of Rock (double LP)	Germany
	Star of Rock 'n' Roll	Holland
1974:	*Brenda Lee Now*	U.K., Japan
	The Brenda Lee Story	Germany
1975:	*Sincerely*	U.K., Japan
	Live in Japan	Japan
	Golden Hits	Japan
	Funny How Time Slips Away	U.K.
	Brenda Lee Gold Record	Belgium
1976:	*The L.A. Sessions*	U.K., Germany
	Little Miss Dynamite	U.K.
	10 Golden Years	Germany, Holland
1977:	*Just for You, Something Nice*	Japan
	Brenda Lee (four-LP set)	Japan
	25th Anniversary	Holland, Germany
1978:	*Sound Elegance*	Japan
	Super Twin	Japan
	The Original Brenda Lee (double LP)	Germany
1979:	*Miss Dynamite*	France
	The Best of Brenda Lee	Holland
	Rock the Bop	Holland
	The Best of Brenda Lee,	Japan

	Excel One	
	Brenda Rocks the Bop	South Africa
1980:	*The Best of Brenda Lee* (double LP)	Japan
	Little Miss Dynamite	U.K.
1981:	*28 Golden Melodies*	Germany
	Dynamite	Holland
	Brenda Lee Super Deluxe	Japan
	25th Anniversary (double LP)	U.K.
1982:	*16 Classic Tracks*	U.K.
	I'm Sorry, but I Am Rockin'	Belgium
1984:	*The Early Years*	U.K.
	Love Songs Just for You	U.K.
	Merry Christmas from Brenda Lee (reissue)	Japan
	Deluxe 2	Japan
1985:	*Wiedersen Ist Wunderschon*	Germany
	Love Songs	U.K.
	The Very Best of Brenda Lee (double LP)	U.K.
	The Golden Decade (double LP)	U.K.
	Best of Christmas	Japan
1986:	*Best 22 Songs*	Japan
1987:	*Brenda's Best* (picture disc)	Holland
	Best 23 Songs, Volume 2	Japan
	Little Miss Dynamite	Italy
1988:	*All Alone Am I* (picture disc)	Holland
1989:	*Country Gold*	Australia
	In Concert	U.K., Australia, Belgium
	A Portrait of Brenda Lee	Belgium
	Brenda Lee	Germany
	Brenda Lee (double LP)	Japan
1990:	*Let the Good Times Roll*	Belgium
	Sings Her Most Beautiful Songs in Concert	Belgium

	Brenda's Best	Belgium
	Greatest Hits Live	Czechoslovakia
1991:	*My Greatest Songs*	Germany
	Best One	Japan
	Brenda Lee	Japan
	A Brenda Lee Christmas	Japan
	Rockin' around the Christmas Tree	U.K.
	Coming On Strong "Live"	Canada
1992:	*Brenda Lee/All the Way*	Belgium
	Emotions/All Alone Am I	Belgium
	Wiedersen Ist Wunderschon (reissue)	Germany
	The Collection	Germany
	Best Collection (double CD)	Japan
	You Don't Have to Say You Love Me	U.K.
1993:	*Love You!*	Germany, France
	Little Miss Dynamite	Germany
	I'm Sorry	Germany
	Brenda, the Best	Japan
	Brenda and Buddy (w Buddy Holly)	Brazil
1994:	*Best of the Best*	U.K.
	The Very Best of Brenda Lee, with Love	U.K.
	Rock the Bop	U.K.
	An Evening with Loretta Lynn and Brenda Lee (w Loretta Lynn)	U.K.
	Emotions	Australia
1995:	*Little Miss Dynamite* (four-CD box set)	Germany
	EP Collection	U.K.
	Presenting Brenda Lee	U.K.
1996:	*Concert Collection*	U.K.
	Brenda Lee	Germany, Holland

1997:	*Live Dynamite*	U.K.
1998:	*Wonderful Music of Brenda Lee Live*	Holland
2000:	*Miss Dynamite Live*	Australia, Universal Masters, Holland
2001:	*Let Me Sing/By Request*	Holland